W9-CRY-021

IAN MACLACHLAN
733-6830

CARLETON UNIVERSITY BOOKSTORE

BB # ............... 008793

Selling $ ............... -60

*Regional Economic Policies in Canada*
Dept. # ............... 7

# Regional Economic Policies in Canada

*T. N. Brewis*

with an appendix by
*T. K. Rymes*

*The Macmillan Company of Canada Limited   Toronto*

© *The Macmillan Company of Canada Limited*
*1969*

All rights reserved – no part of this book may
be reproduced in any form without permission
in writing from the publisher, except by a
reviewer who wishes to quote brief passages in
connection with a review written for inclusion
in a magazine or newspaper.

*Library of Congress Catalogue Card Number*
*69-14543*

*Printed in Canada by Alger Press Ltd.*

# Acknowledgements

In writing the book I have been helped and stimulated by many colleagues, but I am particularly indebted to Mrs. Sheila Y. Isaac who undertook much of the statistical enquiry as well as the task of seeing the manuscript through the press.

Several readers both inside and outside of government offered advice on individual chapters and Miss Ruth Sims of The Macmillan Company of Canada patiently insisted on the desirability of editorial changes. I appreciated the counsel I received even on those occasions when I chose to disregard it.

Finally, I should like to thank my wife who spent many hours in typing drafts of the manuscript.

T.N.B.

*Carleton University*
*Ottawa*

*September, 1968*

# Contents

# List of Figures and Tables

*Regional Economic Policies in Canada*

 *Introduction*

THERE HAS BEEN in recent years a notable growth in the study of regional economic problems. The subject indeed has become a field of academic specialization, albeit one with uncertain boundaries extending into the broad realms of regional science and attracting geographers, sociologists, and demographers, as well as economists.

Among the factors contributing to this expanded interest in regional problems has been a growing discontent with the magnitude of the differences in income and employment opportunity which exist not only between countries but also between various regions of the same country. In the less developed nations especially there is often a widening gap between the growth of a few industrialized urban centres and the stagnation of rural areas, and if not redressed the disparity that results can be a potent cause of political unrest. Though likely to be less extreme, regional differences in prosperity within advanced industrial countries are also a source of concern, and most countries have introduced policies to modify spatial economic patterns. Canada is no exception.

The inequality of income and employment opportunity within as well as between provinces of the country has long been one of the important issues in the Canadian scene. There is widespread agreement that this inequality is too great to be acceptable, and

1

federal, provincial, and local governments have been devoting increasing efforts to the development of programs to reduce it. It is clear that market forces alone cannot be relied upon to redress the situation. Indeed poverty to some extent begets poverty. But as experience in other countries has shown, governments can do much to improve the fortunes of the less favoured communities by appropriate policies.

In his budget speech of 1963, the federal Minister of Finance drew attention to the establishment of a special Area Development Agency (ADA), within the new Department of Industry, designed to assist in the economic development of slow growth areas of the country. In addition, the Atlantic provinces were to be given further assistance through the strengthening of the Atlantic Development Board (ADB). Two years earlier, in June 1961, a very important piece of legislation, known as "ARDA", had been introduced "to provide for the Rehabilitation of Agricultural Lands and the Development of Rural Areas in Canada", and this was followed in 1966 by further legislation to provide a fund for the implementation of comprehensive rural development programs in specially selected rural development areas (FRED). The poverty of many farm and rural workers was more extreme than was commonly realized, and one of the primary purposes of the legislation was to increase their income opportunities. More generally, the Economic Council has been directed in its terms of reference to study how national economic policies can best foster the balanced economic development of all areas of Canada, a task to which the Council has been devoting increasing attention. These various policies and measures are additional to the federal fiscal adjustments which are made in favour of the poorer provinces and which have a long tradition.

What may prove to be of particular importance is the establishment, as this book goes to press, of a new department of government responsible for regional development. The functions of this new department have yet to be spelled out in detail, but its creation reflects the increasing concern of the federal government with regional problems and recognition of the need for closer integration of various policies relating thereto.

Provincial governments for their part have not been at all content to leave the initiative to Ottawa and are themselves developing programs of varying degrees of comprehensiveness and sophistication which are intended to modify the extent and location of economic growth. It is clear that these programs, which typically have as their prime objective the attracting of new industry, are prepared with scant, if any, regard for their implications at the national level. Thus the Committee on Manitoba's Economic Future, in a voluminous report published in 1963, urged among other things that more Manitobans be induced to travel in their own province and that efforts be made to reduce imports from other provinces as well as to increase exports to them. But it is not just at the *national* level that trade patterns are being modified by regional subventions and policies of one sort and another but at the *international* level too. Efforts to liberalize international trade could well be undermined by certain types of regional assistance which have the effect, if not the intent, of subsidizing export industries or reducing imports.

Though for the most part federal assistance is welcomed by those provincial governments which expect to benefit by it, there is not much enthusiasm among the others, and some provincial governments view the regional policies of Ottawa with very mixed feelings, except when they take the form of money with no strings attached. Questions concerning the criteria for assistance, the designation of areas to receive it, and the amount and form such assistance should take are matters of concern to all levels of government, and there are often sharp differences of opinion on policy. Should aid be distributed widely, or concentrated on smaller areas of deep distress? And what criteria of distress should be used? Would it be preferable to assist areas with more potential growth even though their distress is less marked? Is it preferable to concentrate efforts on various measures designed to influence the relocation of industry, or on measures to encourage the migration of people? And which industry and which people do we have in mind? Some favour leaving the main initiative for change to the local communities themselves, even though the process of education and voluntary action may be slow. Others argue that the problems are too pressing and that there is little hope of achieving substantial results within an acceptable time period in this way. The chronic differences in educational achievement across the country, regarded as one of the causes of income inequality, are not likely to disappear if left solely to local initiative. The areas offering the poorest education are precisely those least able to help themselves.

At the township and municipal level prolonged distress may lead to apathy; but often rivalries are keen, and local development associations compete with each other to gain a greater share of the over-all economic expansion, bringing what pressure they can to bear on provincial governments to support them in their efforts.

Recognition of this rivalry, combined with experience in the implementation of specific measures, has led to a belief in the virtues of planning regional development in a more systematic way. Even when they have begun with a modest enough objective, those concerned with the formulation of policies have often found themselves faced with a situation where one step seems to lead inexorably to another. Assistance to the "marginal" farmer, to cite one example, has led to the question of his alternative employment, and from this to the limited opportunities available to rural workers in general. Proposals to expand those opportunities have given rise to recommendations and measures to improve education, encourage the mobility of workers, increase social capital, and provide incentives to induce industry to locate in certain areas. Each of these measures leads to still others. It soon becomes obvious that all of them are interrelated, and that their efficacy depends upon integrating them into a coherent program of development. Judging from the experience of certain other countries, moreover, effective planning for regional development may entail integration in a national plan. The issues involved raise fundamental questions of an ideological nature concerning Canada's social and political objectives, as well as the interrelationship of its various levels of government.

A great variety of policies bear on the subject of area development. Some, designed to encourage the growth of specific sectors of the economy, may have very important regional implications, for sectoral growth has a spatial aspect. By way of illustration, the tariff on manufactured goods and assistance to particular primary industries benefits some areas of the country more than others. Federal defence and other expenditures may also have an uneven regional impact. These spatial effects may be as important as they are fortuitous. The present enquiry, however, is concerned with those policies which are framed specifically to influence regional patterns rather than with those whose regional impact is not deliberately intended.

The proliferating agencies and bodies at the national as well as the provincial level pursue their individual objectives, and overlapping functions as well as serious gaps and conflicts result. ARDA, for example, cannot fulfil the objectives of rural development without support in the form of industrial development, but little is forthcoming since ADA is concerned solely with designated areas and with the reduction of unemployment rather than with measures designed to sustain a viable industrial expansion. With the passage of time, certain bodies such as ARDA have changed and added to their objectives, but however desirable such changes may be, they have added to confusion in the public mind as to the direction in which we are going.

The rapidity with which changes in the structure of the economy are taking place and the magnitude of these changes add an urgency to policy decisions. An instance of this is the trend towards urbanization and the concentration of population in larger centres which necessitates major investment decisions that will affect the location of schools, hospitals, and other forms of social overhead capital. Projections of future population patterns will not only influence but be influenced by these decisions. Whether we intend it or not, capital expenditures on a large scale can be expected to have a significant and perhaps decisive bearing on future population distribution, hastening the decline of some areas and the expansion of others.

One of the basic difficulties in framing regional economic policies is the lack of reliable and adequate data on which to base such policies. The designation of areas for development by the Area Development Agency, to note one example, has turned upon statistical material which is both obsolete and suspect. There is an urgent need for more statistical information on a sub-provincial basis. This would not only make it easier to identify areas requiring assistance, it would also indicate the direction that remedial action might take.

A second and more fundamental difficulty in the designing of policies is the absence of an adequate theoretical framework for the study of regional questions. The works of Hirschman and Perroux, especially, offer revealing insights into the regional growth process, but the regional economist is obliged to rely heavily on his own intuition regarding the steps that should be taken to achieve whatever goals he regards as appropriate. He soon finds himself, moreover, immersed in the speculations of sociologists, in the niceties of inter-governmental administration, and in constitutional questions concerning responsibility for providing certain services such as education. He can, of course, take a detached Olympian view of the whole scene, but if he does this he is likely to find that his contributions to the discussion of policy are not taken very seriously by those on whom the burden of decision must fall.

It is the purpose of this book to look at the above issues, to examine area development policies as they affect the Canadian scene, and to consider some of the factors involved in their formulation. Following a brief sketch of some of the spatial characteristics of the Canadian economy, attention will be turned to the forces influencing industrial location decisions and population movements. Too often policies to influence locational decisions are introduced without sufficient regard for the underlying technological and market forces that are constantly modifying the relative merits of alternative locations. This discussion is followed by an examination of the complex concept of a region, the factors which contribute to regional growth, and the problems involved in its measurement. With the foregoing as background, attention is then directed to the various reasons advanced for the introduction of regional development policies, to the problems of planning and the evaluation of programs, and, more especially, to a discussion of the policies themselves.

The problems of economic development in the large, very sparsely populated areas in the northern parts of the country are discussed briefly in Chapter 11, but otherwise receive only passing mention. Area development policies, as conventionally understood and associated with the Departments of Industry and Forestry and with the Atlantic Development Board, are not designed to open up parts of the country which are largely uninhabited, though provincial governments have at times exerted pressure on the federal government to include some of these areas in its programs of assistance and there have been occasions when the federal government has been obliged to give way.

A final chapter summarizes the main issues. A statistical appendix by Thomas K. Rymes provides the reader with an examination of Regional Accounts.

The main discussion centres on the economic aspects of the subject, but in the full realization that the issues involved in area economic development are more than just "economic", in the narrow sense of that term. As observed at various points in the discussion, political, sociological, and administrative considerations lie at the root of development programs. Those who forget this are likely to find themselves engaged in speculation of little relevance to the world around them. The need for close collaboration between social scientists in different fields is nowhere more obvious than in the consideration of problems of regional development.

The subject is a large and comparatively unexplored one, and this study does little more than review some of the main issues. It is hoped, however, that it will serve as a useful introduction to university students and others concerned with this important aspect of Canadian economic policy, as well as to the many individuals whose work entails a consideration of regional development and who feel the need for a broader perspective.

*1. Spatial Characteristics
of the Economy*

ANY GOVERNMENT which seeks to influence the
spatial patterns of economic activity and encourage development
in the lower income areas of the country must reflect not only on
the present situation but on those trends which can be expected to
bear on the future. Information is necessary on the changing patterns of population distribution and industrial activity, the reasons
underlying those changes, and the regional differences in income
and employment opportunity with which they are associated.
Developments in one region have repercussions on another, and a
study of this interrelationship is desirable and perhaps indispensable. In undertaking such a study, decisions should be reached on
the specific spatial boundaries to be considered, for variations in
those boundaries may influence materially the picture which is
presented as well as the action needed to effect such changes as
appear desirable.

This chapter, sketching in some of the significant spatial characteristics of the economy, is intended as a prelude to the discussion
which follows and is for the benefit of those readers in particular
who may lack familiarity with the Canadian scene.

## The Distribution of Population

The population of Canada is now four times as great as it was at the turn of the century and it is still growing rapidly; but except for the narrow strip north of the United States border extending unevenly across the country from the Atlantic Ocean to the Pacific the country remains sparsely populated and undeveloped, having a population density of nine per square mile, or five if the Yukon and Northwest Territories are included. Inhabitants of the Northwest Territories and the Yukon, which together take in an area of almost one and a half million square miles, total less than forty thousand. Most of this forty thousand, moreover, live in two or three centres, and vast areas of the North are completely uninhabited. Of the total population of the country over sixty per cent live in the two central provinces, Ontario and Quebec, the metropolitan areas of Toronto and Montreal alone accounting for about one fifth. Toronto and Montreal have a population as great as that of all four Atlantic provinces, and fifty times as great as that of the Yukon and the Northwest Territories combined.

The distribution of the population by province for the decennial census years and the factors involved in the growth of that population are shown in Tables 1:1 and 1:2.

It will be observed in these tables that the pace of development has been very uneven. There have been wide differences in the rate of population increase between the provinces and from decade to decade. The population of Saskatchewan increased over five times between 1901 and 1911 with the opening up of the wheat lands, but fell between 1931 and 1951. The population of Prince Edward Island was virtually the same in 1961 as it was at the turn of the century, whereas that of Alberta increased eighteen times. In the Yukon and Northwest Territories, in spite of a doubling of the population between 1941 and 1961, the total population was less in 1961 than in 1901, largely because of a sharp fall in the first decade of the century. Six provinces experienced a net out-migration between 1951 and 1961, while Ontario experienced a heavy inflow of migrants which was more

# Table 1:1
## Distribution of Population and Percentage Change
## Decennial Census Years 1901 to 1961

(numerical distribution in thousands)

| | 1901 | 1911 | 1921 | 1931 | 1941 | 1951 | 1961 |
|---|---|---|---|---|---|---|---|
| Newfoundland* | 220 | 242 | 263 | 281 | 303 | 361 | 458 |
| Prince Edward Island | 103 | 94 | 89 | 88 | 95 | 98 | 105 |
| Nova Scotia | 460 | 492 | 524 | 513 | 578 | 643 | 737 |
| New Brunswick | 331 | 352 | 388 | 408 | 457 | 516 | 598 |
| Quebec | 1,649 | 2,006 | 2,361 | 2,875 | 3,332 | 4,056 | 5,259 |
| Ontario | 2,183 | 2,527 | 2,934 | 3,432 | 3,788 | 4,598 | 6,236 |
| Manitoba | 255 | 461 | 610 | 700 | 730 | 777 | 922 |
| Saskatchewan | 91 | 492 | 758 | 922 | 896 | 832 | 925 |
| Alberta | 73 | 374 | 588 | 732 | 796 | 940 | 1,332 |
| British Columbia | 179 | 392 | 525 | 694 | 818 | 1,165 | 1,629 |
| Yukon Territory | 27 | 9 | 4 | 4 | 5 | 9 | 15 |
| Northwest Territories | 20 | 7 | 8 | 9 | 12 | 16 | 23 |
| CANADA | 5,371 | 7,207 | 8,788 | 10,377 | 11,507 | 14,009 | 18,238 |

(% change from preceding census)

| | | | | | | | |
|---|---|---|---|---|---|---|---|
| Newfoundland | — | — | — | — | — | — | 10.3 |
| Prince Edward Island | − 5.3 | − 9.2 | − 5.5 | − 0.7 | 8.0 | 3.6 | 5.4 |
| Nova Scotia | 2.0 | 7.1 | 6.4 | − 2.1 | 12.7 | 11.2 | 6.1 |
| New Brunswick | 3.1 | 6.3 | 10.2 | 5.2 | 12.0 | 12.7 | 7.8 |
| Quebec | 10.8 | 21.6 | 17.7 | 21.8 | 15.9 | 21.7 | 13.6 |
| Ontario | 3.2 | 15.8 | 16.1 | 17.0 | 10.4 | 21.4 | 15.4 |
| Manitoba | 67.3 | 80.8 | 32.2 | 14.8 | 4.2 | 6.4 | 8.4 |
| Saskatchewan | — | 439.5 | 53.8 | 21.7 | − 2.8 | − 7.2 | 5.1 |
| Alberta | — | 412.6 | 57.2 | 24.3 | 8.8 | 18.0 | 18.6 |
| British Columbia | 82.0 | 119.7 | 33.7 | 32.3 | 17.8 | 42.5 | 16.5 |
| Yukon Territory | — | −68.7 | −51.2 | 1.8 | 16.2 | 85.1 | 20.0 |
| Northwest Territories | −79.7 | −67.7 | 25.1 | 14.4 | 29.1 | 33.1 | 19.1 |
| CANADA | 11.1 | 34.2 | 21.9 | 18.1 | 10.9 | 21.8 | 13.4 |

Note: Figures do not add to totals in all cases because of rounding.
*Populations of Newfoundland (not part of Canada until 1949) were: 1901, 220,984; 1911, 242,619; 1921, 263,033; 1931, 281,500 (estimated); 1941, 303,300 (estimated); and 1945, 321,819.

Source: D.B.S, *Canada Year Book, 1962*, p. 1196.

## Table 1:2
## Factors in the Growth of Population
## 1951-1961

| | 1951 Census | Natural increase | Actual increase | Net migration | 1961 Census |
|---|---|---|---|---|---|
| | | Population (thousands) | | | |
| Newfoundland | 361 | 111 | 96 | − 15 | 458 |
| Prince Edward Island | 98 | 18 | 6 | − 11 | 105 |
| Nova Scotia | 643 | 128 | 94 | − 34 | 737 |
| New Brunswick | 516 | 119 | 82 | − 37 | 598 |
| Quebec | 4,056 | 998 | 1,204 | 205 | 5,259 |
| Ontario | 4,598 | 953 | 1,639 | 685 | 6,236 |
| Manitoba | 777 | 150 | 145 | − 5 | 922 |
| Saskatchewan | 832 | 172 | 93 | − 79 | 925 |
| Alberta | 940 | 265 | 392 | 127 | 1,332 |
| British Columbia | 1,165 | 224 | 464 | 240 | 1,629 |
| Yukon and North-west Territories | 25 | 9 | 13 | 3 | 38 |
| CANADA | 14,009 | 3,148 | 4,229 | 1,081 | 18,238 |

Note: Figures do not add to totals in all cases because of rounding.

Source: D.B.S., *Canada Year Book, 1962*, p. 1196.

than three times as great as that into Quebec.[1] The heavy migration into Ontario has offset the generally greater natural increase
in Quebec, and has contributed to the dominance of Ontario in
the economy of the country, a dominance not without political
overtones.

[1] In his study "Regional Aspects of Canada's Economic Growth 1890–
1929", *Canadian Journal of Economics and Political Science*, XXXIII, no.
2 (May 1967), 232–45, Alan G. Green estimates that by 1929 the Prairie
provinces and British Columbia accounted for approximately 28 per cent of
countrywide gross value added, whereas in 1890 they had accounted for
only about 8 per cent, the bulk of this increase taking place by 1910. He
notes too that the rapid countrywide economic growth between 1890 and
1910 was accompanied by a growing divergence in output per capita
among the provinces.

Although net immigration from other countries has been very heavy at certain periods, internal migration from one province to another and from rural to urban areas has far exceeded it. Net immigration to Canada between 1921 and 1961 totalled almost a million and a half people, but that figure amounted to less than half the movement of people out of farming areas.[1]

The shift from rural to urban living has proceeded extremely rapidly in Canada. In fact the Economic Council has expressed the view that Canada may have had the fastest rate of urban growth among the countries of the Western world in the post-war period as a whole, and it foresees the possibility of a dramatically faster rate of urban growth than that of other industrial economies over the years ahead.[2] In 1901 the rural population accounted for some 60 per cent of the whole, by 1921 it had dropped to a little over 50 per cent, and by 1961 the urban population had risen to over 60 per cent, reversing the position at the turn of the century. The most notable drop was in agricultural labour, which constituted almost half the total work force in the final quarter of the last century and had dropped to less than 8 per cent by 1966.

The degree of urbanization, however, differs greatly among the provinces. As seen from Table 1:3, Prince Edward Island, New Brunswick, and Saskatchewan are predominantly rural, Newfoundland is about equally divided, and Ontario is the most urbanized.

The depressed conditions which prevail in many rural areas have constituted one of the spurs to migration and, as discussed in later chapters, have prompted a number of regionally oriented policies on the part of the government to encourage an improve-

---

[1] See Isabel Anderson, *Internal Migration in Canada, 1921–61* (Economic Council of Canada, Staff Study No. 13 [Ottawa: Queen's Printer, 1966]). Miss Anderson also makes the point that the rates of internal migration in Canada have been even greater than those experienced over long periods in the United States. Foreign born people in Canada seem to be more mobile than native born, and this is true also of their children. Regional differences also manifest themselves, Westerners being readier to move than Easterners who are often native to several generations.

[2] Economic Council of Canada, *Fourth Annual Review: The Canadian Economy from the 1960's to the 1970's* (Ottawa: Queen's Printer, 1967), pp. 177–8.

**Table 1:3**
**Distribution of Rural and Urban Population**
**1961**

| | Rural | | | Urban | | | | | Rural as % of urban |
| | Farm* | Non-farm | Total | Population of Centre | | | | | |
| | | | | 1,000 to 9,999 | 10,000 to 29,999 | 30,000 to 99,999 | 100,000 or over | Total | |
|---|---|---|---|---|---|---|---|---|---|
| | | | (thousands) | | | | | | |
| Newfoundland | 9 | 217 | 226 | 99 | 48 | 85 | — | 232 | 97 |
| Prince Edward Island | 35 | 36 | 71 | 16 | 18 | — | — | 34 | 296 |
| Nova Scotia | 57 | 280 | 336 | 75 | 49 | — | 276 | 401 | 84 |
| New Brunswick | 62 | 258 | 320 | 80 | 62 | 136 | — | 278 | 115 |
| Quebec | 565 | 788 | 1,353 | 606 | 278 | 385 | 2,638 | 3,906 | 35 |
| Ontario | 506 | 907 | 1,413 | 632 | 298 | 935 | 2,959 | 4,824 | 29 |
| Manitoba | 171 | 161 | 333 | 72 | 51 | — | 466 | 589 | 62 |
| Saskatchewan | 305 | 222 | 527 | 109 | 48 | 129 | 112 | 398 | 132 |
| Alberta | 286 | 203 | 489 | 158 | 44 | 35 | 605 | 843 | 58 |
| British Columbia | 78 | 370 | 447 | 161 | 153 | — | 868 | 1,182 | 38 |
| Yukon Territory | — | 10 | 10 | 5 | — | — | — | 5 | 191 |
| Northwest Territories | — | 14 | 14 | 9 | — | — | — | 9 | 157 |
| CANADA | 2,073 | 3,465 | 5,538 | 2,022 | 1,049 | 1,705 | 7,924 | 12,700 | 44 |

Note: Figures do not add to totals in all cases because of rounding.

*Excludes 55,615 persons living on farms in localities classed as urban.

Source: D.B.S., *Canada Year Book, 1965*, p. 165.

ment in economic conditions in those areas.

The urban population has not only increased, it has tended to concentrate in the larger centres. The two largest metropolitan areas may soon have a total population as great as that of all rural areas combined. Over one half of Canada's entire population now lives within 150 miles of the three largest cities. This concentration seems likely to continue unless measures are taken to reduce it.

## The Distribution of Manufacturing Activity

Manufacturing activity is also overwhelmingly concentrated in urban centres. In the decade between 1950 and 1960, the six metropolitan areas of Montreal, Toronto, Hamilton, Vancouver, Windsor, and Winnipeg gained 1,287 establishments; the rest of the country, by contrast, showed a *decline* of 547. In 1961, these same metropolitan areas, with approximately 32 per cent of the national population, accounted together for 48 per cent of the selling value of factory shipments in Canada.[1]

In 1962 the province of Ontario accounted for half the entire value of factory shipments in the country, Quebec for 30 per cent, the Prairies and British Columbia for 8 per cent each, and the combined Atlantic provinces for only 4 per cent. This high degree of concentration is still more marked when attention is paid to sub-provincial areas. For instance, within Ontario manufacturing is heavily concentrated in the Toronto metropolitan area and is very limited in the North.

Table 1:4 casts further light on the distribution of economic activity.[2] From this table, it will be noted that the concentration of

[1] This is a much higher degree of concentration than in the United States where, in 1961, 37.5 per cent of the nation's value added by manufacture was accounted for by *ten* metropolises containing 27 per cent of the 1960 population.

[2] The table is a modification of one prepared by D. W. Slater and presented in his paper "Trends in Industrial Locations in Canada" at the Resources for Tomorrow Conference held in Montreal in 1961. See *Resources for Tomorrow: Conference Background Papers* (Ottawa: Queen's Printer, 1961), I, 410. More recent data have been included here; Newfoundland has been added to the Maritime Provinces, and certain minor changes in classification have been made.

## Table 1:4
## Distribution of Population, Labour Force, and
## Manufacturing Employment
## 1961

| | Atlantic provinces | Quebec | Ontario | Prairies | British Columbia |
|---|---|---|---|---|---|
| | | | (%) | | |
| (a) Population | 10.43 | 28.90 | 34.26 | 17.47 | 8.95 |
| (b) Urban population | 7.44 | 30.79 | 38.02 | 14.43 | 9.32 |
| (c) Labour force | 8.70 | 27.38 | 37.05 | 17.93 | 8.94 |
| (d) Non-primary labour force* | 8.40 | 28.19 | 38.91 | 15.13 | 9.37 |
| (e) Employees in manufacturing | 5.54 | 33.21 | 45.80 | 7.41 | 8.05 |
| (f) Employees in manufacturing (excluding primary and local)† | 2.79 | 37.21 | 50.39 | 6.24 | 3.37 |

*Density measures* (concentration of manufacturing jobs relative to other characteristics):

| | | | | | |
|---|---|---|---|---|---|
| (e) as % of (a) | 53.1 | 114.9 | 133.7 | 42.4 | 89.9 |
| (e) as % of (b) | 74.5 | 107.9 | 120.5 | 51.4 | 86.4 |
| (e) as % of (d) | 66.0 | 117.8 | 117.7 | 49.0 | 85.9 |
| (f) as % of (b) | 37.5 | 120.9 | 132.5 | 43.2 | 36.2 |

Note: Figures do not add to 100% in all cases because of rounding.

*Excluding labour force in agriculture, fishing, forestry, and mining.

†Excluding foods and beverages, wood products, paper products, printing and allied industries, and primary metal.

Source: D.B.S., *1961 Census of Canada*, Vol. I (92-536) and Vol. III (94-518).

manufacturing activity in Ontario and Quebec appears even greater if primary manufacturing and manufacturing for a local market are excluded. Manufacturing for markets outside the Atlantic provinces amounts to less than 3 per cent, in contrast to over 50 per cent for Ontario.

## Table 1:5
## Personal Income* Expressed as a Per Cent of the Canadian Average
## 1926 to 1965 (various years)

(as % of the national average)

| | 1926 | 1929 | 1933 | 1939 | 1946 | 1950 | 1955 | 1959 | 1961 | 1963 | 1965 |
|---|---|---|---|---|---|---|---|---|---|---|---|
| Newfoundland | | | | | | 51 | 54 | 55 | 60 | 58 | 59 |
| Prince Edward Island | 57 | 59 | 51 | 53 | 58 | 56 | 55 | 62 | 62 | 63 | 69 |
| Nova Scotia | 67 | 71 | 77 | 76 | 86 | 74 | 73 | 75 | 77 | 74 | 75 |
| New Brunswick | 64 | 65 | 66 | 65 | 75 | 69 | 65 | 66 | 68 | 66 | 69 |
| Quebec | 85 | 92 | 94 | 88 | 82 | 85 | 85 | 85 | 88 | 87 | 88 |
| Ontario | 114 | 122 | 129 | 124 | 115 | 121 | 120 | 119 | 118 | 117 | 115 |
| Manitoba | 109 | 98 | 93 | 90 | 103 | 100 | 95 | 100 | 97 | 97 | 97 |
| Saskatchewan | 102 | 67 | 47 | 77 | 97 | 87 | 93 | 87 | 78 | 107 | 99 |
| Alberta | 113 | 92 | 74 | 87 | 108 | 103 | 103 | 104 | 102 | 100 | 99 |
| British Columbia† | 121 | 128 | 132 | 125 | 114 | 123 | 122 | 118 | 116 | 114 | 115 |

*Includes all transfer payments and imputed net income of farmers.
†Includes Yukon and Northwest Territories, 1926 to 1950.

Source: Calculated from D.B.S., *National Accounts, Income and Expenditure* (13-201), various years.

This high concentration of manufacturing activity in certain regions of the country is not peculiar to Canada. Throughout the world the output of manufactured goods is heavily concentrated in certain regions or belts of industrial production. Even in very industrialized countries such as the United States or those of western Europe there are extensive areas which contribute little to manufacturing output. A variety of factors account for this, and any attempt to modify the situation must take cognizance of the various forces which have created the present patterns and which can be expected to give rise to further change.

## Disparities in Income and Employment

In a country as large and diversified as Canada, it is to be expected that there will be substantial differences in economic potential between one area and another. As seen from Table 1:5 and Figures 1:1, 1:2(a) and 1:2(b) average incomes are much lower and unemployment is higher in some provinces than in others. The degree of economic stability also varies, though unequivocal conclusions concerning the causes of this and other differences may be difficult – partly because of inadequate data and partly because, as noted below, different concepts of growth produce different results. Levels of income and of unemployment show a striking regional pattern. Marked fluctuations in income are characteristic of Saskatchewan. As might be expected, high unemployment rates tend to be associated with low labour force participation rates, and participation rates for both males and females in the Atlantic provinces are generally well below those in the rest of the country, though the gap is narrowing. Participation rates for Ontario are the highest.

On the issue of income differentials specifically, a distinction can be drawn between gross income and disposable income after taxes. Less income tax is paid by residents in the poorer provinces on the average, and as a result net disposable incomes show a smaller regional variation than do gross incomes. A wider regional variation in income is manifest if attention is confined to income derived from work, transfer payments contributing a somewhat

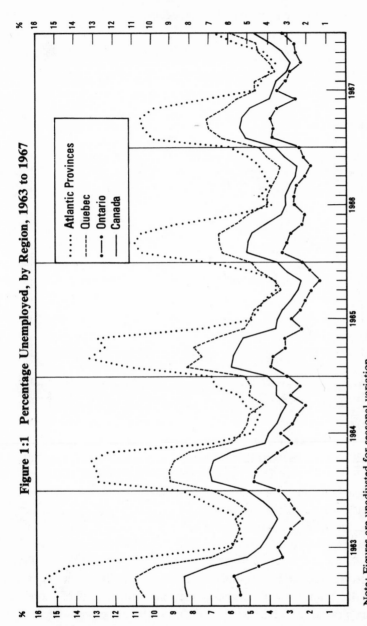

Figure 1:1  Percentage Unemployed, by Region, 1963 to 1967

Note: Figures are unadjusted for seasonal variation.

*Source: D.B.S.,* Canadian Statistical Review *(11-003), various months.*

### Figure 1:2(a)
### Participation Rates* for Males, by Region, 1950 to 1967

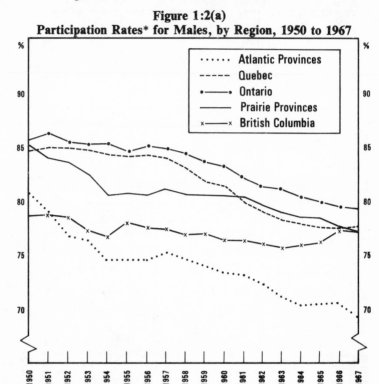

larger proportion of income to the poorer areas of the country. Table 1:6 indicates the magnitudes involved for the year 1966.

It will be observed that while total personal disposable income in Prince Edward Island was 68 per cent of the national average, earned income was only 57 per cent. Nova Scotia and New Brunswick also showed a marked difference between the two measures, with earned income being 8 and 6 percentage points lower respectively.

As for the distinction between real and nominal incomes, the view is sometimes expressed that it is cheaper to live in some parts of the country than in others, and that comparisons of money incomes fail to reflect differences in purchasing power. There is some evidence that the distinction between real and nominal incomes could be an important one in certain cases. The very low

## Figure 1:2(b)
## Participation Rates* for Females, by Region, 1950 to 1967

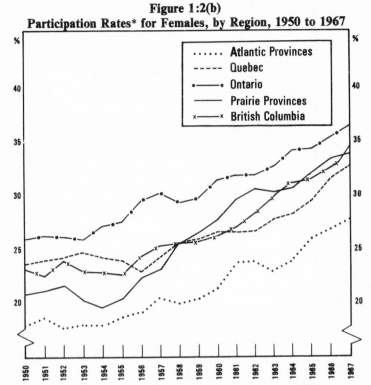

*The labour force as a percentage of the population age 14 and over, excluding inmates of institutions, members of armed forces, and Indians living on reserves.
*Source: D.B.S.*, The Labour Force (*71-001*).

incomes prevailing in Prince Edward Island, for example, imply a lower standard of living than actually seems to be the case. Many recreational amenities which are free in some parts of the country are expensive in others; costs of travel to and from work and the time involved in such travel also vary greatly, as do capacities to supplement income from unrecorded agricultural and related pursuits. These differences in purchasing power, which are not reflected in statistical data, may explain in part the reluctance of many people to migrate to areas where incomes are nominally higher.

## Table 1:6
## Source of Income
## 1966

($ per capita, unless otherwise noted)

| | Newfoundland | Prince Edward Island | Nova Scotia | New Brunswick | Quebec | Ontario | Manitoba | Saskatchewan | Alberta | British Columbia | CANADA |
|---|---|---|---|---|---|---|---|---|---|---|---|
| Wages and salaries (excluding military pay) | 947 | 716 | 1,024 | 1,006 | 1,348 | 1,746 | 1,276 | 956 | 1,335 | 1,736 | 1,465 |
| Net income from farm production | 4 | 101 | 11 | 23 | 33 | 67 | 181 | 702 | 290 | 45 | 102 |
| Net income from unincorporated businesses | 108 | 156 | 147 | 125 | 117 | 155 | 172 | 169 | 171 | 188 | 147 |
| Total earned income | 1,059 | 972 | 1,181 | 1,154 | 1,499 | 1,969 | 1,629 | 1,826 | 1,796 | 1,970 | 1,715 |
| % of national average | 62 | 57 | 69 | 67 | 87 | 115 | 95 | 106 | 105 | 115 | 100 |
| Interest dividends, net rental income | 67 | 101 | 149 | 120 | 190 | 290 | 219 | 203 | 204 | 259 | 227 |
| Government transfer payments | 237 | 284 | 246 | 266 | 244 | 243 | 249 | 253 | 273 | 278 | 250 |
| Balancing item* | −45 | +19 | +7 | −41 | −60 | −71 | −53 | −46 | −56 | −85 | −58 |
| Total personal income | 1,318 | 1,376 | 1,583 | 1,499 | 1,873 | 2,431 | 2,044 | 2,236 | 2,217 | 2,422 | 2,134 |

| % of national average | 62 | 64 | 74 | 70 | 88 | 114 | 96 | 105 | 104 | 113 | 100 |
|---|---|---|---|---|---|---|---|---|---|---|---|
| Direct taxes | −77 | −73 | −112 | −108 | −203 | −286 | −188 | −182 | −177 | −238 | −222 |
| Total personal disposable income | 1,241 | 1,303 | 1,471 | 1,391 | 1,670 | 2,145 | 1,856 | 2,054 | 2,040 | 2,184 | 1,912 |
| % of national average | 65 | 68 | 77 | 73 | 87 | 112 | 97 | 107 | 107 | 114 | 100 |
| Net transfer payments† | 160 | 211 | 134 | 158 | 41 | −43 | 61 | 71 | 96 | 40 | 28 |

Note: Figures do not add to totals in all cases because of rounding.

*Largely composed of military pay and allowances, less employer and employee contributions to social insurance and government pension funds.

†Government transfer payments less direct taxes as shown in the previous columns. Though data by province is not available, 50 per cent of the transfer payments at the national level were federal, 48 per cent provincial, and 2 per cent municipal.

Source: D.B.S., *National Accounts, Income and Expenditure* (13-201).

While in some cases nominal differences in income seem to be greater than real differences, in others the reverse seems to be true. It is common knowledge, for example, that prices of many items are higher in Newfoundland than on the mainland, a consequence of the transport costs involved. Housing, on the other hand, seems to be cheaper. One study made for the Economic Council of Canada indicates that the cost of living is probably highest in Newfoundland, followed by British Columbia, and that prices are generally somewhat higher in the Atlantic provinces than in central Canada and the Prairies.[1] There is considerable doubt, however, as to how much one can safely conclude from the evidence available.[2]

## *The Constancy of Regional Disparities*

Whatever the gaps in real income may be between one area of the country and another, it is of considerable interest to know whether or not the gaps are tending to diminish or to widen. In his study of interregional disparities in income, Chernick concludes that in the period from 1926 to 1964 there has been little or no change, and, moreover, that the ranking among regions remains much the same. The relatively prosperous regions have remained prosperous, and the poor have remained poor.[3] There is little evidence in the Canadian experience to support Kuznets's view that income inequality widens in the early and middle stages of economic development and then narrows as the economy approaches maturity.[4]

[1] Consumer price indexes for Canada and regional cities are made available by the D.B.S., but base year comparisons between cities are not. Technical difficulties in making inter-city comparisons arise out of differences in climate, consumer spending patterns, and the like. In *Interregional Disparities in Income* (Economic Council of Canada, Staff Study No. 14 [Ottawa: Queen's Printer, 1966]), by S. E. Chernick, a sample of items in major regional cities was priced which could serve as a preliminary basis for evaluating real income levels among regions.

[2] The reader who wishes to pursue the subject further is referred to John M. Munro, "The Measurement of Interregional Income Disparities in Canada", a paper presented to the annual meeting of the Canadian Political Science Association in Ottawa, June 1967 (mimeographed).

[3] Chernick, *op. cit.*, p. 65.

[4] Simon Kuznets, "Economic Growth and Income Inequality", *American Economic Review*, XLV (March 1955), 1–28.

In reviewing the historical trend of differences in income among the Canadian regions, other writers have also reached the conclusion that the relative per capita income among the main regions has changed little over the past thirty to forty years. There has been neither secular convergence nor divergence, though the fortunes of certain regions, particularly the Prairies, have varied greatly from one period to another.[1] Such conclusions, however, cannot be divorced from the statistical measures and techniques employed, and not all doubts on the subject have been resolved.[2]

If we are concerned with interregional comparisons of welfare it can be argued that the income per family is in some ways a more appropriate indicator than income per capita. Using the number of families as a denominator shows an increase in the rate of convergence and a reduction in the level of disparity.[3] If we are concerned with productivity rather than welfare, government transfer payments should be excluded from income, and the denominator should be the work force. In this regard, income per worker in agriculture differs widely between the various regions, being two to three times higher in the Prairies than in the Maritimes, and although income per worker in *non*-agricultural occupations differs much less among the various regions, it is none the less substantial, ranging in 1963 from $4,581 in British Columbia to $3,358 in the Maritimes.[4]

The range of difference becomes even wider if smaller areas are selected for comparison. The choice of spatial boundaries is thus

[1] See R. Marvin McInnis, "The Trend of Regional Income Differentials in Canada", a paper presented to the Canadian Political Science Association Conference in Statistics in Ottawa, June 1967 (*The Canadian Journal of Economics*, I, no. 2, May 1968, pp. 440–70). An exception might be made in the case of Newfoundland, which has been improving its position since joining Canada in 1948.

[2] Specifically, the belief that there has been a greater trend towards regional convergence of income in the United States than in Canada has been challenged. See, for example, the comments of Eva Tihanyi in *An Approach to the Study of Regional Labour Absorption; The Case of Saskatchewan, 1941–61* (Saskatoon: Centre for Community Studies, 1966), pp. 134–40. It makes a difference, for instance, whether a weighted or an unweighted index of disparity is used, since a relatively small and decreasing proportion of the Canadian population resides in the low-income provinces. The degree of disparity in the States, moreover, started out at much above the Canadian level (*ibid.*, p. 137). The respective size of the regions selected for comparison is also a significant variable.

[3] Munro, *op. cit.*, p. 41.    [4] Chernick, *op. cit.*, Table 5, p. 32.

of critical importance in evaluating the extent of disparities. Although convention and the availability of statistical data generally lead to the adoption of provincial boundaries or the boundaries of a combination of provinces for purposes of income comparison, the most striking differences in income are to be found at the sub-provincial level, between rural and urban areas and within the urban areas themselves.

In this last connection, there are more families with incomes below $3,000 a year in the prosperous metropolitan centres of Toronto and Montreal than there are in the four Atlantic provinces combined (see Table 1:7). The 1961 census also indicates that incomes in different districts of Montreal vary from $4,515 in Rivière des Prairies to $16,535 in Westmount. This is an important point, for it is not the average differences in income between rural and urban areas which are important to the rural migrant but the income which he personally can expect to enjoy if he makes the move. Urban poverty is not necessarily preferable to rural poverty and in some cases might even be worse.

In attempting to explain the disparities in income and employment opportunities across the country, it is possible to explore many different variables: among these, an investigation can be made of the significance of different age structures. A province with a relatively high proportion of children of school age and under will, other things being equal, have a lower labour force participation rate and per capita income. In some instances, lower income levels may be largely attributable to the industrial mix; for example, a high proportion of the labour force may be in subsistence agriculture. In other cases unemployment may be higher. Such studies, by quantifying the component elements in the disparities between regions, can help to clarify the problem.[1] But if we are to understand the *causes* of the differences, it is necessary to proceed further. Why does the age structure, industrial mix, or level of unemployment vary between regions? Why

[1] See, for example, Frank T. Denton, *An Analysis of Interregional Differences in Manpower Utilization and Earnings* (Economic Council of Canada, Staff Study No. 15 [Ottawa: Queen's Printer, 1966]).

## Table 1:7
## Families with Incomes Less Than $3,000
## a Year, Atlantic Provinces, Toronto, and Montreal
## 1961

| | Number of Families | | | Total under $3,000 | % of total families |
|---|---|---|---|---|---|
| | Under $1,000 | $1,000 to $1,999 | $2,000 to $2,999 | | |
| Newfoundland | 9,886 | 9,892 | 8,682 | 28,460 | 32.9 |
| Prince Edward Island | 1,175 | 1,365 | 1,159 | 3,699 | 25.7 |
| Nova Scotia | 10,409 | 10,382 | 9,894 | 30,685 | 20.9 |
| New Brunswick | 8,043 | 7,924 | 8,284 | 24,251 | 21.9 |
| Total Atlantic provinces | 29,513 | 29,563 | 28,019 | 87,095 | 24.3 |
| City of Toronto | 7,505 | 11,420 | 17,254 | 36,179 | 22.7 |
| City of Montreal | 10,041 | 17,258 | 28,567 | 55,866 | 20.1 |
| Total: Cities of Toronto and Montreal | 17,546 | 28,678 | 45,821 | 92,045 | 21.1 |
| Metropolitan Toronto | 13,192 | 20,176 | 31,525 | 64,893 | 14.1 |
| Metropolitan Montreal | 15,375 | 25,359 | 42,235 | 82,969 | 17.2 |
| Total: Metropolitan areas of Toronto & Montreal | 28,567 | 45,535 | 73,760 | 147,862 | 15.7 |

Source: D.B.S., *1961 Census of Canada*, Vol. IV (98-503).

do inequalities of income persist over such long periods, given the mobility of the factors of production?

Economic geographers in Canada are few in number and have not for the most part concerned themselves with such issues. There is, as a result, little literature on which the student of Canadian economic geography can draw in seeking answers to these questions.[1] The chapter that follows looks at some of the changing patterns of industrial location and the forces underlying them.

[1] A start might be made with the study by P. Camu, E. P. Weeks, and Z. W. Sametz, *Economic Geography of Canada: with an Introduction to the 68-region System* (Toronto: Macmillan, 1964). See also Richard E. Caves and Richard H. Holton, *The Canadian Economy: Prospect and Retrospect* (Cambridge, Mass.: Harvard University Press, 1959), and the study which has become a classic by W. A. Mackinosh, *The Economic Background of Dominion-Provincial Relations* which formed Appendix 3 to the Rowell-Sirois Report (Report of the Royal Commission on Dominion-Provincial Relations) (Ottawa: King's Printer, 1939). Professor Mackintosh is concerned not only with historical economic developments as they affected different parts of the country but also with the regional effects of national policies. The study has since been republished in the Carleton Library Series, No. 13 (Toronto: McClelland & Stewart, 1964).

# 2. Industrial Location
# and Its Determinants

## The Historical Importance of the Staples

SWEEPING CHANGES have taken place in the location of economic activity in Canada over the past century, one of the most notable of these being the rapid growth of output in the West. Associated with these changes has been the ascendancy and decline in the importance of particular industries. Pulp and paper, oil and gas, and the non-ferrous mining industries have expanded rapidly. Other industries have shown little or no expansion or, as in the case of some of the earlier staples, have been characterized by an absolute decline.[1]

The dominant role played in Canadian economic development by the export of products having a large natural resource content is seemingly incontrovertible, and the varying fortunes of particular regions of the country can be explained largely in terms of the changing demand for and supply of these "staples". Fishing attracted settlers to the eastern seaboard; the fur trade encouraged extensive exploration; demand for timber for British ship con-

---

[1] Caves and Holton, *op. cit.*, analyse the historical forces at work which have affected the fortunes of certain industries and regions, drawing attention to the major studies by Innis, Buckley, Easterbrook and Aitken, and others. See also the study by Alan G. Green, *op. cit.*

struction spurred the early development of the Atlantic provinces. These in turn were followed by the enormous production of wheat in the West, by pulp and paper production, and more recently still by non-ferrous metals, oil, and gas. These are the basic developments which provide the broad background to the study of industrial location in Canada. Whether the development of new staples will be the path along which the main lines of expansion occur in the future is, however, by no means certain.[1]

In recent years, as Table 2:1 shows, there has been a striking difference in the extent to which different provinces and regions of the country have shared in this over-all expansion.

British Columbia, in contrast to other parts of the country, has increased output in the agriculture, forestry, and fishing and trapping sectors. All areas have increased their output in mining, construction, and electric power, but the Prairies have achieved by far the greatest gains here, and also in the manufacturing sector. Once again the Prairies are experiencing a period of rapid economic development. In the past the explanation lay in the vast expansion of wheat production; now it lies in the discovery of rich natural resources of oil, gas, and potash.

These recent changes, however, need to be kept in perspective. In terms of net value added by industry per capita, Ontario dominates the manufacturing scene overwhelmingly, and is followed by Quebec and British Columbia. The Prairie provinces are still far behind. Saskatchewan produces by far the greatest output of farm products at $981 per capita in 1963, followed by Alberta at $361. Alberta leads in the value of mineral products per capita at $423. British Columbia is well above its nearest competitor in forestry at $214 per capita.[2]

---

[1] See, in this regard, H. E. English, "The Canadian Industrial Structure: an Essay in its Nature and Efficiency", *Contemporary Canada*, ed. Richard H. Leach (Publication No. 32, Durham, N.C.: Duke University Commonwealth Studies Center, 1967). In discussing aspects of the staple theory, the author observes that the development of staples no longer deserves pride of place in the explanation of Canadian economic growth.

[2] Changes in statistical classifications and definitions make it difficult to trace out details of long-run changes in individual industries with certainty, however.

**Table 2:1**
**Net Value Added by Industry**
**1951 and 1963**

| | Agriculture, forestry, fishing, and trapping | | | Mining, construction electric power | | | Manufactures | | | Total | | |
|---|---|---|---|---|---|---|---|---|---|---|---|---|
| | *($ per capita)* | | *%* | *($ per capita)* | | *%* | *($ per capita)* | | *%* | *($ per capita)* | | *%* |
| | *1951* | *1963* | *Change* | *1951* | *1963* | *Change* | *1951* | *1963* | *Change* | *1951* | *1963* | *Change* |
| Atlantic provinces | 132 | 104 | −21 | 140 | 262 | +87 | 185 | 226 | +22 | 456 | 593 | +30 |
| Quebec | 131 | 82 | −37 | 178 | 283 | +59 | 514 | 656 | +28 | 823 | 1,022 | +24 |
| Ontario | 164 | 112 | −32 | 208 | 318 | +53 | 776 | 1,014 | +31 | 1,148 | 1,445 | +26 |
| Prairie provinces | 580 | 505 | −13 | 231 | 584 | +153 | 155 | 284 | +83 | 967 | 1,373 | +42 |
| British Columbia | 239 | 300 | +26 | 317 | 409 | +29 | 508 | 626 | +23 | 1,064 | 1,335 | +25 |
| CANADA | 233 | 189 | −19 | 205 | 357 | +74 | 495 | 665 | +34 | 933 | 1,121 | +30 |
| Per cent of total | 25.0 | 15.6 | | 22.0 | 29.5 | | 53.1 | 54.9 | | 100.0 | 100.0 | |

Source: D.B.S., *Survey of Production* (61-202).

## *Technological Change and Other Influences Bearing on Locational Decisions*

In reviewing changes in provincial output and the location of industry, the importance of the natural resource base deserves special mention. But although the presence of rich natural resources has been a potent factor attracting various industries, such resources are not a prerequisite to regional growth, nor, as experience in the Canadian North illustrates, does their presence ensure a broadly based expansion in the area of discovery. The resource base is clearly only one of many variables explaining industrial location. Taking the world as a whole, the connection indeed appears a tenuous one; some of the most advanced industrial countries, such as Britain and Switzerland, have very limited natural resources of their own.

Given the great diversity of industry, it is apparent that the factors influencing location decision will differ markedly from one instance to another. There are some industries – the textile industry is one – whose location is strongly influenced by the ready availability of low-cost labour. Others which are heavy users of some particular input – aluminum production being a case in point – are attracted towards the sources of such supplies as water and electric power. The weight of items was at one time regarded as one of the most important variables in determining location patterns. Weber built a theoretical framework around their significance, suggesting that location decisions would be determined in large measure by the relative weights of inputs and outputs. Transportation costs figure more prominently in the determination of the location of industries producing items heavy in weight and low in value than of industries producing goods with a high value to weight ratio. Materials such as coal which lose weight in their conversion to a finished product tend to attract users to them. The development of industry close to the coal-fields in the nineteenth century was a manifestation of this. Processes which add weight tend, in contrast, to be pulled towards the market. In cases where the production of a single commodity involves a combination of a number of different materials, the predominant weight-losing material will be the one that tends to attract production to itself. As Colin Clark points out, however, the theory has now a quite restricted relevance "only in a very limited number of industries does the weight of the products to be transported play any significant part in location decisions". For the great majority of industries other forces are at work.[1]

It is the purpose of location theory to explain why economic activity takes place where it does. Earlier theorists, owing much to the work of Weber, placed emphasis on the least cost location, the market being taken for granted. Each seller was assumed to be faced with the same demand curve and market price regardless of location. More recently, "the market area school" has argued in contrast that if buyers are distributed over an area, they will influence the location of the sellers, who will each attempt to supply a different group of buyers.[2]

Recognition of the many factors influencing location has led to the classification of industries as "power oriented", "labour oriented", "transport oriented", "market oriented", and so on. Some industries which appear to have no strong locational preferences are conventionally described as "foot-loose". As a first step this sort of classification can be useful to those concerned with regional development, but it does not take us very far. For one thing, patterns of location are changing, and changing rapidly. Although inertia may cause an industry to remain in a certain location even though the considerations which gave rise to the choice of that location in the first place have disappeared, other

---

[1] See "Industrial Location and Economic Potential", *Lloyd's Bank Review*, No. 82 (October 1966), 6. Typically it is only in the early processing stages of production that the weight loss is a significant factor. Thereafter, loss of weight is only of minor importance in determining the choice of location.

[2] A survey of the landmarks in the theory of industrial location is provided by Melvin L. Greenhut in his study *Plant Location in Theory and in Practice* (Chapel Hill: University of North Carolina Press, 1956), Chapter 11. Professor Greenhut comments on the contributions of von Thünen, Weber, and Lösch, and also draws attention to more recent works by Fetter, Hotelling, Chamberlin, and others. See also the study of Peter Haggett, *Locational Analysis in Human Geography* (London: Edward Arnold, 1965). Haggett's study is one of the pioneering works of a new generation of geographers, and constitutes a complete departure from the descriptive type of survey that used to be characteristic of the field of economic geography.

forces may encourage its increasing concentration elsewhere. Continuing changes in technology, transportation, and cost structures result in the patterns of industrial location being in a constant state of flux. Illustrations of this abound: the iron and steel industry, automobile manufacture and assembly, and oil refining are cases which come immediately to mind.[1]

In the iron and steel industry, technological progress has permitted large reductions in the amount of coking coal needed to produce a ton of pig iron, and the "pull" of coking coal in the siting of blast furnaces has been correspondingly reduced. Similarly, the introduction of electricity in the production of steel has attracted furnaces to the sources of large supplies of cheap electric power. As for other inputs, the expanded use of scrap metal in steel production has also had an important bearing on the choice of location, pulling the industry towards the large industrial centres where such scrap is readily available. In general, the greater the economies achieved in raw material inputs, and such economies are continually being achieved, the greater the pull of the market is likely to be.

Oil refining, like the steel industry, has been subject to a variety of changing forces which have powerfully influenced its location. Improvements in technology have been especially prominent among these; they have made possible a much fuller utilization of crude oil and opened up markets for end products which formerly did not exist. During the early years of the oil industry, which is little more than a hundred years old, the disposal of waste products posed a serious problem and led to the location of refineries near the oil wells. Now, since virtually the whole of the crude oil can be used, the market has exerted a much more powerful pull on the siting of refineries. The economies in refining made possible by very large-scale operations have contributed to the disappearance of smaller plants and the concentration of

[1] For a discussion of these, see Robert C. Estall and R. O. Buchanan, *Industrial Activity and Economic Geography* (London: Hutchinson, 1961), and Edgar M. Hoover, *The Location of Economic Activity* (New York: McGraw Hill, 1948) – especially Chapter 10, "Technology and Locational Change".

output in larger ones, and in the last few years further important developments have been introduced. Pipelines and giant tankers have reduced transport costs, and both have influenced the siting.[1]

If we are to influence effectively the location of industry, a knowledge of what technological and other forces bear on locational decisions is indispensable, since, in the absence of such knowledge, there is a risk that policies will prove misguided. It is not enough just to extrapolate past trends; an estimate of probable future trends must be made. For example, increasing refinery complexity calls for even larger amounts of water in the cooling process and adds to the volume of waste load per barrel. But there are also offsetting factors of greater magnitude which arise from the integration of refinery processes and can lead to savings in an individual refinery of several thousand gallons per minute of cooling water capacity. A marked increase in refinery capacity is thus most unlikely to result in a corresponding demand for fresh-water intake, a factor having an obvious bearing on location decisions. Similarly, in the case of the pulp and paper industry, the rising proportion of coloured paper products has led to a marked increase in the amount of water needed to produce a given output, but offsetting this increase are very great economies which have been achieved through closed cooling systems, reduction in waste, and the re-use of water.

The fact that it is often difficult to foresee the net effect of such technological changes is not, however, a reason for failing to obtain as much information on the subject as one can. Planning for regional development needs to be conducted in the light of the underlying forces at work. Attempts to encourage industry to locate in areas at variance with strong underlying trends are likely to lead to failure and frustration.

The prime consideration of the entrepreneur in deciding upon a particular location for production is the estimation of profit over a period of time. It is true that other considerations than expected profit will also weigh with him, but it is a safe initial generalization

[1] See the discussion on this by Peter R. Odell, *An Economic Geography of Oil* (London: Bell, 1965), especially Chapter 7.

that he will choose a locality where profit potentials appear to be greatest. One important qualification, however, needs to be borne in mind. Few entrepreneurs will make an extensive study of different locations when searching for an optimum location; most, rather, will choose between two or three which seem promising, since investigation is costly and time-consuming. To some extent decisions have to be made in the dark: the future cannot be foreseen with certainty, nor is it possible to know the advantages and disadvantages of all locations that might be available. Changes in technology leading to changes in the cost of production and distribution may completely upset earlier estimates. There is little point, therefore, in attempting minute calculations. Production costs, tastes and location of customers, transportation costs, are all variables.

Given the degree of uncertainty, a producer may well select a locality which offers him an opportunity to make modest rather than maximum profits but which also allows him to hedge against losses. In a locality with a large and varied market, for example, it may not be difficult to make substantial changes in the product mix. Such a locality may then be preferred to another whose locational advantages look better in the short run. The fact that costs appear to be lower in one locality than in another may thus be only one factor in the location decision; it is not necessarily the prime factor. Considerations involved in the distribution of products may weigh more heavily; the prompt availability of supplies or technical knowledge may be considered of particular importance; or the presence or absence of actual or potential competition may be decisive. A consideration of the institutional factors which influence location broadens the field of enquiry still further, introducing as it does the implications of variations in taxation, public policy, freight-rate structures and subventions, attitudes of the labour force, provision of public services, and the like.

Of particular importance in the explanation of location patterns are the external economies associated with close inter-industry relationships. Vertical, horizontal, and diagonal linkages can make possible very substantial savings in operating costs, or firms engaged in the same or related activities may contribute to and share services to their mutual benefit. Isolated firms can be at a great disadvantage in this respect. It is harder for them to keep in touch with developments, and they are apt to lack quick access to the specialized services more readily available to others. The interchange of ideas among firms engaged in the same and related fields is a spur to innovation. The grouping of firms also permits a higher degree of specialization in production, with attendant economies. Isolated firms are more dependent on their own resources and are obliged to undertake functions on their own which less isolated firms would allocate to others with more specialized knowledge.[1]

The nature and extent of the linkages between different industries is one of the most important elements to be considered in planning for regional development. If an industry has weak local linkages, it will import the great bulk of its inputs from other regions and send its outputs for further processing to distant points. If it has strong ones, it will tend to strengthen related industries in the area. As a result, the greater the local linkages one industry has with another, the greater will be the impact of its establishment on the regional economy.

In recommending the lines along which a region might be developed, a knowledge of the technical and economic relationships existing between industries and processes is thus of great value. Production engineers and industrial economists familiar with these relationships can frequently draw up a chain of potential forward and backward linkages, indicating the types of activity which are likely to prove feasible given the particular industries and the factor inputs currently available. A large part

[1] Case studies of the location of firms in the United Kingdom are very revealing of the way decisions are made and of the factors that are considered. It was noted in one of these that proximity to suppliers had not proved as important as was originally expected. Such proximity tended to lead to carelessness in the keeping of inventories and to frequent deliveries involving significant additions to cost even though the distances involved were small. See, for example, W. F. Luttrell, *Factory Location and Industrial Movement: a Study of Recent Experience in Great Britain* (London: The National Institute of Economic and Social Research, 1962), 2 vols.

of industrial investment arises directly out of the potential which one industry creates for another. By way of illustration, cotton ginning can lead to oilseed pressing and from there to the production of explosives, soap, animal feeds, and edible oils. These in turn can provide inputs for other industries as well as create a demand for various supplies which are necessary to their own production. If the interrelationship of particular industries and processes is not known, it is virtually impossible to focus assistance on those types of development which are likely to show the greatest promise. Here input-output studies can furnish a certain guide.

Associated with the phenomenon of linkages is the impact of location leaders. Location leaders are somewhat analogous to "price leaders", certain industries whose price policies set a pattern for others. Location leaders also set a pattern, in this case for the location of many related industries. Characteristically these are major industries whose linkages extend widely and deeply. In most industrial countries this would include heavy chemicals, engineering, iron and steel, oil refining, and automobile manufacture. Though there are exceptions, their location typically acts as a powerful magnet.[1] Either they provide raw materials or services to other industries or they use their end products on an extensive scale. They often form the nodal points around which industrial complexes have developed. As a result, their location is of particular importance to governments concerned with regional development policies. In the case of the United Kingdom, concern with the location of such industrial leaders has led to action forbidding car manufacturers to expand in certain areas of the country and to decisions determining the location of the steel industry. Since such industries are characteristically those in which there are overwhelming advantages to large-scale production, the number of plants is likely to be small and their location becomes of cardinal importance in development policies.

In an attempt to quantify the effect of different locations on

[1] This can work for better and for worse. If they fail, they are likely to bring down many other firms with them.

production costs, some efforts have been made to assess the relative production costs of particular types of industry in various parts of Canada. One such study comparing the manufacturing costs of certain firms in Nova Scotia with others in Ontario and Quebec suggested that the differences were not large. The costs of metal and chemical groups showed up as 5 per cent higher in Nova Scotia, and food and miscellaneous groups as 2 per cent lower.[1] The lower costs of the food-producing firms could be explained by the labour costs in Nova Scotia, which were 30 per cent lower and more than offset the higher costs of materials and other factors. In the case of the metal and chemical groups, the lower labour costs in Nova Scotia were not sufficient to offset the higher costs of other factors of production and transport. Taking all firms together, the cost of producing exclusively in Nova Scotia was calculated to be 2 per cent higher than the cost of producing that same output in a similar plant in Ontario or Quebec, a difference too small to account for the pull of these two provinces.

The difficulties in making studies of comparative costs are, of course, considerable. Apart from the problem of collecting information which may be regarded as confidential, costing procedures may differ from one firm to another. The matter is further complicated by different product mixes in output so that unit costs are hard to identify. While there is considerable uncertainty about the extent of cost differentials across the country, such studies are worth pursuing and provide a firmer basis for decisions on location policy than unsubstantiated assertions about the relative merits of different areas as locations for manufacturing activity.

The very fact that population is concentrated in certain areas is itself a factor which influences industrial location. Communities of different sizes, from the smallest rural settlement to the largest metropolitan area, are interconnected through a network of economic relationships, a matter which forms the substance of

[1] Roy E. George, "Costs of Manufacturing in Alternative Locations: Nova Scotia Compared with Ontario and Quebec" (mimeographed; Halifax: Dalhousie University, Department of Commerce, 1966), p. 29.

the literature on Christaller's central-place theory. The smaller the community, the narrower the range of services and goods that will be available in it. Highly specialized consumption goods and services are generally found only in the largest centres. The question thus arises as to what size a centre needs to be to attract a particular type of service or consumption outlet. And what are the probable future trends in an area, given a particular communications network and pattern of population distribution? Some very illuminating studies on these issues have been made, and more can be expected in future.[1] With the ease of travelling and the reduction in time required to reach larger centres, many smaller towns which at one time catered to local needs are now being by-passed. Some indication of the communities which seem likely to grow or to diminish in importance can be a valuable guide to those who are faced with the responsibility of recommending where efforts to encourage growth can most effectively be concentrated.

## Location Decision and International Influences

The existence of international boundaries greatly influences locational patterns of industry, and the higher the barriers to trade, the greater is their influence. Were Canada and the United States to reduce the tariff barriers between each other, a higher degree of economic specialization would become possible in Canada, and considerable change would occur in the location, structure, and relative expansion of particular industries. Plans to influence industrial locational patterns thus need to be viewed within the broader context of commercial policy.

In a recent study of the potential economic effects of free trade between the United States and Canada, the investigators divided the North American economy into eighteen regions and examined sixteen manufacturing sectors. Among other things, they compared total costs (labour, transportation, resource, and capital)

[1] One of the many excellent studies is *Service Centres* (Report No. 12 of the Royal Commission on Agriculture and Rural Life [Regina: Queen's Printer, 1957]), submitted to the Government of Saskatchewan.

in the metal products and chemical industries by region, ranking them as percentages that are higher or lower than in Ontario. Their investigation cast a helpful light on the question of which regions would most likely be attractive to industry. Quebec, Ontario, and British Columbia appear to have little to fear, but the Maritimes and Prairies compared unfavourably.[1]

Though less important in some ways, mention might also be made of a study of the determinants of the location of United States subsidiaries in Canada.[2] There are marked contrasts between eastern Ontario and the rapidly growing metropolitan areas of south-western Ontario, and the disparate rates of growth seemingly cannot be explained by internal factors such as labour costs or accessibility to the Canadian market. In this study, Michael Ray has argued that the failure of eastern Ontario to develop more rapidly can be explained largely in terms of the location of branch plants of United States subsidiaries. Since half the total of Canadian manufacturing industry is either owned outright or controlled by United States nationals, decisions on branch plant location made by parent companies in the United States can be expected to have an important bearing on the location of economic activity in Canada. Those decisions are influenced strongly by the desire of parent companies to maintain close contacts with branch plants, especially during the early days of a plant's operation when its need for outside technical and managerial services is especially great. Such plants tend, therefore, to be located where they are readily accessible to the parent company and, given the heavy concentration of manufacturing activity in the United States midwest, there is a corresponding concentration of subsidiaries in nearby southern Ontario. Investigation disclosed that the number of Ontario subsidiaries controlled from

[1] Ronald J. Wonnacott and Paul Wonnacott, *Free Trade Between the United States and Canada: the Potential Economic Effects* (Cambridge, Mass.: Harvard University Press, 1967).

[2] D. Michael Ray, *Market Potential and Economic Shadow* (Department of Geography, Research Paper No. 101 [University of Chicago Press, 1965]). See also his "Regional Aspects of Foreign Ownership of Manufacturing in Canada" (mimeographed; Waterloo: University of Waterloo, 1967).

any United States city was directly proportional to the number of establishments in that city and inversely proportional to its distance from the province, a relationship which could be expressed in an interactance or gravity model. Pressing the enquiry further, Professor Ray noted the strong pull that Toronto exerted on United States subsidiaries. Those localities lying at the far side of the city as seen from the parent company were in an "economic shadow" unattractive for the establishment of branch plants. While parent companies might choose other Canadian cities to locate in because of their proximity, the more distant they were from Ontario, the greater was the proportion of their Ontario subsidiaries located in Toronto. Thus a Detroit manufacturer would tend to select Windsor as a location for a branch plant, because of its accessibility, even though this was not the centre of the market, whereas a west coast manufacturer would tend to select Toronto. In contrast to southern Ontario, other parts of Ontario attract few United States subsidiaries and the Atlantic provinces attract even fewer.

The explanation for the location of United States subsidiaries in Canada is clearly worth investigation. It must not be forgotten, however, that the preferred locations for such subsidiaries are also the preferred locations of a great many Canadian firms. By explaining why Canadian industry locates where it does, we may find we have gone a long way towards accounting for the location patterns of United States subsidiaries in Canada.

One further point deserves emphasis. To the extent that regional subventions of one sort and another are given to influence the location of industry, their impact may extend well beyond national boundaries and it would seem from experience in Europe that some international regulation of regional aid is desirable.[1]

[1] In some instances, aid to industries in the poorer regions of a country is advocated not only because of the local employment and income effect but also because of the desire to reduce imports and increase exports. Were it not for the fact that most countries provide regional incentives and that it is difficult to identify the export subsidy involved, more complaints would probably be heard on this score.

# 3. The Demarcation
# of Regions

## The Concept and Classification of Regions

IT IS POSSIBLE to speak in general terms about "regional" or "area" problems without explaining precisely what we mean by a region or an area, and for many purposes, a specific delineation of the boundaries – or agreement on the criteria for drawing them – is not essential to useful discussion. In the same way, it is possible to talk about "rural" or "urban" problems in Canada without becoming enmeshed in the statistical definitions which distinguish urban areas from rural ones in the census classifications. None the less, boundaries which may be appropriate for one purpose may be inappropriate for another, and precision is essential when administrative action is involved. If a particular program applies only to "rural" areas, the administrator of the program needs to know precisely which communities will qualify under the program and which will not.

As observed in Chapter 1 on the spatial characteristics of the economy, the way in which particular boundaries are drawn modifies and in some cases transforms impressions of the extent of the disparities that prevail in income and employment. By varying the boundaries it is possible to either reveal or conceal

43

evidence of distress. If the Prairie provinces or the Atlantic provinces are treated as a unity, marked differences in prosperity and unemployment between the individual provinces are concealed. Similarly, if each province is treated as a whole, the data will conceal sharp differences at the sub-provincial level. There are pockets of distress and high unemployment even in the most prosperous provinces, and the high average income of certain cities veils the poverty that exists within individual districts. Sometimes quite modest changes in area boundaries will transform the picture which the statistics present and lead to a quite different impression of the need for remedial action. In general, the smaller the area selected, the greater will be its divergence from national averages in growth, stability, and level of income. Larger regions, in contrast, tend to reflect more closely the national picture.

The selection of boundaries in one way rather than another not only changes our perspective of the situation, it also influences the form that policy is likely to take.[1] The demarcation of boundaries to show up the isolated pockets of distress that may exist in an otherwise prosperous area can be expected to have different implications for policy than the demarcation of large regions in which there may be widespread but less acute distress.

As might be expected, it is the geographers who have devoted the greatest effort to the delineation of regions and the determination of spatial boundaries. Geographical literature abounds on the subject,[2] but much of it is of limited relevance for the economist concerned primarily with programs designed to encourage economic growth in less prosperous areas of the country, since geographers tend for the most part to be concerned with the description of the physical or social environment and not with the dynamics of development.

---

[1] There is a parallel on the political front. A relatively minor change in constituencies' boundaries can greatly influence electoral results.

[2] See, for example, David Grigg, "The Logic of Regional Systems", *Annals of the Association of American Geographers*, Vol. 55 (1965), 465–91, which contains many references to the literature. For a view of Canadian regions, see N. L. Nicholson and Z. W. Sametz, "Regions of Canada and the Regional Concept", *Resources for Tomorrow: Conference Background Papers* (Ottawa: Queen's Printer, 1961), I, 367–83.

According to the definition used by the American Association of Geographers, "a region is not an object either self-determined or nature given. It is an intellectual concept, an entity for the purposes of thought, created by the selection of certain features that are relevant to a real interest or problem, and by the disregard of all features that are considered to be irrelevant."[1] Such a definition emphasizes the subjectivity of the concept. In a staff study undertaken for the United Nations, a similar approach is taken in referring to "Types of Developmental Regions".[2] The authors of this study observe that many different types of development regions have been designated by governments and "there is no particular mystique about identifying them. . . . They are ordinary, common, practical, geographic areas for which social and economic improvement plans have been conceived, planned and undertaken." They went on to say that the boundaries may be determined by natural features, trading or metropolitan areas, labour markets, ethnic groupings, or political jurisdictions.[3]

It would, however, be a mistake to conclude from the foregoing that the way in which regions are conceived is a matter of indifference. In determining both whether economic development is necessary and what type of development is best suited to an area some boundaries are much more appropriate than others. In choosing between them, some guidance can be gained by looking at the ways in which regions are commonly classified.[4]

[1] Quoted in *Regional Economic Planning* (Paris: Organisation for European Economic Co-operation, 1961), p. 379.

[2] *Design for a Worldwide Study of Regional Development: a Report to the United Nations on a Proposed Research-Training Program* (Washington, D.C.: Resources for the Future, distributed by Johns Hopkins Press, Baltimore, Md., 1966), pp. 3–4.

[3] The authors classified regions under the following headings for the purpose they had in mind: Single-purpose or limited-purpose regions normally involving the intensive development of a specific natural resource; Frontier regions; Depressed regions; Metropolitan regions and hinterlands; and Economic regions or political jurisdictions established under a nationwide plan of regionalization.

[4] In practice those responsible for the framing of development policies are likely to have to work with ready-made administrative boundaries established with other objectives in mind. It is rarely possible to start with a clean slate; in addition to which, the choice of boundaries may be circumscribed by the lack of adequate data.

## Some Regional Classifications

*Homogeneous Regions.* One of the most common criteria for classification is homogeneity. A homogeneous economic region has one or more significant characteristics in common; such characteristics in the case of a "lagging" region, for example, may include a low income level, a high percentage of unemployment, a low growth rate, and an abnormally high percentage of people with less than average education. Regions differ, however, in the extent to which they display these various characteristics, and the determination of homogeneity becomes, as a result, a matter of judgment. In a dynamic context, moreover, a region may have high incomes which are declining, or be depressed economically but be growing rapidly.

The federal government has relied extensively on the homogeneity criterion in designating regions and in deciding which qualify for special assistance, the variables selected being mainly levels of unemployment and income. But although homogeneity is a useful concept in identifying areas of economic stress, it is much less useful in framing policies to eliminate it. Here quite different boundaries may be needed.

*Nodal Regions.* Nodal regions, in contrast to homogeneous ones, are based on focal points of economic activity and entail functional relationships. For this reason they are sometimes known as "functional" or "polarized" regions. A town or city may be the main source of demand for an agricultural hinterland, and provide employment opportunity as well as goods and services for the surrounding rural area. The increasing output of the rural area may be dependent almost entirely on the growth of population and income in the town. Any project for rural development should thus take account of such relationships. As in the case of the homogeneous regions, the boundaries of the nodal region will depend upon the particular matter under study. Commuting patterns may suggest one boundary, marketing patterns a second, and administrative controls a third. The strength of the links will tend to vary inversely with the distances involved, and an index of intensity may need to be assigned. The combination of the various links into one index – if such is to be attempted – is necessarily complex. In spite of its obvious relevance for development policies, the concept of nodality has not played a significant role in federal policies, in part because it is a more sophisticated concept to work with than homogeneity, requiring a recognition of functional relationships rather than just the statistical measurement of such factors as unemployment and income levels in determining regional boundaries.

*Administrative Regions.* Administrative coherence might suggest a simpler method of classifying regions, but in practice such coherence is often lacking. Administrative responsibility for roads, education, industrial development, employment services, or local taxes is likely to be shared by a variety of public bodies whose bailiwicks do not necessarily coincide. The confusion to which these overlapping jurisdictions have given rise has led to suggestions for providing a more unified framework within which development can take place. In this connection provincial governments are exerting increasing pressure on municipalities to cooperate with each other in the provision of water supplies, education, and roads.

Many of the administrative boundaries established to deal with a set of circumstances a generation ago have become anachronisms today, and they need substantial changes. Discussions of various forms of regional planning have added force to the arguments of those advocating such changes, for the task of preparing a coherent plan of development is rendered much more difficult when a multiplicity of bodies, each responsible for a different area, have to be consulted. In many instances municipalities and townships are too small to undertake the action necessary to create the sort of environment that encourages economic expansion, and their integration with or absorption into a larger administrative unit may have many advantages. At the very least, some co-ordination of their action is necessary, though this is a matter for the provincial rather than the federal government.

So far as the federal government is concerned, it has relied in the main on existing administrative and political boundaries in the implementation of its regional policies.[1] ADA has depended upon existing Canada Manpower Centres, the boundaries of which were originally determined with other objectives in mind. Rural development programs under ARDA are drawn up in co-operation with the provinces, and the selection of the boundaries calls for agreement between the two levels of government. A more comprehensive approach in the selection of boundaries is that associated with the Atlantic Development Board, whose responsibilities cover the whole of the four Atlantic provinces.

*Regions of Potential Growth.* Since a major objective of regional economic policies is to encourage economic growth, it is natural that the potential for such growth should be advocated as one of the more important determinants in the selection of boundaries. Regions might be set up to centre on some natural feature such as a watershed, which could be a source for hydro power and irrigation, or on urban centres, which could serve as focal points for industrial expansion.

The importance of cities in regional planning has been stressed by many writers. In the United States, John Friedmann observes, the post-war years have seen a shift of emphasis from the watershed to the metropolitan region as the major planning area. He expresses the view that "No effective regional planning can be done – in the sense of resource and economic development – without considering the role of cities, without considering the *core* of economic progress."[2]

---

[1] Reliance on areas defined by administrative boundaries has been encouraged because of the availability of statistical data for them and the lack of data for other types of areas. Admittedly, as observed in Appendix A, the figures do not always present an adequate picture and in some cases may be of uncertain reliability, but at least they provide a foundation of sorts on which to base policies.

[2] See John Friedmann, "The Concept of a Planning Region – the Evolution of an Idea in the United States" in *Regional Development and Planning: A Reader*, eds. John Friedmann and William Alonso (Cambridge, Mass.: M.I.T. Press, 1964), pp. 497–518; quotation on p. 500. This book by Friedmann and Alonso is a most valuable guide to the subject matter of regional development.

Whether or not Friedmann's view is equally applicable to Canada, the concept of a "planning region" is clearly a more fruitful one than that of homogeneity if the prime concern of policy is economic development rather than just the relief of distress. But if we are to have confidence in the drawing of the planning boundaries, there is an urgent need for more knowledge of the determinants of growth. This indeed is crucial, for the choice of boundaries will depend upon what we know about the growth process. A policy designed to accelerate the rate of growth in those parts of the country which are not realizing their full potential will stand or fall on our ability to recognize the most fruitful forms that development might take and to focus on those measures most likely to be effective in their achievement.

As might be expected, federal and provincial officials concerned with regional programs are faced repeatedly with the problem of area designation, and increasingly in recent years they have made a serious effort to grapple with the issues involved. It has long been recognized, for example, that the boundaries employed by the Area Development Agency are unsatisfactory in many respects, and studies have been commissioned to see if a more appropriate basis for area identification can be found. It is encouraging to note that some of these studies have been undertaken with the purpose of developing, not just identifying, distressed areas.[1]

In his discussion of the problems of delineating regions, L. H. Klaassen points out among other things that boundaries should be selected with a view to the kind of investment envisaged.[2] As in private industry, certain types of public service cannot be undertaken efficiently on a small scale, and the larger scale presupposes an adequate demand. Under these circumstances, if a

[1] See, for example, Richard S. Thoman and Maurice H. Yeates, "Delimitation of Development Regions in Canada (With Special Attention to the Georgian Bay Vicinity)", a report submitted to the Area Development Agency, Department of Industry, in 1966 (mimeographed). The authors place the emphasis on urban-centred regions.

[2] L. H. Klaassen, *Area Economic and Social Redevelopment: Guidelines for Programmes* (Paris: Organisation for Economic Co-operation and Development, 1965), pp. 27–8.

service is to be supplied, the area needs to be large enough to justify it.[1] There is merit too in his view that an area should be large enough to contain at least one growth point and be able to meet the bulk of its own demand for labour.

*A Canadian Synthesis.* Among the more important studies of the delineation of regions in Canada is that contained in the *Economic Geography of Canada* by Camu, Weeks, and Sametz. Their delineation involves a synthesis of the four variables stated below.

As the authors observe, "Canada is the second largest country in the world, and comprises such a wide variety of geographic situations that it cannot properly be understood except as a series of regions much smaller and more homogeneous than the five major economic regions to which reference is usually made."[2]

Drawing on the work of three pioneers in location theory, Lösch, Vining, and Florence, they divide the country into sixty-eight economic regions, and subdivide them into smaller and more homogeneous area units. The utility of the zoning from the standpoint of economic enquiry was the prime consideration. Four variables were considered and combined, each being given a weight deemed to be appropriate. The four variables considered in the zoning were:

a) Structural factors, such as the physiographic bases and the population and capital structure. Structure refers to the basic organization of stable elements, and structural factors are those involving the location of key natural resources (raw materials and power). The homogeneity of an area based on a common resource would be an important consideration.

b) Functional factors such as the transportation and communications network, that is, those activities that tend to tie an area together in a community of common interest notwithstanding varying structural factors. In addition to transportation and communications, functional factors were taken to include a unitary

---

[1] The substantial technical economies of large-scale power production have weighed heavily in some of the investment decisions of the Atlantic Development Board. It would have resulted in serious diseconomies to have provided individual areas with their own sources of supply.

[2] Camu, Weeks, Sametz, *op. cit.*, p. 262.

labour market such as is reflected in the area serviced by a Canada Manpower Centre.

c) Production factors, in respect to both their homogeneity and their relationship to each other. Homogeneity of the structure of production was stressed, together with certain functional relationships such as that of a forest hinterland to a pulp industry.

d) Marketing factors, such as internal consumption patterns and marketing relationships with other areas.

As the authors of this particular classification realized, however, there are difficulties in trying to devise a system for classifying regions that combines homogeneity of structure with a consideration of functional relationships. Functional regions necessarily comprise heterogeneous sub-regions as where, for example, a rural area provides the agricultural produce for a market town, which in turn provides recreational facilities for the rural population. In common with all forms of regional classification, therefore, the technique has limitations which will be greater or less, depending upon what one hopes to accomplish with it.[1]

## The Political Element

The reader may wonder at this stage how much bearing the views of economists and geographers have in the determination of regional boundaries and whether the dominant force underlying that determination has not in fact been political.

It is obvious that if certain areas of the country are to be singled out for special assistance, the decision is not going to be left to geographers and economists, though their advice may be influential. For one thing, as the foregoing discussion indicates, the drawing of boundaries is a matter of judgment. Even at the technical level, there are too many variables in the way in which a region can be conceived to expect a unanimous view as to where

[1] For a fuller discussion of this subject see Camu, Weeks, and Sametz, *op. cit.*, Chapter 10, and for a criticism of it see D. Michael Ray and J. L. Berry, "Multivariate Socio-Economic Regionalization: a Pilot Study in Central Canada" in *Papers on Regional Statistical Studies* (Canadian Political Science Association Conference on Statistics, 1964), eds. Sylvia Ostry and T. K. Rymes (Toronto: University of Toronto Press, 1966).

the boundaries should be drawn in any particular case. Often, moreover, the available statistical data on which judgments must be based is sketchy and impressionistic. Different assessments can be expected of growth potential and the process by which growth might be most effectively achieved: the economist who pins his faith on the growth potential of urbanization will not be likely to suggest the same boundaries as one who, viewing the same situation, sees the solution in the development of some natural resource.[1]

The views of the inhabitants of the area under discussion also have to be given due consideration. Some ethnic groups in Canada, especially French-speaking ones, form well-defined communities, and in such instances feelings of group identity may weigh heavily in a final decision as to where the boundaries should lie.

In decisions on regional and especially sub-provincial boundaries, provincial governments are unlikely to leave final decisions to Ottawa. It is to the provincial governments, therefore, rather than to Ottawa that one must turn for information on the steps being taken. Ontario, to mention a case in point, is divided into ten regions. It so happens that these regions were decided by the provincial government largely on the basis of the studies of Camu, Weeks, and Sametz to which reference has been made above.

A fundamental problem in any system of regional classification, however, is that regional boundaries appropriate for one purpose are not necessarily appropriate for another. The geographical delineation of small pockets of chronic poverty is indicated if the prime concern of the government is social welfare, but not if it is regional economic growth.[2] It follows that the drawing of the boundaries cannot be divorced from the priorities which the policy maker sets himself. The areas with the greatest potential for development are not likely to be the same ones as those with the

[1] Economists have only recently addressed themselves to regional questions; as a result the theory of regional growth is far less well developed than the more traditional areas of economics.

[2] A somewhat similar dilemma exists in the matter of foreign aid programs. Should aid be channelled primarily to those countries where the need is greatest or to those where the need is less but where the greatest potential is shown for self-sustaining growth?

most poverty and unemployment, but to help areas where the need is less because of their potential for growth may seem unjust when there are others where misfortune is greater and the future bleaker.

The criteria to be used in drawing up boundaries have been much debated in all countries that have introduced regional policies. Depending on the course that debate has taken and the specific objectives being pursued, boundaries have been shifted, often several times. Local pockets of distress have been singled out for assistance at one time and large areas of the country at another. In the United Kingdom the pendulum has swung from large regions to small ones covered by employment exchanges, and back again to large.

The fact that some areas qualify for assistance while adjacent ones do not, also makes the issue a politically sensitive one. If the areas to receive special assistance are extensive and include a large proportion of the population, aid will be spread thinly; but if the areas are small, aid will be much more concentrated and the distinction between those that receive special assistance and those that do not becomes sharper, increasing the political sensitivity associated with the drawing of the boundary.

# 4. The Assessment and Determinants of Regional Economic Growth

## The Varied Interpretations of Growth

IN CHAPTER 1 attention was drawn to some of the significant differences between the Canadian provinces in terms of population, employment, and income. It is the purpose of this chapter to consider more specifically the determinants and measurement of economic growth, and to discuss some of the ways in which the spatial differences in income might be explained.[1]

There are various ways in which growth can be conceived and measured, and their differences are significant. The three most common concepts are those related to total volume of output,

[1] Following current practice, the term "growth" is used synonymously with "expansion" and "development." There are times when the risk of ambiguity makes it desirable to distinguish between these terms, confining the meaning of "growth" to important structural changes occurring over a long period of time, "expansion" to temporary and reversible increases in output, and "development" to changes over a broad front, involving not only economic factors but also political, social, and administrative ones which effect a profound change in the structure of society. Such distinctions are not always easy to draw in practice, however, and except where otherwise stated, the terms have been used interchangeably, leaving it to the context to make the intention clear.

54

welfare, and productivity. If we are concerned with welfare, we are primarily interested in per capita or family income. If productivity per worker is our concern, then output per member of the labour force is the relevant indicator, adjusted perhaps for hours worked.

Wide variations in apparent growth rates can result from using one approach or one time period rather than another.[1] For example, while the total income of one province may rise less rapidly than that of another if its rate of population growth is lower due to net out-migration, this might well result in an increased per capita income for those who remain. As a result, measurement according to total provincial income could show a slower rate, and measurement according to per capita income a more rapid one.[2]

At the provincial or sub-provincial level the statistical problems involved in measuring growth, however conceived, increase considerably, the data on provincial output being less complete and certain than on national output. In the short run these uncertainties are compounded by unrecorded population movements. The danger of drawing unwarranted conclusions regarding secular growth rates is increased, moreover, by the marked instability of income from one year to the next in certain provinces.

The distinction between total income and per capita income at the regional level is an important one for policy purposes. As discussed in Chapter 5 on the grounds for regional development policies, some groups place the emphasis on total income, and look with disfavour on policies that may have the effect of reducing

[1] For further discussion of the subject, see T. N. Brewis, "Economic Growth Concepts and Objectives" in T. N. Brewis *et al., Growth and the Canadian Economy* (Toronto: McClelland & Stewart, 1968). In terms of total output, provincial growth rates show phenomenal differences because of the magnitude of the shifts which have taken place in population distribution. Thus, the population of Prince Edward Island has remained virtually unchanged over this century, whereas that of Alberta has increased almost twenty times.

[2] The migration of the population from a very poor part of the country to a richer one may tend to depress per capita incomes in the richer area more than it raises them in the poorer one. It does not necessarily follow from this, however, that national average per capita income will fall. It might still rise.

total income by out-migration of population, even where such action seems likely to raise the average per capita income of those who remain. Political leaders are apt to attach considerable weight to population size and are encouraged to do so by those federal grants that are determined on a per capita basis. Real estate, transportation, utility groups, and others whose income depends largely on aggregate demand are likely to share the view that total regional income should be the criterion for growth. Their vested interest in such an interpretation needs to be recognized.

## Interregional Relationships and Population Movements

The subject of growth at the national level has been much discussed in recent years, and this has been accompanied by an increased concern with growth at the provincial and sub-provincial level, for growth at the national level is an aggregation of regional changes. By and large, the outputs of various regions rise and fall together, though the extent of the rise and fall can differ sharply and the swings in economic activity are much greater in some parts of the country than others, a phenomenon which has implications for stabilization and regional development policies. Theoretical and empirical studies have cast some light on the growth process and have prompted measures at the policy level to hasten it; none the less, our understanding of the nature and causes of growth, both regionally and nationally, remains very incomplete, and uncertainty characterizes much public discussion of the subject.

The repercussions of growth or lack of growth in one region spill over into others, affecting them favourably or adversely.[1] The favourable effects result from a growing region's increasing purchases from other regions and possibly from its increased investment in them – "trickling-down" effects, to use the termino-

---

[1] Contrary to what one would have expected, Alan Green (*op. cit.*) has observed that the rapid expansion in population and output in the Prairies between 1890 and 1910 was *not* accompanied by a relative rise in per capita incomes, although it was the primary growth area of the period. Nor does the migration appear to have been a response to the fact that income differentials favoured the Prairies.

logy of Hirschman.[1] But the extent to which higher incomes in the growing region spill over into another will vary. Higher incomes will not be expended in a poorer region if it is producing goods and services for which there is a negative income elasticity of demand. The smaller the income elasticity of demand, the smaller will be the gains of the poorer region.

In some cases the gains of the growing region may be directly at the expense of those regions that are prospering less, as where improved technology or a change in taste shifts demand from the region which is not growing to the one that is. Oil and gas production in Alberta, for example, diminishes the demand for Nova Scotian coal. The higher incomes that result in Alberta are most unlikely to lead to an increase in purchases from Nova Scotia sufficient to compensate for adverse effects on this province's economy through the loss of its market for coal. Here, the trickling-down effects will be more than offset by "polarization" effects, that is, by the magnetic pull of labour and resources towards the stronger growth centre, in this instance, Alberta. The more extensive the growth of a particular region, the more likely it is to attract migrants from other parts of the country. Such migration, moreover, is selective and tends to draw workers, generally the younger and more competent ones, out of the lagging regions. If, in addition to such migration, the growing region also attracts capital from the less promising regions, the inequalities between the regions become even greater,[2] and once this trend becomes marked the situation is still further aggravated by the tendency of industry to locate in areas promising the greatest rate of growth and to avoid the depressed areas.

Whether the trickling-down effects will more than offset such

[1] Albert O. Hirschman, *The Strategy of Economic Development* (Yale Studies in Economics 10; New Haven, Conn.: Yale University Press, 1958), pp. 187–90.

[2] See the discussion by Gunnar Myrdal in *Rich Lands and Poor Lands* (New York: Harper & Row, 1957), Chapters 2 and 3 – "The Drift towards Regional Inequalities in a Country" and "The Principle of Circular and Cumulative Causation". Similar views are expressed by Caves and Holton in "The Economics of Retarded Regional Growth", *op. cit.*, pp. 164–9.

polarization effects depends on individual circumstances. Generalizations on the subject are of dubious value, but recognition of the prolonged period during which incomes in the Atlantic provinces have remained below those elsewhere suggests that the forces tending towards equality across the country are relatively weak, and that government intervention is necessary if greater equality is to be achieved.

The same sort of discussion applies to the influence of urban centres on regional growth. No one will question the extremely important role that towns play in the growth process and the stimulus that they give to innovation and enterprise, but how far are they likely to have a "spin-off" effect encouraging growth in outlying areas and how far are they likely to attract industry away from those areas? "Growth Centre" advocates are apt to assume the former effect will be dominant but this may not always be the case. In many instances, rather than inducing growth in the region as a whole, expanding urban centres will rob other localities of what growth they had and lead to a decline in their industry and the migration of their population.

Few aspects of regional development have attracted more attention or given rise to more conflicting opinions than the subject of migration and population growth. Some see a rapidly increasing population as one of the prime determinants of economic expansion; others see it as one of the reasons for the distress of certain areas. It is easy to find illustrations in support of both points of view. Any substantial increase in the population of Eskimos dependent on hunting and trapping may lead to disaster, especially if there is a concomitant increase in capital equipment which increases the efficacy of their operation and reduces the stock of wildlife. At the other extreme, the surge in Toronto's population has made Toronto an increasingly powerful magnet for new enterprises, drawing new industry and population away from other possible locations.[1]

---

[1] In like manner, one can see at the national level great advantages accruing to such countries as Canada or Australia and great disadvantages accruing to other countries such as India because of an increase in population.

The difficulty with arriving at conclusions on this subject is that the assumptions underlying them are not spelled out in detail. There is no point in trying to decide whether population movements of themselves will raise or lower per capita incomes in individual regions or areas of Canada without looking at the individual circumstances in question and considering the availability or potential supply of other factors of production. Because an increase in population may benefit British Columbia, it does not follow that an increase in population will be to the economic advantage of Newfoundland. The very opposite may be the case.[1]

## Factors Contributing to Regional Disparities

Without passing judgment on the desirability of one criterion of growth rather than another, for this will depend on the purpose in mind, it is possible to examine the forces that are likely to influence the total output of a region and to seek explanations for regional disparities. In some cases explanations for differing growth rates suggest themselves immediately; in others the explanation may require extensive probing.

The regions of Canada differ greatly in the advantages that they offer for various types of economic activity, and their potential for growth lies along diverse paths. Some have an absolute advantage in the production of a wide range of goods, others in a very narrow one. To maintain high levels of employment, the latter may be obliged to rely heavily on the production of those goods in which their comparative disadvantage is least, and for those who work there to accept lower returns.

Among the many variables that contribute to regional differences in income and growth, the following are singled out for discussion: capital formation, the labour force and its education, the industrial mix, and regional exports. As will be apparent, there is

[1] The difficulty in reaching agreement on the effects of population change is that there are so many variables and unknowns involved. A change in technology or international trading patterns, for example, can transform an "over-populated" region into an "under-populated" one, or vice versa. The time horizon is also important. An increase in population may reduce per capita incomes in the short run but raise them in the long run.

a high degree of interdependence between these variables and others. Thus the presence of rich natural resources will encourage investment; investment will influence the industrial mix and levels of employment, and thereby incomes.[1] But it is not clear just how all these are related; and just how the growth process works remains obscure. As a result, the lines along which policy might be pursued to hasten the growth process also remain uncertain, and we are left with the need to guess.

It is often thought that development follows a primary, secondary, and tertiary sequence; that is, that it begins with production at the primary or basic level, out of which develop secondary industries, and, as the population increases, tertiary or service industries. As Perloff has observed, however, there is nothing inexorable about this sequence.[2] By way of illustration he noted that growth in Florida resulted from a quest for amenities rather than economic opportunity. The growth of population led to the growth of service industries which in turn led to an expansion of secondary manufacturing and finally to primary production as the demand for food supplies increased. In some cases, growth may start in secondary manufacturing, where there is a pool of unemployed labour, for example, and spread out from there to primary and tertiary activity.

The very fact that some regions are developing and others are not may in itself be important in perpetuating differences. New firms are not attracted to an area where the rate of economic expansion is patently less than elsewhere. A region which has gained a reputation for rapid growth will find it easier to attract new industry than one with a less favourable reputation. Whatever the underlying reasons may be, there is certainly a strong tendency for industries seeking a new location to follow the crowd.

[1] For a discussion of the role of natural resources in growth, see Harvey S. Perloff and Lowdon Wingo, Jr., "Natural Resources Endowment and Regional Economic Growth" in *Regional Development and Planning*, eds. John Friedmann and William Alonso, pp. 215–39.

[2] See Harvey S. Perloff and Vera W. Dodds, *How a Region Grows: Area Development in the U.S. Economy* (Supplementary Paper No. 17; New York: Committee for Economic Development, 1963).

## Table 4:1
## Capital and Repair Expenditures
## 1955 to 1966

($ per capita)

| | 1955 | 1956 | 1957 | 1958 | 1959 | 1960 | 1961 | 1962 | 1963 | 1964 | 1965 | 1966* |
|---|---|---|---|---|---|---|---|---|---|---|---|---|
| Newfoundland | 288 | 299 | 316 | 315 | 342 | 422 | 500 | 649 | 601 | 611 | 633 | 844 |
| Prince Edward Island | 300 | 343 | 303 | 390 | 465 | 466 | 476 | 528 | 553 | 486 | 676 | 734 |
| Nova Scotia | 324 | 370 | 382 | 365 | 437 | 451 | 429 | 421 | 440 | 495 | 570 | 688 |
| New Brunswick | 419 | 449 | 402 | 433 | 473 | 431 | 415 | 417 | 440 | 558 | 687 | 748 |
| Atlantic provinces | 344 | 376 | 368 | 376 | 427 | 439 | 444 | 481 | 485 | 543 | 628 | 749 |
| Quebec | 462 | 530 | 557 | 550 | 549 | 530 | 522 | 549 | 572 | 663 | 732 | 782 |
| Ontario | 586 | 689 | 754 | 701 | 668 | 648 | 624 | 662 | 698 | 774 | 869 | 969 |
| Manitoba | 497 | 582 | 593 | 629 | 731 | 726 | 634 | 637 | 711 | 751 | 763 | 899 |
| Saskatchewan | 536 | 707 | 685 | 699 | 698 | 701 | 671 | 735 | 847 | 895 | 1,023 | 1,200 |
| Alberta | 841 | 994 | 920 | 935 | 975 | 946 | 953 | 903 | 1,073 | 993 | 1,147 | 1,277 |
| Prairie provinces | 643 | 783 | 752 | 774 | 821 | 810 | 779 | 778 | 845 | 896 | 1,002 | 1,148 |
| British Columbia† | 686 | 952 | 1,054 | 777 | 788 | 748 | 745 | 759 | 807 | 976 | 1,192 | 1,317 |
| CANADA | 542 | 649 | 683 | 643 | 646 | 629 | 614 | 640 | 675 | 758 | 858 | 957 |

*Preliminary Actual 1966.   †Includes Yukon and Northwest Territories.

Source: Calculated from D.B.S. and Department of Trade and Commerce, *Private and Public Investment in Canada: Outlook and Regional Estimates* (61-205), various years.

*Capital Formation.* Capital formation plays a prominent role in most theories of growth and the fact that it has been much higher in some parts of the country than in others leads one to expect significant regional differences in output. Table 4:1 indicates the extent to which capital expenditures per capita have varied by province. Although in percentage terms there has been a greater rise in investment in the Atlantic provinces over the past decade than in Canada as a whole, the difference in dollar terms shows little change, being still some $200 per head per annum below the Canadian average. Capital expenditures in Ontario have been consistently higher than in Quebec, and in both British Columbia and Alberta have greatly exceeded the national average – in Alberta especially. These prolonged disparities in capital formation between the various provinces strongly suggest that the stock of capital must also be unevenly distributed across the country, although data on capital stock specifically are not available.

In the early post-war years, capital formation was seen as the chief determinant of economic growth, and this view coloured development policies in highly developed as well as in less developed countries. Since then, there has been a growing recognition that growth is an elusive goal requiring action on a broad front, and the emphasis on capital formation has now shifted to the more subtle and less readily quantified factors of technological change, research and innovation, education, and social attitudes. To the extent that capital formation is stressed, it is the technological change embodied in it rather than simply its magnitude that is regarded as important. A consideration of Table 4:1 suggests that there is some correlation between capital formation and income at the regional level. Both capital formation and incomes are higher in Ontario than in Quebec or the Atlantic provinces, and in Alberta than in Manitoba; but although the Prairie provinces as a whole have experienced higher investment levels per capita than Ontario, incomes have been appreciably lower over the past decade. Capital output ratios – the amount of capital required to produce an extra unit of income – have been the subject of much enquiry among growth theorists and those concerned with the implementation of development programs, but the discussion has only underlined the complexity of the relationship between capital and output, and has not furnished answers. It is apparent that what a given increment of capital adds to income will vary with the individual industry, the input of other factors, and the technique of production, as well as with the extent to which the new capital replaces one type of production with another. Attempts, by Wassily Leontief in the United States and others, have been made to ascertain the ratios for different industries, and studies show the range is a broad one. In the case of such types of social capital as roads and housing the ratio is very high, whereas for certain service industries it tends to be low. Given these varying relationships, capital formation and income cannot always be expected to show similar trends across the country. Nevertheless, other things being equal, provinces experiencing a significantly lower level of capital formation per head than others over a period of years are also likely to experience lower levels of output and income.

The Area Development Agency and the Atlantic Development Board have devoted the greater part of their efforts to increasing capital formation, the latter concentrating on infra-structure and the former on direct assistance to industry. To the extent that economic growth is the objective in view, the implicit assumption is that increased capital formation will contribute to its attainment.

So far as the Atlantic region is concerned, there is a prevalent belief, which the Atlantic Development Board shares, that the region is undercapitalized and that additional private and social capital are both needed. Which one of these, social capital or private capital, is likely to be more effective in inducing growth has been a matter of some debate, but generalizations on the subject are of questionable value. Apart from the fact that they are likely to be interrelated, the pay-off period in the case of many social capital investments is often very long-term and any quantification of the benefits is apt to be highly conjectural. What can be said with certainty is that while expenditures on infra-structure may be a pre-condition of growth, they are rarely a sufficient con-

## Table 4:2
## Population Ten Years of Age and Over, not Attending School, with no Secondary Education
### 1961

(% of total)

| | Rural farm population | Rural non-farm population | Urban population | Male population | Female population | % of total population |
|---|---|---|---|---|---|---|
| Newfoundland | 64.3 | 70.5 | 47.5 | 62.5 | 54.3 | 58.6 |
| Prince Edward Island | 54.4 | 56.3 | 34.0 | 57.2 | 38.7 | 48.2 |
| Nova Scotia | 49.6 | 50.5 | 36.0 | 48.7 | 36.1 | 42.5 |
| New Brunswick | 71.0 | 68.4 | 44.2 | 63.0 | 50.6 | 56.8 |
| Quebec | 79.6 | 71.2 | 49.7 | 56.9 | 54.0 | 55.4 |
| Ontario | 61.9 | 54.8 | 40.5 | 47.2 | 41.1 | 44.0 |
| Manitoba | 64.3 | 58.8 | 34.3 | 47.1 | 39.9 | 43.5 |
| Saskatchewan | 60.1 | 56.7 | 39.3 | 55.0 | 44.8 | 50.0 |
| Alberta | 55.8 | 49.6 | 32.4 | 44.0 | 35.2 | 39.6 |
| British Columbia | 46.8 | 41.7 | 30.9 | 37.6 | 30.1 | 33.8 |
| CANADA* | 64.7 | 58.6 | 41.5 | 50.1 | 43.9 | 47.0 |

*Includes Yukon Territory and Northwest Territories.

Source: Calculated from D.B.S., *1961 Census of Canada*, Vol. I, (92-557).

dition, and at times are undertaken with more concern for political than economic expediency.

*The Labour Force and Education.* Spatial differences in the quality and skills of the labour force also contribute to interregional differences in employment and income. A number of studies in recent years have drawn attention to the changing composition of the labour market and the increasing demand for skilled personnel. These have attracted attention in turn to the wide disparities in educational attainment which exist within as well as between provinces and to the relation between education and economic growth.[1]

Table 4:2 shows that the percentages for the rural non-farm and farm population with no secondary school education are much higher than for the urban population, and this is true of every province. What is also striking is that the percentage of males who have had no secondary education is larger than the percentage of females.[2] Table 4:3 shows that in Newfoundland, New Brunswick, and Quebec the percentages of those who have not even attained Grade Five at the elementary level are well above the national average.[3]

Data on the changing composition of labour force requirements reveal immediately the significance of the foregoing. There has been a notable shift to more skilled occupations, accompanied by a great increase in the employment of women (see Table 4:4). Though Group 1 may contain a number of people with less education and skill than Group 2, by and large it is characterized by higher education levels, a situation which has tended to increase the relative number of job opportunities available to women.

[1] See, for example, Gordon W. Bertram, *The Contribution of Education to Economic Growth* (Economic Council of Canada, Staff Study No. 12 [Ottawa: Queen's Printer, 1966]). While it is generally agreed that education makes a significant contribution to growth, there is less agreement on how the relation between education and growth should be quantified.

[2] See D. M. Connor and D. W. Magill, *The Role of Education in Rural Development* (Ottawa: Queen's Printer, 1966), a study undertaken for ARDA.

[3] It is only in recent years that Quebec has introduced free high school education, which generally starts at Grade Nine in Canada.

### Table 4:3
### Population Ten Years of Age and Over, not Attending School, by Highest Grade Attended
### 1961

(%)

| | No school | Elementary | | Secondary | | | Some university | University degree |
|---|---|---|---|---|---|---|---|---|
| | | 5 | 5+ | 1-2 | 3 | 4-5 | | |
| Newfoundland | 5.6 | 18.5 | 34.5 | 21.5 | 11.9 | 4.9 | 2.4 | 0.8 |
| Prince Edward Island | 1.0 | 6.3 | 40.9 | 30.3 | 7.7 | 9.4 | 2.9 | 1.5 |
| Nova Scotia | 1.5 | 6.6 | 34.4 | 28.9 | 13.6 | 9.8 | 2.8 | 2.3 |
| New Brunswick | 2.8 | 10.6 | 43.4 | 19.3 | 9.9 | 9.4 | 2.8 | 1.8 |
| Quebec | 1.1 | 11.8 | 42.5 | 19.2 | 6.2 | 13.7 | 2.7 | 2.9 |
| Ontario | 1.2 | 5.0 | 37.8 | 21.7 | 9.2 | 18.9 | 2.8 | 3.4 |
| Manitoba | 3.0 | 8.0 | 32.5 | 23.0 | 14.0 | 13.3 | 3.6 | 2.6 |
| Saskatchewan | 3.1 | 7.8 | 39.1 | 21.3 | 9.1 | 14.5 | 3.1 | 2.0 |
| Alberta | 2.0 | 5.4 | 32.2 | 24.2 | 11.2 | 17.7 | 4.0 | 3.1 |
| British Columbia | 1.6 | 4.2 | 28.0 | 23.8 | 10.4 | 23.6 | 5.1 | 3.3 |
| CANADA* | 1.7 | 7.7 | 37.6 | 21.7 | 9.1 | 16.2 | 3.1 | 2.9 |

Notes: A person was considered as attending school if his main daytime activity at any time between September 1960 and the census date of June 1, 1961, was attending an elementary or secondary school, university, or an institution providing an equivalent type of general education. The age classification is based on a definition which specifies completed years of age at last birthday prior to the census date of June 1, 1961.

Figures do not add to 100% in all cases because of rounding.

*Canada includes Yukon and Northwest Territories.          Source:  Calculated from D.B.S., *1961 Census of Canada*, Vol. I (92-557).

**Table 4:4(a)**
**Structure of Occupational Groups, by Sex**
**1951 and 1961***

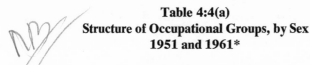

### GROUP 1

(*Managerial, professional, technical, clerical, sales, commercial*)

|  | 1951 | | 1961 | | 1951-1961 |
|---|---|---|---|---|---|
|  | (*thousands*) | (%) | (*thousands*) | (%) | (*% change*) |
| Males | 1,045 | 62 | 1,436 | 59 | +37 |
| Females | 645 | 38 | 1,011 | 41 | +57 |
| Total | 1,690 | 100 | 2,447 | 100 | +45 |

### GROUP 2

(*Agriculture, fishing, logging, mining, manufacturing,
construction, transport, labourers, and service
and recreation†*)

| Males | 3,018 | 86 | 3,134 | 82 | + 4 |
|---|---|---|---|---|---|
| Females | 505 | 14 | 711 | 18 | +41 |
| Total | 3,523 | 100 | 3,845 | 100 | + 9 |

*1951 occupational classification.
†Includes protective services, housekeepers, cooks, athletes, entertainers, barbers, launderers, cleaners, janitors, bartenders, etc.

Source: D.B.S., *1961 Census of Canada*, Vol. IV (94-501), excluding "occupations not specified".

Employment in Group 1 increased by 37 per cent for males and 57 per cent for females between 1951 and 1961, while the increase in Group 2 was much less, 4 per cent and 41 per cent respectively.

It would be dangerous to apply to individual circumstances the generalization that there has been a shift in recent years from occupations with low educational requirements to ones with high ones, but there can be no denying the significance of this trend as a factor in existing spatial disparities in income and employment.

## Table 4:4(b)
## Structure of Occupational Groups, by Education
## 1961

| | GROUP 1 | | GROUP 2 | |
| --- | --- | --- | --- | --- |
| Secondary education | (*Managerial, professional, technical, clerical, sales, commercial*) | | (*Agriculture, fishing, logging, mining, manufacturing, construction, transport, labourers, service and recreation*) | |
| *Males:* | (*thousands*) | (%) | (*thousands*) | (%) |
| None | 258 | *18* | 1,789 | *57* |
| 1-3 years | 431 | *30* | 987 | *31* |
| 4 or more years | 738 | *52* | 380 | *12* |
| Total | 1,427 | *100* | 3,156 | *100* |
| *Females:* | | | | |
| None | 113 | *11* | 404 | *55* |
| 1-3 years | 365 | *37* | 253 | *34* |
| 4 or more years | 509 | *52* | 79 | *11* |
| Total | 987 | *100* | 736 | *100* |

Source: D.B.S., *1961 Census of Canada*, Vol. IV (94-509), excluding "occupations not specified".

Table 4:5 shows there is a strong correlation between education and income.

As might be expected, there is also a striking difference between expenditures per child on education from one province to another. Table 4:6 shows the expenditures per school child in 1961, which varied from $141 in Newfoundland[1] to $396 in Alberta.

[1] The leeway in education that Newfoundland has had to make up is indicated by the fact that two thirds of the 1,200 schools in operation in 1947–8 were one-room schools and the annual median salary of teachers was $920. It was only in 1942 that the School Attendance Act made education free and compulsory between the ages of 7 and 14, and even then education depended on the appropriate denominational school being available.

Ontario spent over eighty dollars more per child than Quebec. Though the situation is changing rapidly, education in Quebec until the late 1950s was given a very low priority, a circumstance which has contributed substantially to the dearth of French Canadians in the more rewarding occupations and positions, and given rise to feelings of ethnic discrimination. It will be observed that New Brunswick gave a higher priority to educational expenditures (expressed as a per cent of personal income) than all other provinces except Alberta and Saskatchewan, although the actual expenditures in New Brunswick were lower than in any other province except Prince Edward Island and Newfoundland.[1]

The variations in expenditure per school child are to some extent a cause and to some extent a consequence of variations in personal income. The richer provinces find it easier to spend more than the poorer ones, and the higher educational expenditures contribute in turn to higher incomes.

A lack of education is also characteristic of certain ethnic groups that are concentrated in particular areas of the country. The resultant low incomes may suggest an area or an ethnic problem, but the fundamental issue is essentially one of education and associated occupational opportunity.[2]

It is worth noting, however, that while incomes increase with education, provincial differences in income for comparable educational levels are still considerable: to take the extremes, the average income of male graduates in 1961 was $6,823 in Prince Edward Island and $9,370 in Ontario. For all levels of education, incomes in the Atlantic provinces are lower than the national average. Lower incomes in such provinces as Newfoundland, eastern Quebec, or northern New Brunswick cannot be attributed solely to the general lack of educational attainment and skills of

[1] With regard to vocational training, specifically, there has been a notable increase in federal expenditure in recent years, but the bulk of the expenditure has gone to the wealthier provinces. Some of the schools that have been built have been poorly attended, especially by unemployed workers, partly because of the limited financial inducement to attend the schools.

[2] I am indebted to Jenny R. Podoluk for drawing my attention to significant data on the relation between ethnicity, education, and occupation. The fact that certain ethnic groups receive lower incomes can largely be explained by their lower educational levels.

## Table 4:5

## Income of Non-Farm Males, Fifteen Years of Age and Over, by Education
## 1961

($ per capita)

| | No schooling | Kindergarten and elementary | 1-3 years high school | 4-5 years high school | Some university | University degree |
|---|---|---|---|---|---|---|
| Newfoundland | 1,449 | 2,210 | 3,179 | 3,886 | 4,109 | 8,133 |
| Prince Edward Island | — | 2,185 | 3,150 | 3,889 | 3,840 | 6,823 |
| Nova Scotia | 1,448 | 2,378 | 3,425 | 4,265 | 4,527 | 7,722 |
| New Brunswick | 1,467 | 2,476 | 3,654 | 3,722 | 4,087 | 7,569 |
| Quebec | 1,746 | 3,065 | 3,793 | 4,938 | 5,325 | 9,001 |
| Ontario | 2,218 | 3,438 | 4,136 | 5,070 | 5,301 | 9,370 |
| Manitoba | 1,477 | 2,943 | 4,039 | 4,492 | 4,574 | 8,545 |
| Saskatchewan | 1,235 | 2,869 | 3,729 | 4,256 | 4,223 | 8,625 |
| Alberta | 1,471 | 3,236 | 4,032 | 4,582 | 4,749 | 9,309 |
| British Columbia | 1,731 | 3,340 | 4,074 | 4,509 | 4,597 | 8,796 |
| CANADA | 1,715 | 3,134 | 3,943 | 4,825 | 4,995 | 9,048 |

Source: D.B.S., *1961 Census of Canada*, Vol. IV (98-501).

## Table 4:6
## Expenditures on Education
## 1961

| | Personal income ($000,000) | Expenditures provincially controlled schools ($000,000) | Public school attendance (thousands) | Expenditures as % of personal income | Expenditures per school child ($) | Children in school as % of the labour force | % Increase per annum in expenditures 1951-61 |
|---|---|---|---|---|---|---|---|
| Newfoundland | 428 | 18.1 | 128.7 | 4.2 | 141 | 114.6 | 14.5 |
| Prince Edward Island | 101 | 3.9 | 25.7 | 3.9 | 152 | 75.1 | 13.1 |
| Nova Scotia | 882 | 38.9 | 186.3 | 4.4 | 209 | 78.6 | 12.1 |
| New Brunswick | 636 | 30.2 | 154.6 | 4.7 | 195 | 86.7 | 10.0 |
| Quebec | 7,272 | 307.6 | 1,226.4 | 4.2 | 251 | 69.4 | 15.9 |
| Ontario | 11,490 | 478.8 | 1,429.6 | 4.2 | 335 | 59.7 | 12.7 |
| Manitoba | 1,395 | 60.4 | 211.6 | 4.3 | 285 | 61.8 | 11.7 |
| Saskatchewan | 1,130 | 75.8 | 218.1 | 6.7* | 347 | 67.0 | 10.6 |
| Alberta | 2,125 | 122.9 | 310.1 | 5.8 | 396 | 63.3 | 13.5 |
| British Columbia | 2,953 | 126.7 | 353.7 | 4.3 | 358 | 61.2 | 11.2 |

*1961 was an abnormally low year for personal income in Saskatchewan. The percentage of the average of personal income for 1960, 1961, and 1962 is 5.6%.

Sources: D.B.S., unpublished data, *National Accounts, Income and Expenditure* (13-201), and *1961 Census of Canada*, Vol. I (92-550) and Vol. III (94-518).

the labour force, though it has certainly been a major factor – combined with the failure of demand for labour in primary occupations to grow – for it has inhibited change to other occupations and closed the door to more remunerative employment. The shift away from employment in primary occupations raises the issue of the industrial mix.

*The Industrial Mix.* The growth of a region reflects the fortunes of the individual industries within its borders. Since some industries are expanding more rapidly and are characterized by greater stability than others, the industrial mix in an area affects not just the level of incomes, but also the distribution and stability of incomes, the growth of the population, and land use. In some cases, the concentration of production in particular fields of activity which are subject to sharp fluctuations in demand and technological change leads to a high degree of economic instability; in others, the industrial mix may offer limited scope for the employment of females or of workers with limited skills. As a result, many problems in depressed areas stem directly from the kind of industry that has located there. If a region depends upon an industry undergoing secular decline, diversification of economic activity offers the only alternative to out-migration.

The following table shows that "slow" and "fast" growth industries are very unevenly distributed in Canada. According to this study, a much larger percentage of slow growth industries is to be found in the Atlantic provinces than anywhere else in Canada, with the exception of British Columbia. The lowest percentage is in Ontario. The relation is reversed for the fast growth industries, with the lowest percentages in the Atlantic provinces and the highest in Ontario, Saskatchewan, and Alberta.

The situation of British Columbia is anomalous. Contrary to expectations, this study showed it to have a high percentage of slow growth industries and a low percentage of fast growth industries, although the province as a whole is clearly prosperous. This called for further enquiry, and an analysis was made of the value of manufacturing shipments in two slow growth industries where employment in British Columbia was substantial, namely, in the

## Table 4:7
## 1961 Labour Force in Manufacturing Industries, Rated by
## Growth of Industry from 1949 to 1965

|  | (%) | | |
|---|---|---|---|
|  | Fast-growth industries | Slow-growth industries | Other industries |
| Ontario | 35.2 | 26.2 | 38.6 |
| Saskatchewan | 34.7 | 50.9 | 14.4 |
| Alberta | 31.8 | 42.9 | 25.3 |
| Quebec | 25.9 | 44.0 | 30.1 |
| Manitoba | 22.4 | 47.9 | 29.7 |
| British Columbia | 16.7 | 60.0 | 23.3 |
| Nova Scotia | 16.2 | 56.8 | 27.0 |
| Prince Edward Island | 12.8 | 77.8 | 9.4 |
| New Brunswick | 12.5 | 75.6 | 11.9 |
| Newfoundland | 12.2 | 80.9 | 6.9 |

Note: Fast-growth industries – Index 286 or more
Slow-growth industries – Index 200 or less
Other industries – Index 201-85

Index refers to the December 1965 index of industrial production, seasonally adjusted; 1949 = 100.

Source: D.B.S., *1961 Census of Canada*, Vol. III (94-518) and *Annual Supplement to the Monthly Index of Industrial Production* (61-005).

wood products and paper industries. It was discovered that the growth rate of each of these two manufacturing sectors differed sharply between provinces. British Columbia was gaining a larger share of these slow growth industries, while the Atlantic provinces showed a declining share. The wood and paper industries were not growing rapidly as a whole, but British Columbia experienced a greater increase than the national average for the industry. In the competition with British Columbia, the Atlantic provinces were left with a smaller share of these industries, and the weakness of their position was thus compounded.[1]

*Regional Exports.* Of the various attempts that have been made to explain regional growth, those associated with the view that exports from a region play a primary role in determining its growth have exerted a considerable influence on those concerned with regional questions. In this connection, a distinction is drawn between goods and services exported from the area and those absorbed internally. The output sold externally constitutes "the economic base". The significance of this distinction resides in the fact that exports out of the region are considered the prime mover of the local economy. It follows from this that if internal consumption bears a known relation to external demand, a forecast of the economic base will permit a forecast of the total economic activity within the region.[2]

The rapid growth and decline of uranium mining at Elliot Lake provides a simple illustration of the dependence of internal consumption and imports on exports. The discovery of a rich ore body there led to the establishment of a thriving town providing goods and services to the mining community. The subsequent collapse of the mining boom, and the cessation of the basic activity of mining and exporting the ore, led to the concomitant collapse of the non-basic activities that had grown up around it. The dependence of these activities on the mining industry was little less than that of the miners themselves. Conceptually, in any region there will tend to be "carrier" industries that determine

[1] The Atlantic provinces' share of the value of manufacturing shipments of wood products dropped from 6.5 per cent to 4 per cent between 1952 and 1962 and that of British Columbia rose from 37.6 per cent to 42.1 per cent. A similar change occurred in paper products, the Atlantic provinces' share dropping from 11.6 to 9.2 per cent and that of British Columbia rising from 10.1 to 15.1 per cent.

[2] The analytical framework for such regional forecasting bears a resemblance to that used at the national level. Gross National Expenditure is the total of expenditures on consumption, investment, and exports, less imports. Investment and exports are considered the prime determinants of the level of economic activity. Consumption and imports are dependent variables. Given a knowledge of how consumption and imports vary with income, a forecast of investment and exports will permit the determination of Gross National Expenditure.

the level of activity in the "passive" industries. It is not always easy to draw distinctions between "carrier" and "passive" industries, however, and the conclusions drawn on a region's economic activity will depend on the quality of the data available and the methods of statistical analysis used.

In recent years, much has been written on the economic base theory. In part this has been concerned with a discussion of the theory's validity and in part with the practical problems of applying it to actual situations. The ways in which regional boundaries are designated is likely to make a marked difference to the proportion of goods which are "exported"; the smaller the area, the larger the proportion of exports, and vice versa: a large area tends to have a greater proportion of internal trade than a smaller one and this internal trade is likely to assume increased importance as a determinant of growth.

It is apparent too that many services, while not "exports" in themselves, are indispensable to those industries which are exporting from the area. Power and water supplies are cases in point; they become in effect *indirect* exports. But once the notion of indirect exports is introduced, the problem of deciding what should and should not be included in the "export base" becomes more complex and the quantification of the base requires a much more elaborate investigation. The whole problem of measurement is in fact a complicated one.

Depending upon the relative availability of the basic data, income, employment, sales, or value added may be selected as the unit of measurement of the economic base, but the results may differ somewhat depending on which is chosen. Because of the ready availability of data on employment, this is a convenient measure to use, though adjustment for hours worked may be necessary where they show substantial fluctuation.

Since attempts to measure the export sectors by field investigation are costly, indirect measures are generally preferred. One of the most commonly used is the location quotient, or coefficient of specialization. The underlying assumption is that if the proportion of employment in the production of a particular commodity within the region in question exceeds that in the nation as a whole, the excess employment indicates exports. If the proportion of employment is less than in the nation as a whole, the difference indicates imports into the region. This measure is a simple one with much to commend it as an indicator of the economic base, taking account as it does of indirect as well as direct exports. But apart from the fact that the technique presupposes uniform demand throughout the country as well as uniform output per employee, there is a serious difficulty in that the results depend on the amount of detail available in the classification of industries according to the Standard Industrial Classification of the Dominion Bureau of Statistics. Shoe factories may, for example, concentrate on the production of certain types of footwear, the bulk of which may be exported from the region. Other types of footwear may be imported. A composite figure for shoe factories within the region might then fail to reveal any exports at all. The size of the base, in short, will be determined by the degree of statistical sub-classification.

There remains the question of the real importance of exports in the growth of the region. To the extent that local investment is determined by forces other than the level of local income, independent or autonomous investment is, like exports, a factor influencing local income, the effect depending on the size of the local investment multiplier. It thus becomes necessary to distinguish between investment which reflects merely the level and rate of growth of local income and investment which is independent of it. The same considerations apply to government expenditure in the region. Tiebout, however, expresses the view that while in the short run other sectors besides exports can be considered as basic, local housing being a case in point, "Over the longer time span only the export sectors appear as basic. The locally oriented industries will grow or decline along with the growth or decline of the export sectors."[1]

---

[1] Charles M. Tiebout, *The Community Economic Base Study* (Supplementary Paper No. 16; New York: Committee for Economic Development, 1962), pp. 74–5.

As Tiebout himself observes, however, it needs to be emphasized that "The concept of the base is essentially a short run tool of analysis. If the desire is to explain future growth possibilities both in terms of the expansion of existing basic activities as well as the possibility of attracting new industry, then an approach via location theory and the economies of regional development are called for. All the base type of analysis can do is point out what happens if you add more independent activities. It cannot say whether or not you *will* grow in independent activities."[1]

## A Summing Up

The uncertainty surrounding the forces which contribute to disparities in regional incomes is well brought out by Frank Denton in his *Analysis of Interregional Differences*. Having examined the factors contributing to the differences in income between the Atlantic provinces and other regions of the country, Denton observes that seemingly "one cannot go far in accounting for basic differences in levels of earnings in terms of mere statistical differences in industrial and occupational distribution, age composition, hours and weeks of work, average levels of education, and rural-urban population distributions". After drawing attention to the interdependence of the variables and the risk of double counting which this entails, he notes that "The significant conclusion is a negative one: even at the level of mere statistical distribution, the factors examined do not account for much of the observable variation in earnings; something more basic must be sought."[2] To the student of regional economics this conclusion is a most important one, a reminder of the dangers of facile popularizations of current discussions on the importance of some particular variable, such as education. Moreover, as Denton points out, even if one were able to account for earnings differences in terms of some

[1] Charles M. Tiebout, "The Urban Economic Base Reconsidered" in *The Techniques of Urban Economic Analysis*, ed. Ralph W. Pfouts (West Trenton, N.J.: Chandler Davis, 1960), pp. 288–9. See also Gerald Sirkin, "The Theory of the Regional Economic Base", *The Review of Economics and Statistics*, XLI (1959), 426–9.

[2] Denton, *op. cit.*, p. 13.

specific factor or factors, one would still be left with the need to explain the circumstances which give rise to it.

While it may be possible to discover that unemployment accounts for a certain percentage of the difference between incomes in region A and in region B, and that the industrial mix or some other variable accounts for another percentage of the difference, this does not explain *why* the unemployment is higher in the first place or *why* the industrial mix is what it is. Ideally this is what one would like to know.

*5. The Grounds for*
*Regional*
*Development Policies*

REGIONAL DEVELOPMENT POLICIES have been introduced in recent years by a great many countries, and there has
been considerable experimentation. In some of these countries,
especially in Britain, governments have been exerting an influence on the location of industry and employment for the past
several decades. The debates and enquiries pertaining to the
British scene provide a rich source of information on the issues
involved. One of the most important pre-war studies was that
undertaken by the Royal Commission on the Distribution of the
Industrial Population. The report, commonly known as "The
Barlow Report", was presented to Parliament in January 1940,
shortly after the outbreak of war.[1] The Commissioners enquired
into the causes underlying the distribution of the industrial population and into the social, economic, and other disadvantages to
which that distribution gave rise. They then proceeded to an
examination of regionalism and the problem of the depressed
areas, and concluded with recommendations for remedial action.

[1] Royal Commission on the Distribution of the Industrial Population,
*Report* (London: H.M.S.O., 1940, reprinted 1963, Cmd. 6153).

Like the Rowell-Sirois Report in Canada, the Barlow Report in Britain contains much that is still relevant and furnishes a useful background to current discussion.

In common with Britain, and to some extent following her lead, most of the countries in western Europe have pursued regional development policies, and here again many of the relevant studies will repay investigation by the student of Canadian affairs.[1] These studies provide a broader perspective than is likely to be gained by concentrating exclusively on the Canadian situation, and some European innovations might well be adopted in Canada.

Regional economic policies in Europe vary, but the problems that gave rise to them are in many instances the same. Prominent among them are:

a) concentration of unemployment, instability of employment, and the threat of future unemployment in certain parts of the country;

b) marked regional disparities or increasing disparities in per capita income, resulting in a sense of social injustice;

c) extreme concentration of the population in some areas and the depopulation of others;

d) retarded growth at the national level leading to the need to expand output in lagging regions where potential for such expansion exists.

Though attitudes differ from one country to another, the view is widely held in Europe that *laissez-faire* policies of market equilibrium will not achieve the regional distribution of income and employment opportunity which is desired and that governments have a responsibility to influence regional patterns of economic activity. Even where they operate in the desired direction, market forces are likely to be too slow and uncertain. At the worst they may contribute to a cumulative disequilibrium in which local unemployment increases and income differentials widen. As a

---

[1] See, for example, U.S. Department of Commerce, Area Redevelopment Administration, *Area Redevelopment Policies in Britain and the Countries of the Common Market* (Washington, D.C.: Government Printing Office, 1965), and numerous country studies published by the O.E.C.D., Paris.

case in point, migration is selective and hence is likely to reduce the quality of the labour force that stays behind and contribute to an adverse age structure. In the absence of counterbalancing steps, population may also become even more concentrated in certain areas already regarded as overcrowded.

While the governments of most countries attempt to modify regional economic patterns along the lines indicated above, the manner in which the objectives are construed and the form the policies take differ in many respects. The government of France, for example, has moved towards an integration of regional objectives in its national plan and, like Britain, has restricted building in congested areas. Italy has undertaken a number of measures to encourage industrial development in the impoverished south, requiring certain mixed and public holding companies to invest there. Programs in Germany, in contrast, have been comparatively modest.

In a number of cases it is clear that European policies have tended to be bolder than those in Canada. This can be explained at least in part by a lack of clear purpose on the part of the Canadian government. This is related in turn to the division of jurisdiction between Ottawa and the provinces and the desire of Ottawa not to alienate provincial support. As a result, the federal structure of government has led to extreme caution in implementing national policies designed to redistribute population or industry. In some respects, however, the federal structure of Canadian government has been a spur to implementing regional policies, and among these spurs has been the need to maintain national unity.

## Unemployment and Under-employment

As noted in Chapter 1, unemployment shows a striking regional pattern, and so does under-employment as it is reflected in labour force participation rates. In Canada, as elsewhere, chronic high levels of regional unemployment have been one of the most powerful forces in giving rise to policies of regional development. The causes of that unemployment may be due to several factors: the decline of a basic industry in the area, the exhaustion of natural resources, or technological change resulting in sharply reduced demands for manpower.

Some areas of the country are heavily dependent on only one or two industries and are especially vulnerable to declines in them – opportunities for employment in other types of occupation may not exist. At any given moment there may be prosperity and high levels of employment in such areas, but the position is a precarious one, with a risk of sharp reversals. Under these circumstances, a policy of assisting areas to establish new industry only when the threat of unemployment has materialized is an inadequate one. If unemployment is to be a reason for the implementation of regional policies, it is not enough just to look at current or past figures. What is at stake is not the past but the future.[1]

As observed in an International Labour Office study,[2] the impact of the decline of an industry on a particular region will vary not only with the extent of the region's dependency on the industry in question, but also with the rate of its decline and the severity of its repercussions on other forms of economic activity. If it is a base industry, the secondary effects may be far-reaching. These effects may manifest themselves in two ways. Workers who lose their jobs will cut down their consumption of local goods and services; and the declining industry will reduce its demands for material and service inputs (the so-called structural effect). Other local industries will also be affected to the extent that they have supplied these demands. Transfer payments designed to maintain levels of consumption and thereby ensure the survival of the service industries may do little to solve the problems of the supplying industries. In general, the smaller the geographical area under consideration the greater the risks of instability are likely to be, though this is not always the case, for it may be able to transfer much of its instability to other areas.

One of the reasons for concern with the regional aspects of

[1] As discussed in Chapter 8, Canadian policy is very deficient in this regard.
[2] "The Regional Problem" in *Unemployment and Structural Change* (Studies and Reports, New Series, No. 65; Geneva: International Labour Office, 1962), pp. 43–50.

unemployment, and not just with the national average, is that when unemployment is concentrated in certain localities, it is more disruptive to the social fabric – particularly if it is not only heavy but chronic – a number of public services are likely to suffer, social capital deteriorates, and the mood of pessimism and futility which is engendered greatly complicates the task of recovery. Areas which have suffered long periods of heavy unemployment are among the most difficult to restore; skills and work patterns have suffered and apathy replaces enterprise.

It is not intended to suggest, however, that measures to deal with regional unemployment should necessarily be regional in character. It is commonly argued, and with justification, that the primary measures required to increase regional employment must lie in the maintenance of high levels of aggregate demand through the adoption of appropriate fiscal and monetary policies. That is, while deficient demand at the national level may manifest itself in an exacerbation of regional unemployment figures, this does not warrant the conclusion that such unemployment calls for specifically regional measures. None the less, it is apparent from Canadian experience as well as from that of many other countries, that high levels of aggregate demand may still leave extensive areas of the country suffering from a deficiency in employment opportunity. Beyond a certain point, moreover, an increase in aggregate demand will contribute to inflationary forces and necessitate curbing expansion. That point may be reached at a time when unemployment still remains at unacceptably high levels in particular regions. Under these circumstances, the solution has to be found in policies permitting a *selective* expansion at the regional level. On certain occasions in Canada, the need to curb a boom has occurred when unemployment in some provinces has been 6 per cent or higher.[1]

Regional monetary policies have never been attempted in Canada, and it is difficult to see how they could be implemented

[1] For instance in 1965, when the national level of unemployment was under 4 per cent and deflationary policies were being introduced, unemployment in the Atlantic provinces was almost double at 7½ per cent. A similar situation arose in 1956.

with any prospect of success, nor has any particular effort been made by the Minister of Finance to introduce counter-cyclical fiscal policies on a regional basis, though some efforts have been made recently to exclude the poorer regions from expenditure cuts.[1]

## Disparities of Income

After unemployment, lower levels of income in certain areas of the country are frequently regarded as the prime reason for the introduction of regional development policies. High unemployment and low levels of income are generally found together, although there are exceptions to this. In British Columbia, for example, unemployment rates tend to be higher than the national average, though incomes are higher there too.

The case for the provision of special assistance to less prosperous communities has been argued on a variety of grounds, including the need for social justice as well as for a more efficient use of economic resources. Most consider it to be neither desirable nor just to permit the perpetuation of islands of distress in a nation which enjoys as a whole one of the highest levels of living in the world. For many communities the prospects of participating fully in a growing national income are bleak, and the perpetuation and even the widening of the gap between their fortunes and those of others gives rise to feelings of resentment. Their acceptance of poverty is made more difficult when they see many others prospering. Unless it is argued that the inherent quality of the labour force differs from one part of the country to another, rewards should also tend to be equal, and if marked disparities persist over the long run, there are strong grounds for presuming that resources are not being allocated efficiently.

It is clear, for example, that educational opportunities differ

[1] For a report on the effects of monetary policy on the economy of the Atlantic provinces and a recommendation of methods by which it might be made flexible so as to meet the particular needs of those provinces, see the study by A. K. Cairncross, *Economic Development and the Atlantic Provinces* (Fredericton, N.B.: Atlantic Provinces Research Board, February 1961).

widely from one part of the country to another and that human resources are going to waste in some of the poorer areas. The survival of obsolescent industries, concentrated in certain areas, results in depressed incomes there, and is a further manifestation of inefficient resource allocation. The fact that more people do not migrate out of such areas is not to be interpreted so much as evidence of a desire to stay there and continue working in declining industries as of a deficiency in training and skill which would permit them to make a significantly better living elsewhere.[1]

It has long been a practice of the federal government in Canada to transfer funds to the poorer provinces as a means of reducing income inequalities, though the task of actually quantifying total net transfers to individual provinces is an almost impossible one. The total amount of the allocation of federal government revenues and expenditures by province has been questioned from time to time, but as the Minister of Finance explained on one occasion,[2] it is impossible in view of the nature of the problem to provide a simple answer. There is bound to be a large element of uncertainty, and impressions of what should and should not be included will vary. One cannot, for example, do much more than guess the extent to which individual areas benefit from certain federal payments for goods and services. Government receipts from indirect taxes paid by firms located in a particular area do not represent a net burden on that area, for the taxes are largely passed on to others. The question also arises as to whether one ought to include or exclude the receipts and payments of crown corporations.

Table 5:1, for 1962 to 1963, furnishes information on certain aspects of federal transfer payments, which are designed specifically to assist the poorer provinces.

Apart from the difficulty of quantifying the federal assistance that is given, there is the problem noted in Chapter 1 of defining

---

[1] This is not to deny that prolonged periods of poverty may also create psychological and other barriers to movement, so that some people are content to receive lower incomes because of the psychic satisfaction in living where they do or because the costs of movement appear excessive.

[2] "Reply of the Minister of Finance, tabled November 6, 1964, to Question No. 741 asked by Mr. Balcer, July 22, 1964", *Hansard*, 1964, Vol. VI, p. 5809.

## Table 5:1
## Federal Transfers to Provinces
## 1962-1963

($ per capita)

| | Newfoundland | Prince Edward Island | Nova Scotia | New Brunswick | Quebec | Ontario | Manitoba | Saskatchewan | Alberta | British Columbia |
|---|---|---|---|---|---|---|---|---|---|---|
| **Unconditional transfers** | | | | | | | | | | |
| Equalization | 29.14 | 34.10 | 23.71 | 25.39 | 13.46 | — | 14.87 | 24.37 | 8.62 | — |
| Statutory subsidies | 3.52 | 6.20 | 2.86 | 2.87 | 0.75 | 0.73 | 2.23 | 2.28 | 2.06 | 1.01 |
| Atlantic provinces adjustment | 22.34 | 33.08 | 14.08 | 17.30 | — | — | — | — | — | — |
| Additional, Newfoundland | 17.02 | — | — | — | — | — | — | — | — | — |
| Total | 72.03 | 73.32 | 40.65 | 45.56 | 14.21 | 0.73 | 17.10 | 26.64 | 10.67 | 1.01 |
| Conditional transfers | 67.53 | 52.09 | 38.05 | 40.31 | 39.17 | 50.78 | 39.20 | 41.27 | 51.45 | 47.21 |

Note: Figures do not add to totals in all cases because of rounding.

Source: D.B.S., *Provincial Government Finance* (68-207).

and measuring the disparities themselves. Various measures can be used, such as per capita income, family income, income per worker, or even the aggregate income, in so far as it can be ascertained, of the area as a whole.

## Migration and Population Distribution

While rising per capita incomes are desired, they may not be desired at the expense of heavy out-migration and a decline in the total output of the area. In the minds of some, this applies no less at the provincial than at the national level. It is highly unlikely, for example, that measures designed to increase per capita income in Quebec would be acceptable to that province if they entailed an out-migration to Ontario of people from the impoverished Gaspé peninsula. Indeed, many provincial governments regard out-migration to another province as too high a price to pay for a rise in per capita incomes. This imposes a distinct restraint on the policies that can be pursued at times.

It can be argued that if the per capita income of a community rises as a result of out-migration, such migration should be encouraged even though it results in a decline in the aggregate income of the community. But out-migration will not be favoured by those individuals in the community who are likely to benefit more from a rapidly growing population than from a slowly growing population, or by those who see their livelihood threatened by the exodus. Such groups favour a concept of growth which stresses the total rather than the per capita income of the region. Together they may well form an influential pressure group, but there is no reason why their views should prevail over those of others who think differently. Local retail merchants, real estate salesmen, local construction firms, and the suppliers of services, whose incomes all depend largely on population size, are likely to agree that declines in population should be avoided. Their views will also be shared by others who fear that while out-migration is likely to result in a rise in income for those who leave, it is also likely to result in a decline not only in the total income but also in the per capita income of those who stay. It can also be argued that the per capita gains of those who migrate are more than offset by the losses of those who remain. This underlying fear undeniably motivates many local attempts to avoid a loss of population, and it must be conceded that the fear is not always without some justification. There may well come a time in the life of a region or community where a cumulative decline sets in, threatening the livelihood of those who remain.

A further reservation about the desirability of migration from less prosperous areas is that it tends to be selective. Almost invariably it is the younger members in the labour force who move, and the consequences of this can be especially unfortunate for the declining regions. There is thus no assurance that a smaller population will be a more favoured one economically. Furthermore, gains may be more than offset where expensive social services have to be shared among smaller numbers.

It is worth noting that in a number of European countries the out-migration of people is a circumstance which justifies the granting of assistance under programs of regional aid. While there is no desire to maintain the present population distribution without change, the depopulation of certain areas of the country and the heavy concentration of population in others is discouraged as a matter of national policy. Canada still has to come to grips with this problem. Unlike many European countries, Canada so far has not been faced with the problems arising out of extreme population concentration in one or two localities, but this will not always be the case, and provincial and national policies on the matter can be expected to lead to sharp differences of opinion. In this as in many other aspects of regional policy there is need for more data on the costs and benefits entailed in certain patterns of population distribution. Toronto and Montreal, with some two million inhabitants each, are still relatively small when compared with many other cities in the world, and the economies arising from their further growth may prove to be substantial. The point has certainly not yet been reached where the disadvantages of living and working in these cities are so great as to result in any significant decline in their rate of growth. It is clear that in the minds of many people the net advantages lie the other way, and the cities continue to attract newcomers. There is, however, some disposition in Canada to adopt policies akin to those in Britain, where deliberate efforts have been made to siphon population away from the largest urban centres and create new employment centres.

Governments are, of course, aware that while migration of population may have repercussions which are undesirable, there are some situations where there are overwhelming advantages in encouraging it. When an area cannot readily be revived and nothing is to be gained by attempting to resist the process of decay, the sooner people can be encouraged to leave, the better. As one writer observed, there is no point in applying artificial respiration to economic dinosaurs.

In reviewing the issues of migration and unemployment, the Special Committee of the Senate on Manpower and Employment drew attention in its Report to the enduring difficulties of certain areas and regions, especially the Atlantic region, and suggested that over the long run there were only two solutions: "either the people move out to better opportunities elsewhere, or better opportunities are made available to them where they are". The Committee then added: "The massive migration of the population is neither socially nor economically desirable, *and we reject this possibility*. Therefore, the other course, namely of providing better opportunities for these people in the areas concerned, must be undertaken with determined effort." Commenting further on the various policies that would be necessary, the Committee continued:

> The consequences of technological changes and the effects of declining industries are so large that little can be accomplished with marginal and small-scale remedies. New industries which have a good prospect of prospering in these locations must be established. For this purpose a co-ordinated programme must be undertaken which includes all the steps that are necessary – research and study to determine the best economic potentialities of the areas concerned, the provision of capital on attractive terms to build new productive facilities, retraining of manpower

along the appropriate lines, and the provision of social capital in the form of utilities and other public services. Sporadic incursions into this problem and random flourishes are not going to bring results. The Federal Government, with the co-operation of the Provincial Governments, must take the initiative in developing a co-ordinated series of efforts which get to grips with the task involved.[1]

## Contribution to National Output

In its Second Annual Review, the Economic Council of Canada referred to two main, interrelated considerations involved in moving towards "a better regional balance". The first was the importance of reducing the relative disparities in average levels of income as they presently existed among the regions, and the second was the need to assure that each region contributed to total national output and to the sustained, long-run growth of that output, on the basis of the fullest and most efficient use of the human and material resources available to the region.[2]

The desire to expand output at the national level has stimulated enquiry on the implications of retarded growth at the regional level. Two schools of thought have emerged. Some favour specific assistance to the lagging regions, arguing that substantial gains in total output can be expected by concentrating on their problems. Others are sceptical about the net effects of such assistance on national output, arguing that growth should be encouraged only in the more promising regions of the country. The national objective of more rapid growth, they contend, will be easier to achieve if attempts are not made to bolster up the less favoured regions. In effect they apply to the national scene the

[1] Special Committee of the Senate on Manpower and Employment, *Final Report* (Ottawa: Queen's Printer, 1961), No. 25, p. 6. (The *Proceedings* of the Special Committee, Nos. 1–24, contain a wealth of information on unemployment in Canada, at the regional as well as the national level.) See also: S. F. Kaliski, "Structural Unemployment in Canada: Towards a Definition of the Geographic Dimension", *The Canadian Journal of Economics*, I, no. 3, August 1968, pp. 551–65.

[2] *Towards Sustained and Balanced Economic Growth* (Ottawa: Queen's Printer, 1965), pp. 98–9.

same argument that many apply to the regional scene. They insist on the importance of concentrating attention on "growth points".

That both schools of thought have their adherents in part reflects the inadequacy of the evidence. Depending on the assumptions made, it is possible to argue either way. There may be some cases where assistance to the less favoured regions appears to be at the expense of the country as a whole or to produce only meagre returns. There may be others where such assistance will benefit the nation. Whatever uncertainty there may be on this score, lagging regions are characterized by unused resources of manpower which may take several forms: unemployment, low labour force participation rates, and low output per worker. There is no denying that such a situation results in a significant loss in national output, and unless it is clear beyond reasonable doubt that other measures will be more effective in redressing this situation, it would seem sensible to tackle the regional weakness directly.

As a final observation, it should be added that whatever the economic rationale of regional development policies may be, political rather than economic considerations are likely to weigh with governments, and this indeed is true to some extent of all policies. Governments are subject to constant pressures of one sort and another, and the final decisions on the action to be taken will be coloured by the expected effects on the political fortunes of the party in power. Although the consequences of economic measures which prove to be ill-conceived are likely to manifest themselves and to lead to reappraisals, a bad situation may have been rendered worse and more intractable in the interim. Cases are not uncommon where attempts to assure the survival of a key industry in a depressed locality lead to ever-increasing subventions. To the extent that the fortunes of that industry determine the well-being of others which have been encouraged to locate or expand there, the more difficult it becomes to discontinue aid to it.

Political attitudes also colour the type of government measures likely to be introduced. Direct assistance to specific industries, encouraging them to establish in certain areas, tends to be viewed with less favour than public expenditures on social capital of one sort or another which are designed to accomplish the same end and which have a longer tradition behind them.

## Concern with National Unity

The maintenance of national unity has been a prime concern of federal government in Canada from the time of Confederation on. The forces leading to friction between the provincial and federal governments have varied in importance from one period to another, but there has never been a time when the federal government could ignore them.

Among the most important issues in federal-provincial relations have been the disparities in income and employment opportunity that exist throughout the country. These disparities have been a never-ending source of concern and have led to innumerable federal-provincial conferences and adjustments of one sort and another, varying from freight-rate subventions to direct transfer payments. The Report of the Royal Commission on Dominion-Provincial Relations in 1939 is one of the outstanding documents on the subject, having relevance especially to the inter-war years. There is no better historical source from which to begin a survey of subsequent developments.

The Commissioners were instructed to examine in particular the constitutional allocation of revenue sources and governmental burdens to the federal and provincial governments, the past results of this allocation, and its suitability to present conditions as well as to the conditions likely to prevail in the future. In addition, the Commissioners were to determine whether the division of the burden of government was equitable as it stood, and whether the federal and provincial governments were able to discharge their responsibilities within the framework of the present allocation of public functions and powers or would be able to do so within the framework of some new allocation.

Many of the issues that were discussed remain as relevant today as they were then, and discussions on the sources and distribution of revenue and the allocation of economic and other responsibilities continue to dominate present debate. An illustration of this is the statement made by the Minister of Finance to the Tax Structure Committee on September 14, 1966. In referring to the need for a new equalization formula, he said:

> Equalization arrangements are one of the four central features of federal-provincial fiscal relations. They represent one of the dividends of Canadian unity, designed as they are to enable all Canadians to enjoy an adequate level of provincial public services. Where circumstances – whether natural or man-made – have channelled a larger than average share of the nation's wealth into certain sections of the country, there should be a redistribution of that wealth so that all provinces are able to provide to their citizens a reasonably comparable level of basic services, without resorting to unduly burdensome levels of taxation.

The federal structure of Canadian government has been one of the most important factors in the formation and development of regional development policies. The regional Canadian scene cannot be comprehended except in the context of the federal-provincial structure, for it is a safe assumption that national unity would not survive for long stresses and strains that would be created by large and growing disparities in economic development. At the same time, any attempt by the federal government to foster economic development in one part of the country at the possible expense of another can be expected to meet with strong opposition from those whose interest is likely to be jeopardized. The government thus finds itself walking a tight-rope and the delicacy of the situation is reflected in the caution of ministerial statements.

While differences in culture and language seem to constitute the primary reason for feelings of regional disunity, some provincial premiers have made it clear that they attach greater importance to economic disparities. In general, French-speaking Canadians concentrated in Quebec and some parts of New Brunswick tend to be at the lower end of the income scale. Whatever the explanation for their lower incomes, the very fact that they are lower is a source of discontent. Were such disparities less, other aspects of dissatisfaction might prove more tractable.

Concern with national unity has not usually been specifically mentioned in debates on regional policy, however. It is often an implicit rather than an express objective of policy. For the most part, regional policies in Canada have been couched in terms of relieving local unemployment and poverty. Whether the emphasis will shift under the direction of the new department for regional development remains to be seen. There are suggestions of a reassessment of priorities that would give increased attention to long-run structural changes designed to create a more efficient economy in the future rather than to measures designed to reduce immediate unemployment and poverty.

# 6. *Rural Poverty and the Agricultural and Rural Development Program*

THERE ARE THREE main programs designed to bear directly on area or regional economic development for which the federal government is responsible. The earliest of these programs, which will be discussed in this chapter, was set up under the Agricultural and Rural Development Act and is administered by the Rural Development Branch of the Department of Forestry and Rural Development. The other two, administered by the Area Development Agency in the Department of Industry and by the Atlantic Development Board, will be discussed in the chapters following.[1]

## *The Origins of* ARDA

It has been obvious for a long time that agricultural and rural poverty is particularly marked in certain areas of the country, and

[1] Since this was written, these programs have all been brought under the wing of the department for regional affairs. This department has also been given the responsibility for the Prairie Farm Rehabilitation Administration, the Cape Breton Development Corporation, and certain other bodies. The reorganization should be a great improvement.

## Table 6:1
## Analysis of Farms by Economic Type*
### 1961

| | Commercial farms† | | | | Part-time farms‡ | | Small-scale farms§ | | Total farms |
| | Sales $2,500 and over | | Sales $1,200 to $2,499 | | | | | | |
| | (number) | (%) | (number) | (%) | (number) | (%) | (number) | (%) | (number) |
|---|---|---|---|---|---|---|---|---|---|
| Newfoundland | 281 | 26 | 175 | 16 | 335 | 31 | 289 | 27 | 1,080 |
| Prince Edward Island | 2,886 | 45 | 1,644 | 25 | 793 | 12 | 1,160 | 18 | 6,483 |
| Nova Scotia | 3,016 | 32 | 1,923 | 20 | 2,466 | 26 | 2,085 | 22 | 9,490 |
| New Brunswick | 3,073 | 33 | 2,043 | 22 | 2,150 | 23 | 1,939 | 21 | 9,205 |
| Atlantic provinces | 9,256 | 35 | 5,785 | 22 | 5,744 | 22 | 5,473 | 21 | 26,258 |
| Quebec | 38,927 | 46 | 23,570 | 28 | 10,249 | 12 | 11,889 | 14 | 84,635 |
| Ontario | 69,667 | 64 | 20,678 | 19 | 9,920 | 9 | 9,371 | 9 | 109,636 |

| | | | | | | | | |
|---|---|---|---|---|---|---|---|---|
| Manitoba | 24,286 | 60 | 9,236 | 23 | 2,402 | 6 | 4,563 | 11 | 40,487 |
| Saskatchewan | 63,546 | 70 | 18,739 | 21 | 2,515 | 3 | 6,276 | 7 | 91,076 |
| Alberta | 45,203 | 66 | 13,495 | 20 | 3,807 | 6 | 5,933 | 9 | 68,438 |
| Prairie provinces | 133,035 | 67 | 41,470 | 21 | 8,724 | 4 | 16,722 | 8 | 200,001 |
| British Columbia | 8,150 | 52 | 2,752 | 18 | 3,002 | 19 | 1,791 | 11 | 15,695 |
| CANADA** | 259,037 | 59 | 94,256 | 22 | 37,645 | 9 | 45,301 | 10 | 436,239 |

*Excluding residential farms (farms with annual sales of less than $250) and institutional farms.

†Farms with annual sales of agricultural products of $1,200 and over.

‡Farms with annual sales of from $250 to $1,199, and 100 days or more of off-farm work *or* off-farm income of the operator and his family is greater than the income from the sale of agricultural products.

§Farms with annual sales of from $250 to $1,199, and less than 100 days of off-farm work and off-farm income of the operator and his family is less than the income from the sales of agricultural products.

**Includes Yukon and Northwest Territories.

Source: D.B.S., *1961 Census of Canada*, Vol. V (96-530).

over the years there have been numerous policies designed to reduce it. The ARDA program is one of the most comprehensive of these.

According to Table 6:1, 41 per cent of all farms in Canada had annual sales of less than $2,500 in 1961. Of this 41 per cent, 10 per cent had sales of between $250 and $1,199, and the revenue exceeded the farmers' income from other sources. In Quebec 54 per cent of the farms had sales of less than $2,500, a figure it will be noted, that does not include so-called "residential farms" having sales of less than $250, that is, constituting only a supplementary source of income. In one survey of the farm situation in eastern Canada it was estimated that approximately half the farmers were redundant, in the sense that they could leave agriculture to the benefit of themselves as well as of the remaining farm community and the national economy.[1]

In November 1956, in a speech delivered in Toronto, the Prime Minister drew attention to the fact that certain land in eastern Canada was quite unfit for its current use in farming. He expressed his conviction that such land should be returned to forestry and water conservation and that those attempting to live on it should be resettled in more rewarding surroundings. The succeeding Prime Minister followed this recommendation by a statement to Parliament, in August 1958, that his government was considering a program designed to improve the standard of living of farmers on small farms. This was to be achieved by means of better land use, technical training for farmers including those who wished to enter new occupations, and encouraging the formation of economic farm units.[2] Subsequently the Minister of Agriculture asserted that the objective of the national program was to give agriculture a reasonably fair share of the national income, not by charity but by providing opportunities for the

[1] Hedlin, Menzies & Associates Ltd., *Report of the Eastern Canada Farm Survey* (Ottawa: ARDA, May 1963). There is a very extensive literature on the problems facing small-scale farmers and the broader issues of rural poverty in general. See, for example, *Rural Canada in Transition*, eds. Marc Adelard Tremblay and Walton J. Anderson (Ottawa: Agricultural Economics Research Council of Canada, 1966).

[2] Hansard, 1958, Vol. IV, p. 4347.

farmers to help themselves.[1]

Reflecting this concern over agricultural incomes, a special committee of the Senate was authorized in January 1957 to consider and report on land use in Canada. Consideration was to extend to the action necessary to ensure that land resources would be most effectively utilized for the benefit of the Canadian economy and the Canadian people and, in particular, to increase both agricultural production and the incomes of those engaged in it. In introducing the motion, the leader of the government in the Senate stated that "It is . . . the challenging task of this proposed Senate Committee, (*a*) to make a broad survey of land use in Canada, (*b*) to focus public attention on all aspects of this problem, and (*c*) to invite the best minds in the country to set out their views as to the appropriate solutions, and particularly as these would benefit the farmer and tend to raise farm incomes."[2]

Witnesses representing national, regional, and local interests were called on to testify before the Senate Committee, and their testimony was made public. In this testimony, frequent references were made to the plight of impoverished farmers, the unsuitability of their land for farming, poor managerial practices, and the deficiencies arising out of inadequate farm size and finance. The view was expressed repeatedly that the best opportunities for many in the farming community were to be found outside the field of agriculture because technological changes had reduced the need for manpower on the farms by permitting great increases in output per man.

It was clear that there was widespread distress among small-scale farmers, though precise quantification of the problem was impossible, partly because of the difficulty in deciding who should be counted as a farmer and partly because a great many farmers supplement their income with outside earnings on which there are few data. There was also underlying uncertainty as to how poverty could be measured. Poverty is a concept which is difficult

---

[1] Hansard, 1961, Vol. II, p. 1403.
[2] Senate of Canada, *Report of the Special Committee on Land Use in Canada* (Ottawa: Queen's Printer, 1964), pp. 9–10.

to pin down in numerical terms.[1] A farmer living in semi-retirement or farming only part time might have only a very modest income from his farm, yet not be "poor" in the sense in which most people interpret it. In other cases, family incomes may not be particularly low, but may only have been achieved by the younger members of the family leaving school to work. Individual and family needs also tend to vary over time, as does the notion of what constitutes poverty. Whatever the magnitude ascribed to poverty among farmers specifically, however, it was clear that their plight was only one aspect of the much larger problem of rural poverty in general. As seen from Table 6:2 following, some 300,000, or over 40 per cent of the rural non-farm families had annual incomes below $3,000 in 1961. In the Atlantic provinces the figure rose to 58 per cent, with Newfoundland heading the list at 70 per cent. In Quebec the percentage was 47 per cent, 2 per cent higher than in the Prairie provinces, and in British Columbia it was the lowest at 29 per cent. Farm families with "low" incomes fared better, according to the definition used – only 22 per cent falling within this category – though again the concentration was in the Atlantic provinces and Quebec.[2]

A comparison of the incomes of rural non-farm families with those of families from urban or metropolitan areas showed that urban families have incomes that are considerably higher than rural ones, and those in metropolitan areas have substantially more again. The following table indicates the magnitudes involved. Prince Edward Island and Saskatchewan have no metropolitan areas, but urban incomes in those provinces were about 50 per cent higher than incomes in rural non-farm areas.

[1] See Jenny R. Podoluk, "The Characteristics of Low Income Families" in *Incomes of Canadians* (to be published, Ottawa: Queen's Printer, 1968). This monograph, which is a valuable source of reference, includes a statistical study of regional income distribution and an examination of the economic returns in education.

[2] By using 1961 census data and employing a definition of a "low income farm family" as one whose farm has a total capital value of less than $25,000, gross sales of agricultural products of less than $2,500 a year, and off-farm work by the operator of less than 25 days a year, it was calculated that some 95,000 farms fell within this category, more than one fifth of all farms in Canada. Low income farms in the Atlantic provinces and Quebec were 33 per cent and 29 per cent respectively.

### Table 6:2
### Rural Non-Farm Families with Incomes of $3,000 a Year
### or Less
### 1961

|  | (a) Total rural non-farm families | (b) Families with annual incomes of $3,000 or less | (a) as % of (b) |
|---|---|---|---|
| Newfoundland | 41,152 | 28,900 | 70 |
| Prince Edward Island | 6,898 | 4,035 | 58 |
| Nova Scotia | 59,601 | 31,063 | 52 |
| New Brunswick | 50,583 | 27,476 | 54 |
| Atlantic provinces | 158,234 | 91,474 | 58 |
| Quebec | 145,547 | 69,010 | 47 |
| Ontario | 194,765 | 59,440 | 31 |
| Manitoba | 33,227 | 15,680 | 47 |
| Saskatchewan | 47,615 | 23,598 | 50 |
| Alberta | 41,240 | 15,963 | 39 |
| Prairie provinces | 122,082 | 55,241 | 45 |
| British Columbia | 81,215 | 23,312 | 29 |
| CANADA* | 703,513 | 298,821 | 42 |

*Includes Yukon and Northwest Territories.

Source: D.B.S., *1961 Census of Canada*, Vol. IV (98-503), Table C.2.

### Table 6:3
### Average Income of Rural Non-Farm, Urban, and
### Metropolitan Families
### 1961

| | Rural non-farm | Urban (excluding metropolitan) | | Census metropolitan areas | |
|---|---|---|---|---|---|
| | | | (b) as % of (a) | | (c) as % of (a) |
| | (a) | (b) | | (c) | |
| Newfoundland | 2,612 | 4,455 | *171* | 4,921 | *188* |
| Prince Edward Island | 3,130 | 4,646 | *148* | — | — |
| Nova Scotia | 3,338 | 4,237 | *127* | 5,685 | *170* |
| New Brunswick | 3,351 | 4,707 | *140* | 5,067 | *151* |
| Quebec | 3,829 | 4,974 | *130* | 6,015 | *157* |
| Ontario | 4,598 | 5,491 | *119* | 6,357 | *138* |
| Manitoba | 3,564 | 4,745 | *133* | 5,874 | *165* |
| Saskatchewan | 3,584 | 5,417 | *151* | — | — |
| Alberta | 4,198 | 5,181 | *123* | 6,160 | *147* |
| British Columbia | 4,744 | 5,815 | *123* | 5,877 | *124* |

Source: Calculated from D.B.S., *1961 Census of Canada*, Vol. IV (98-503).

In the matter of land use, one of the most frequent and strongly advocated proposals made to the Committee was for the development of a national land use policy. Decisions, it was said, should be made as to which areas should be withdrawn from agriculture, which should remain, and which should be developed and in what ways. Some of the submissions contained a strong element of geographic determinism. Suggestions were also made that an inventory of land be compiled and studied to permit the most desirable uses to be recommended.

Admittedly, the poor quality of the land was not the small-scale farmer's only handicap. Many were unable to keep up with the technological revolution in farming because of the very heavy expenditures required and their inability to finance the purchase of modern equipment or to undertake the responsibility such financing entailed. This inability was often linked with inadequate education and skills, which had led not only to poor farming practices in the first place but also to resistance to change. Chronic poverty had contributed to inertia, apathy, and immobility; and in areas where poverty was most concentrated, social problems and inadequate services also resulted, and exacerbated the situation.

A variety of remedial measures were clearly needed to overcome the resultant distress; and the Senate Committee recommended that policies take three forms: the creation of an economic climate to facilitate and improve off-farm income and employment, better land use, and more efficient production on farms remaining in agriculture. The latter called for more than just an increase in marketing information, crop insurance, and credit facilities, for such measures in practice did little to help the poorest farmers. It was the more enterprising, successful farmer who tended to benefit most from technical advice and assistance. The farmer in the greatest need of help was often the one least able to take advantage of the services available to him. Similarly, production subsidies were far more likely to benefit the large commercial farmer than the one eking out a marginal subsistence.

There was general agreement that welfare payments of one sort and another were not the solution, a view also expressed by the Minister of Agriculture when, as noted above, he stated that the objective of the national agricultural program was to give agriculture a reasonably fair share of the national income, not by charity but by providing opportunities for the farmers to help themselves.

The concern of the Committee with inappropriate land use and the poverty that resulted led it to a concern with the related question of rural development, a term broadly defined as "the organized consideration and programming of required resource adjustments in rural areas of Canada".[1] Witnesses appearing

[1] *Report of the Special Committee on Land Use in Canada*, p. 37.

before the Committee had recommended that a concerted program
be undertaken by provincial and federal government groups that
would be particularly concerned with rural development. The
sequel to the Senate enquiry was the creation of a program for
rural development set up under ARDA.

In December 1960, the Minister of Agriculture introduced the
following Resolution:

> That it is expedient to introduce a measure to authorize the
> Minister of Agriculture to enter into agreements with provincial
> governments or agencies thereof for the undertaking jointly
> with those governments or agencies of projects for the alter-
> native uses of lands that are marginal or of low productivity,
> projects for the development of income and employment oppor-
> tunities in rural agricultural areas, and projects for the develop-
> ment and conservation of the soil and water resources of
> Canada; for the payment to the provinces of contributions in
> respect of the cost of such projects undertaken by a province
> or agency thereof; to authorize the Minister of Agriculture to
> undertake programs of research and investigation in respect
> of these matters; to provide for the establishment of advisory
> committees and the appointment of their members, and to
> provide for other related and incidental matters.[1]

The Resolution reflected a view that much of the poverty of
small-scale farmers could be traced to the inadequacies of the
land they were cultivating.[2]

The debate in the Commons that followed the Resolution did
little to contribute to an understanding of the basic issues and
problems involved. Considerable time was devoted to such
irrelevancies as whether the Opposition might appropriately take
credit for the underlying idea.[3] In the debate, the Minister of
Agriculture asserted that "it is not the purpose of ARDA to reduce

---

[1] Hansard, 1960–61, Vol. 1, p. 819.

[2] The emphasis placed on the importance of land utilization seems to have
owed its origin to experience with earlier programs designed to improve
land use, especially those under the Prairie Farm Rehabilitation Act of
1935 (PFRA) and the Maritime Marshland Rehabilitation Act of 1948
(MMRA).

[3] Some of the more important aspects of the debate are contained in Hansard, 1960–61, Vol. II, pp. 1403–23; Vol. III, pp. 3255–84; Vol. IV, pp.
4183–4201, and Vol. V, pp. 5193–5212, 5584–93, and 5644–52.

the number of farms. Those who feel that the small farm problem can be resolved by uprooting people arbitrarily from their farms, do not understand the deep attachment of rural people to their home surroundings. ARDA is designed, rather, to help by various means to improve the income and standard of living of the smaller and more marginal farms, and in that way help improve the over-all position of agriculture."[1]

On the second reading of the bill he underlined the point again, stating, "I should like to mention in passing that the idea, the philosophy of this new act, is to build up income and not to push farmers off the land;"[2] though in a different vein he did recognize on the third reading, May 31, 1961, that there was a risk of over-production of food in the world and that this was the real heart of the bill – to get at this fundamental difficulty. Tech-nology, he noted, had permitted the supply of food to outpace the demand so that the income of farmers was being forced down. The consequence was a race between technology and action to discover the proper uses of land.

Underlying much of the debate was a difference in opinion between those who saw remedies to the plight of the small farmer in measures assisting him to increase his output and those who saw remedies in measures encouraging him to leave his farm and seek new employment either locally or elsewhere. While nothing would be gained by encouraging older people to quit the farms unless they were capable of doing something else, there were obvious advantages in inducing many of the younger ones to leave. Given the great increase in the use of farm machinery and the declining demand for manpower on the farms, the best employment opportunities were likely to be found outside the agri-cultural economy. Those who argued this way emphasized the importance of vocational and technical training and the encour-agement of out-migration through assistance to move. Depending on the circumstances, it was conceded, some encouragement might be given to industry to establish in rural communities.

[1] Hansard, 1960–61, Vol. II, p. 1406.
[2] Hansard, 1960–61, Vol. V, p. 5195.

The legislation, "an Act to Provide for the Rehabilitation of Agricultural Lands and the Development of Rural Areas in Canada" was given assent on June 22, 1961.[1] Whatever reservations the Minister of Agriculture may have had about the purpose of the legislation, his earlier statements regarding the lack of any intention to push farmers off the land influenced the climate in which ARDA began its operations. A related influence, and one of great significance, derived from the concern shown in the Senate enquiry with the physical properties of land and their implications for land use. As a result of both these influences, and especially of the latter, the emphasis of ARDA programs tended, at the outset, to be on the manner in which land use could be improved, particularly as it affected agriculture,[2] and geographers and soil scientists, who are generally disposed to attach considerable weight to the study of the physical environment as a key to the type of development that should take place, dominated actions initially taken under ARDA. They gave a slant to early policies which has since been regretted. Their emphasis on the physical properties of land distracted attention from the more fundamental causes of distress in rural areas.

It was considered that programs of land adjustment and regional economic development would be both fallible and costly unless there was, first of all, a sound basis for decisions on the type of land use that was most desirable; and it was decided that a comprehensive land capability survey would provide the best basis for such decisions. Very large sums of money have been spent on studies of land use in Canada, in particular on the Canada Land Inventory, which was begun under the auspices of ARDA in 1963.[3] It assesses land capability and use for a variety of

1 In shorter form the title was "the Agricultural Rehabilitation and Development Act". Subsequently, on April 6, 1966, reflecting a significant shift in emphasis, the title was changed to "the Agricultural and Rural Development Act".

2 The recent introduction of a program for land improvement in the United States was a further factor influencing the climate of opinion, though later investigation was to show that developments there were of greater value as a warning than as a model to be followed.

3 For details see ARDA, *The Canada Land Inventory: Objectives, Scope, and Organization*, Report No. 1 (Department of Forestry Publication No. 1088

purposes, including agriculture, forestry, recreation, and wild life, as well as for social and economic factors relative to land use, and covers all the agriculturally settled portions of rural Canada and the areas adjoining them where questions of the alternative use of land have a strong bearing on rural development. This inventory has thus had a direct bearing on land resource development planning at the three levels of government: federal, provincial, and municipal.

## Federal-Provincial Agreements under ARDA

ARDA policies, unlike those pursued by the Area Development Agency, require formal co-operation between the federal and provincial governments and entail a sharing of costs. The provincial governments accept a large measure of responsibility for the direction that policy takes and for expenditures within their own boundaries. The federal government may advise and recommend, but the provinces make their own selection of programs among those authorized under the agreements signed pursuant to the legislation, and only if the federal government has serious reservations which cannot be resolved about the expenditures proposed will it withhold its own contribution to them.[1] The provinces initiate plans for projects and conduct and administer almost all of them. Research projects, which the federal government may initiate and carry out on its own where it considers this necessary, are the only exception.

The first General Agreements with the provinces, spelling out the operating procedures and authorizing specific types of joint action, were signed in 1962. These were followed by other basic project agreements in the fiscal year 1963–4. Projects which would qualify under the various agreements included those aimed

---

[Ottawa: Queen's Printer, January 1965]). The computer mapping which is involved will make it possible to collect, store, and analyse far greater quantities of information than has been possible in the past.

[1] That such reservations have none the less been serious at times is obvious from the number of rejections of programs submitted by certain provinces. See the discussion below on the evaluation of ARDA programs.

at developing more efficient use and economic productivity of marginal or sub-marginal land in rural areas, soil and water conservation, and research into rural development. The agreements on research were thrown in as something of an afterthought; no one foresaw at the time the importance that was eventually to be given to them. The federal government made available $50 million towards the cost of the entire program, a modest sum in view of all that needed to be done, but small though the sum was, only two-thirds was utilized, partly because of the inability of the poorer provinces to contribute their share of the cost. The Atlantic provinces were a case in point; but Ontario, Alberta, and British Columbia also failed to take full advantage of the program, and a lack of funds was not the explanation in their case. Belief that rural poverty was not serious may have played a part, combined with uncertainty about the specific programs that should be encouraged.[1] In many cases there seemed to be a reluctance to favour one area rather than another, and this led to a multiplicity of minor projects scattered here and there, or to none at all.

The first agreements terminated in March 1965 and shortly thereafter were succeeded by new and more extensive agreements covering the five years up to March 31, 1970. The new agreements increased the federal contribution to $25 million a year for five years, making a total of $125 million over five years, compared with $50 million over two and a half years under the original ones. Each province was allotted a share of this sum according to a formula designed to reflect the extent of farm and rural poverty within its borders. The following year $50 million, subsequently increased to $300 million, was provided as a special Fund for Rural Economic Development (FRED) to permit the implementation of comprehensive rural development programs in specifically designated areas characterized by widespread low incomes and major problems of adjustment, but considered to have develop-

---

[1] Contrary to what might be expected, there is widespread poverty among farmers even in the wealthier provinces. As will be noted from Table 6:1 above, farms in Ontario with sales between $1,200 and $2,499 a year numbered between three and four times as many as those in the Atlantic provinces, but as a percentage of the total there were not significantly less. Ontario is now a major beneficiary under the ARDA program.

ment potential.[1] This has proved to be one of the most important features of the ARDA program. No such fund existed under the first agreements.[2] Except under FRED, federal expenditures are usually matched by those of the provincial governments.

Much of the early action taken by officials under the ARDA program was experimental in nature, for there was little experience to guide them. It was obvious that there was a great deal to learn, and direction was rendered more difficult by differences of opinion at both the provincial and the federal level as to where the main emphasis should lie. Thus it was a while before the emphasis shifted in some quarters from attempts to increase farm incomes by improved land use to attempts to reduce the number of farmers. As might be expected, such a shift did not come easily to those who had been encouraged to believe that the main effort of ARDA would be directed to the improvement of land resources and thereby farm incomes. It was apparent from numerous speeches on the subject by the federal director of the ARDA program that some re-orientation was considered desirable, but in the early years provincial governments concentrated on projects which would improve the productivity of land, and some still do. As in many other aspects of economic policy, major shifts in direction have not brought about without delay. It is inevitable that there will be substantial time lags before new trends supersede the old. The predominant opinion now is that while all farmers with a capacity for management skill and ability should be assisted where necessary to become highly efficient and productive, those who lack the capacity should be given the opportunity to engage in other productive work in their area. If such work is not available, they should either be assisted to acquire new skills and relocate elsewhere or, if in older age groups, be guaranteed a minimum income.

Ministerial changes added to the uncertainty of those respon-

[1] The Fund for Rural Economic Development Act (14–15 Elizabeth II, c. 41) was passed by Parliament in May 1966.
[2] Copies of the forms for the General Agreements made with the provinces may be obtained from the Department of Forestry and Rural Development in Ottawa.

sible for the management of the program. Not only was there a change of government at the federal level, but also a change of ministers responsible for the ARDA program within the government. On February 3, 1964, responsibility for ARDA was transferred from the Minister of Agriculture to the Minister of Forestry; it reverted to the Minister of Agriculture seventeen days later, only to return once again to the Minister of Forestry on March 5.[1] The lack of consistent and strong direction at the federal level was not without its provincial counterpart. Provincial governments are encouraged to have their own ideas on what they would like to see done or not done under the program, and their views have been changing too. In some cases their proposals did not greatly appeal to Ottawa. There have been instances where provincial governments have sought federal assistance for developing very large tracts of sparsely populated land, or areas which suffer no particular distress. On occasion, considerable pressure has been brought to bear on Ottawa to acquiesce in new resource development in the pioneer fringe rather than in the rehabilitation of currently occupied but impoverished areas, and there have been times when Ottawa has felt obliged to give way. Though cost benefit studies are required by Ottawa, a careful cost benefit analysis of projects is comparatively rare, and provincial governments do not always welcome advice and criticism from Ottawa. Since the federal government usually foots half the bill under ARDA, many projects are proposed by provinces without sufficient regard for over-all costs and benefits. Admittedly, these are often hard to quantify – especially where they form part of a larger program, the fulfilment of which may demand expenditures over a broad front.

[1] The reasons for the change in the ministry were not made public. Some geographical division in the responsibilities of the Minister of Agriculture had been contemplated, involving the appointment of an additional minister, so that one could have responsibility for agriculture in the East, and one in the West, but this was not pursued. There was a feeling in some quarters that rural problems entailed a more comprehensive approach than was conventionally associated with the Department of Agriculture. The Minister of Forestry in particular took this stand, having in mind the special problems of Quebec and the potential which ARDA seemed to offer for solving them. As for the provincial governments, most of these allocate responsibility for ARDA to ministers of agriculture.

Various "rules of thumb" have been developed to aid the administrator in reaching a decision as to whether or not a particular investment project is worth while. Thus, in one province, if an investment of $36 will produce a crop worth $108 a year, the project is considered a reasonable one.

In deciding upon the boundaries of a rural development area, there are bound to be differences of opinion on how these should be drawn up. As mentioned in Chapter 3, one can consider physical or socio-economic characteristics, administrative boundaries, or potential for development. Unemployment was the only criterion used in the first ARDA agreement; low income or underemployment, as well as unemployment, are the criteria in the second.

The new agreements contain a number of changes that reflect experience gained in the first three years, and they are broader in scope. The first agreements placed the main emphasis on agriculture, on projects for soil and water conservation, and on alternative uses of land; but it soon became obvious that a much more comprehensive approach had to be taken towards the problems of rural poverty and that a major effort would have to be directed towards the development of the human resources in rural areas. The second agreements thus increased the emphasis on programs to assist rural people to re-establish themselves in new employment or to resettle in areas where improved opportunities exist, programs that require co-operation with other government departments, the Department of Manpower in particular. The need for greater efforts to encourage farm consolidation has also become apparent. In recent years, one quarter of the farm population has produced three quarters of the farm output. This output has been increasing, and in the face of only modest increases in demand, the prospects for the small-scale farmer appeared bleak and still do. Some way to hasten and regulate the flow out of farming was clearly needed. Accordingly the new agreements contained provisions for federal cost-sharing in programs of farm consolidation, and training and re-establishing those who leave the land for other occupations. In addition to these changes, provision was made for intensive programs of development in the most seriously impoverished areas. Residents in such areas are least likely to be able to help themselves.

The new agreements consist of eight parts, covering research, land use and farm adjustment (involving the establishment of viable farms through enlargement or regrouping as well as the withdrawal from agriculture of farmland areas unsuitable for farming), rehabilitation of the under-employed, provision of rural development staff and training services, increased assistance to areas in need of special assistance, carrying out of comprehensive rural development programs in specially selected rural development areas, expansion of public information services to encourage community interest and support, and soil and water conservation. As will be apparent from the above, the scope for action under ARDA is very broad. Most aspects of resource use as well as the training of individuals and the economic development of communities fall within its purview. The difficulties facing many rural communities and individual farmers are not just technical. They also include social problems, lack of education, and limited labour mobility. This is especially true of some of the isolated French-speaking communities, and nowhere is it more obvious than in the case of some Indian communities whose objectives and attitudes towards life differ fundamentally from those of most other Canadians.

The breadth of the program is both its strength and its weakness. That rural poverty needs to be attacked on a broad front seems self-evident. No matter where a start is made on a solution, one measure leads almost inexorably to other measures. For example, the unsuitability of certain land for farming may suggest the desirability of converting it to forestry and finding alternative employment for those engaged in farming it. This raises the question of providing training for new employment either locally or elsewhere, and if elsewhere of assisting in the costs of moving where this appears necessary. These measures in turn have implications for others. Training for alternative employment may require a preliminary improvement in general education as well as vocational skills, and entail the construction or expansion of schools. Improvements in education may depend upon a school consolidation program, the success of which may depend on improvements in road access. To create new employment opportunities locally, incentives may be needed to attract new industry to the area, and additional expenditures on various forms of social capital such as roads, power, and water supply may be required. The financial incapacity of many impoverished local authorities in rural areas to undertake such improvements may suggest the need for some reorganization of local government powers.

The number of bodies involved in the fulfilment of the foregoing objectives is almost certain to lead to complex problems of co-ordination and overlapping powers, and to recommendations for coherent plans of development. This, in fact, is very largely what has happened. What started with a concern over the poverty of the marginal farmer has already developed into a broad network of programs extending widely over the economic problems of rural communities and has led, as discussed below, to the introduction of specific plans for certain areas.[1] Co-ordination of efforts is clearly necessary. Agriculture, power, lands and forests, fisheries, roads, health and welfare, manpower, labour, housing, and municipal affairs are among the various bodies responsible for individual aspects of development; and not infrequently rivalries and differences of opinion arise. These differences exist not only between governments but also within governments. The broader the program envisaged under ARDA, the more serious the problems of co-operation are likely to be. One of the main difficulties is the lack of common purpose with the Department of Industry.

The Director of ARDA once said, "Generally speaking, the underlying aim of the new agreement is to focus the most intensive

[1] That the end result of such a process may be far removed from anything envisaged at the outset is a common experience. Striking illustrations of this appear in Arnold J. Toynbee, "The Psychology of Encounters" in *The World and the West* (London: Oxford University Press, 1953), pp. 66–84.

ARDA programs on areas where the problem of rural low income is particularly grave."[1] The reasons for this are easy enough to see, but it has to be faced that expenditures in such areas are likely to contribute less to growth than those made elsewhere. Areas with the lowest incomes are generally those with the least potential. This is a quandary at the root of almost all projects designed to stimulate production in the poorer regions. Some compromise has to be found between assisting the least promising areas where distress is deepest, and areas where prospects are brighter and the distress is less acute. The essential point is to keep conceptually distinct those measures which are designed primarily to induce growth in an area and those which are envisaged primarily as a kind of social welfare. The fact that the latter may not contribute most effectively to economic growth is not a sufficient reason in itself for rejecting them. But even if the policy itself is clear on this point, administrative decisions still have to be made.

The general intent of the federal legislation to encourage projects for the alternative use of agricultural lands that are marginal or of low productivity leaves little doubt as to the goal pursued, but what constitutes marginal land may be much less obvious. There is a difference, for example, between "marginal land" as decided by various physical criteria and "marginal farms", which may reflect not so much the quality of the physical resources as the quality of the farmer; and what is marginal or sub-marginal land in one locality may be regarded as quite superior in another. The "quality" of the farmer has led ARDA to enquire into the broad subject of managerial competence.

## Rural Development Areas and Development Plans

The General Agreements make a distinction between development areas which is likely to be confusing to the outsider. Part V refers to "Rural Development Areas", Part VI to "Special Rural Development Areas". In both cases the area boundaries must be

[1] A. T. Davidson, "Notes for a Talk to the Saskatchewan Institute of Agrologists", at Regina, December 4, 1964 (mimeographed).

agreed on by the federal and provincial ministers concerned, and remedial action is provided for on a broad front. Part V, however, generally covers unrelated projects requiring cost benefit studies, while Part VI covers formal, comprehensive development plans that will qualify areas for assistance under FRED. The other essential difference is mainly one of emphasis. That in Part V on bringing work to those who are immobile is social welfare; Part VI emphasizes the movement of people and the achievement of sustainable growth. In the designation of areas under both Part V and Part VI, such factors are considered as earnings of families or individuals, the extent of unemployment or under-employment, the record of social assistance payments, levels of education, and the like; but Special Rural Development Areas must have recognized development potential. The distinction between areas which do have such potential and those which do not is necessarily a matter of judgment, and the basis for decision is clearer in some cases than it is in others, the distinction being one of degree rather than of kind. Earlier development plans under ARDA focused on areas where poverty was concentrated and extreme rather than on those where the potential for development existed. Areas of concentrated distress are less likely to be self-correcting than those where distress is more dispersed.

Several plans have now been formulated or are in course of formulation under Part VI.[1] The first of these, made possible by the Fund for Rural Economic Development, was the subject of agreement between the Government of Canada and the Province of New Brunswick in September 1966 and concerned the development of the north-east region of the province. The population of the area numbers approximately 106,000 and the labour force 29,000, of whom over a third are either unemployed or seriously under-employed. Incomes average just over $600, only half the average for the province as a whole and a third that of Canada. The designation of the area was the result of discussions between

[1] The areas covered by these plans include north-east New Brunswick, Mactaquac, the Interlake Region of Manitoba, Newfoundland, Prince Edward Island, and the northern half of Nova Scotia. The nature and process of planning is the subject of Chapter 9.

the federal and provincial governments, a task made easier by the clear demographic break between the Acadian population and the population in the rest of the province. In the initial stages, a federal-provincial task force was appointed to examine the problems of the region and submit proposals for a strategy of development, including plans and programs, but subsequently this task force was disbanded and ARDA administrators took over the responsibility for developing the final plan since they were more familiar with the issues involved and were keenly aware of the potentialities of planning under FRED. The rural development agreement which was reached following a period of research and enquiry committed the two governments to an expenditure of close to $90 million, the federal government's contribution being approximately two thirds of this.[1] Some $45 million is to be spent on education and training, $25 million on land acquisition and resettlement, and $8 million on transportation. The very heavy expenditures on education and training resulted from several studies, all of which indicated that the greatest single obstacle to the achievement of a higher standard of living in the area was the extremely low level of education and skill of the labour force. Many of the school-teachers themselves had not gone beyond Grade Nine, and over one third of the labour force had only reached an educational level of Grade Four or less.

As part of the educational program for the area, population is to be concentrated in specified centres offering the most favourable prospects for sustained development, and one hundred school districts are to be reduced to six, centred in the major communities to be developed. The province rather than the local community, as was the case in the past, will assume the major responsibility for financing and operating the schools.

The provincial government was unable to meet the necessary increase in educational expenditures and needed federal help, but since education is a provincial responsibility under the con-

---

[1] For details see Department of Forestry and Rural Development, *Northeast New Brunswick Federal-Provincial Rural Development Agreement, 1966* (Ottawa: Queen's Printer, 1966).

stitution, the matter of federal aid to education is a sensitive one politically. For this reason, such assistance tends to be classified under the heading of "Manpower" policies, which are a responsibility of the federal government. The funds for such policies are made available by the Department of Manpower and supplement the financial assistance given under ARDA.

It is interesting to speculate on the probable effect these improvements in education will have on migration. There seems to be a very close correlation between education and movement, a correlation not peculiar to Canada. The higher the degree of education, the more mobile people become. Education, in its turn, is correlated with religion, and religion with language. In Canada, for example, English-speaking Protestants are more mobile and have had more formal education, on the average, than French-speaking Catholics. In the eastern Canada farm survey they carried out for ARDA, Hedlin and Menzies drew attention to the inadequate level of public school education among young farm people which was making it difficult for them to fit the changing economic environment. They affirmed that in Quebec this problem was significantly worse, with rural young people in Quebec being a generation behind other provinces in educational attainment. Blue-collar workers find it more difficult to change their place of occupation than do white-collar workers. A study made in Sweden of migration frequency at different levels of education also showed that geographic mobility was related to education. This was the case for both general education and vocational training: the higher the level of education, the higher the frequency of migration.[1] The raising of levels of education in the poorer rural areas of Canada seems almost certain to lead to an exodus from them. Understandably, some of the provinces which have exerted very great efforts to improve educational standards are hopeful that such improvements will also increase

[1] Ejnar Neymark, *Migration Differentials in Education, Intelligence and Social Background: Analyses of a Cohort of Swedish Males,* a paper delivered at the 34th Session of the International Statistical Institute in Ottawa, August 21–9, 1963 (Stockholm, Sweden: Kungl Arbetsmarknadsstyrelsen).

employment potential within their boundaries – New Brunswick is a case in point. Certainly the nation as a whole will benefit from such expenditures, and it is not unreasonable, therefore, to expect the federal government to share the cost.

To encourage the movement of people out of the least promising into the more promising areas, some provinces purchase uneconomic farms and convert the land to other uses or sell it to other farmers to permit an expansion of their operations. Those individuals between the ages of fifty-five and sixty-five who cannot be trained profitably for other employment, and who sell their land, are guaranteed a minimum income of $1,200 per year out of the proceeds. Expenditure on social capital is to be concentrated in those towns which seem likely to remain viable, and efforts are made to assist movement of scattered populations into them, some of the inducements taking the form of subsidized housing. Re-establishment grants of up to $2,400 are also made available to families who sell their land and move to approved growth centres, and compensation is provided to property owners in centres which are virtually abandoned as a result of the move. Roads are to be improved, an industrial park is to be developed, and other measures are to be taken, such as the rationalization of inshore fisheries.

The north-east New Brunswick plan has been the forerunner of several others. Indeed the Mactaquac plan, also in New Brunswick, was announced at the same time. Though requiring a smaller expenditure, this plan is similar in type and shares a number of features such as the establishment of a town site in the central part of the region which will provide a centre for the relocation of displaced families and the establishment of future wood-using industries. A voluntary land-purchase program, financed initially by a revolving fund of one million dollars, will be used to consolidate small holdings and permit their conversion to other uses, particularly forestry.

In implementing these plans, an effort has been made to achieve effective participation at all levels, from the local community and private industry through the provincial to the national government. This is anything but easy. There are conflicts of interest and opinion all along the line, and a consensus will not be easy to reach. It would be naïve, perhaps, to expect uniform agreement as to which people should qualify for special assistance, which forms of development should be given priority, or which body should assume responsibility for what. Where a substantial readjustment of local government boundaries is envisaged, as in the case of New Brunswick, differences of opinion are sharpened; and at all levels government departments long accustomed to being responsible for certain types of program look distrustfully on new bodies likely to usurp their functions or encroach on them. As far as the federal government is concerned, administrative measures to integrate regional policies over a broad front are only just beginning. The administrative structure of the federal government militates against unified action. As discussed in the following chapter, industrial location incentives associated with the Area Development Agency are not integrated with the ARDA programs, and the policies pursued by that agency are conducted without any effort to develop a regional plan. The Atlantic provinces frequently and justifiably complain that the proliferation of government agencies has led to political and planning inconsistencies and delay in finding solutions to basic economic problems.[1]

Given the current climate of opinion, which has led to the increasing transfer of responsibilities to the provincial governments, it seems likely that the initiative for development under ARDA will continue to come from the provinces rather than the federal government. Since experience has indicated that responsibility for management of rural development plans must lie with a competent body working in the region, the federal government has insisted that the provinces establish effective program development and management groups to work alongside the federal administrative staff, and has contributed to the costs. At all stages in this process the active participation of the people living in the

[1] This point was stressed at the annual meeting of the Atlantic Provinces Economic Council (APEC) held in Halifax in October 1967.

## Table 6:4
### Federal Shares of ARDA Projects to March 31, 1965

| | (a) Amount approved, federal | (b) Amount spent, federal | (b) as % of (a) | Amount approved per head of 1961 rural population | Research as % of total amount approved | Rank by $ per head of rural population |
|---|---|---|---|---|---|---|
| | ($000) | ($000) | (%) | ($) | (%) | |
| Newfoundland | 1,080 | 463 | 43 | 4.8 | 49 | 5 |
| Prince Edward Island | 330 | 204 | 62 | 4.7 | 27 | 6 |
| Nova Scotia | 974 | 376 | 39 | 2.9 | 26 | 8 |
| New Brunswick | 753 | 581 | 77 | 2.4 | 45 | 9 |
| Atlantic provinces | 3,137 | 1,624 | 52 | | | |
| Quebec | 11,851 | 4,422 | 37 | 8.8 | 9 | 3 |
| Ontario | 2,672 | 311 | 12 | 1.9 | 7 | 10 |

| | | | | | |
|---|---|---|---|---|---|
| Manitoba | 3,741 | 1,578 | 42 | 11.2 | 17 | 2 |
| Saskatchewan | 7,304 | 3,642 | 50 | 13.9 | 14 | 1 |
| Alberta | 2,537 | 791 | 31 | 5.2 | 11 | 4 |
| Prairie provinces | 13,582 | 6,011 | 44 | | | |
| British Columbia | 2,033 | 367 | 18 | 4.5 | 15 | 7 |
| CANADA* | 34,518 | 13,484 | 39 | 6.2 | 17 | |

Note: The Atlantic provinces have not done as well as Quebec or the Prairies and are lower than the national average. Amounts in any case are very small. Some of the provinces, among them Manitoba and Saskatchewan, had projects under way at the time ARDA began operating and were thus able to take advantage of the new legislation without delay.

*Includes research not allocated to any province.

Sources: ARDA, Department of Forestry, *Annual Report 1965-1966* (Ottawa: Queen's Printer, 1966), "The ARDA Catalogue, 1965" (mimeographed), and D.B.S., *1961 Census of Canada*, Vol. I (92-536).

region is encouraged.[1] While admirable as an objective, the difficulty with such participation is the lack of local skilled talent on which to draw. The exceptionally low levels of education prevailing in some of the poorest, most remote areas create communication problems for which special skills are needed, and in some cases a scattered population may lack leaders with whom effective liaison can be made.

Particular difficulties arise in the case of Indians and Métis, who constitute one of the largest low-income and under-employed groups in Canada as a whole. In the Interlake Area in Manitoba, it has been estimated that at least 50 per cent of the Métis labour force and nearly all the registered Indians lack full-time jobs. Their traditional occupations provide an inadequate livelihood, and they have not developed the skills required for other occupations. As a result, welfare payments are high and are still rising with the growth in population numbers. ARDA is now concerning itself with their problems under one of the FRED programs. To only a very limited extent, however, has the situation of the North American Indian attracted the interest of economists. Professional enquiry into their well-being has been much more widespread among sociologists and anthropologists. Economists, especially outside the civil service, have contributed very little to the debate on their future.

## ARDA *Programs: An Appraisal*

An appraisal of the ARDA program has to depend in large measure upon the quality and volume of the statistical data available, but there is not yet sufficient data, at least in published form, to permit the outsider to form more than general impressions.[2] Provincial governments do not supply the federal government with appraisals of the efficacy of what they are doing, and the federal government

---

[1] See L. E. Poetschke, *Regional Planning for Depressed Rural Areas: the Canadian Experience* (Ottawa: Queen's Printer, 1968), p. 7.
[2] Reference should be made, however, to Helen Buckley and Eva Tihanyi, *Canadian Policies for Rural Adjustment: a Study of the Economic Impact of ARDA, PFRA, and MMRA* (the Economic Council of Canada, Special Study No. 7 [Ottawa: Queen's Printer, 1967]). This is a most welcome addition to the literature on the subject.

has lacked the staff to undertake systematic studies of its own. This lack of current evaluation is a serious deficiency which needs to be remedied. We do not know, for example, how many farmers have sold their land as part of the farm consolidation program, or what consequences increased farm sizes have had on incomes. Nor is there much evidence on whether the exodus from agriculture has increased as a result of ARDA programs or not. The time period, of course, has been short for such an evaluation, and the isolation of responsible factors may be difficult. To cite one instance of this, it is common knowledge that when the economy is operating at high levels and unemployment is minimal, the exodus from farming increases. Conversely, when unemployment is high, the movement slows down.

Under the first agreements, 729 ARDA projects were initiated with a total shareable cost of $61 million, of which the federal government contributed more than half.[1] Table 6:4 shows the cumulative federal contributions by province up to March 31, 1965, the date when the first agreements expired. The approval of larger amounts per head of the rural population in Manitoba and Saskatchewan than in other provinces is explained by the fact that Manitoba and Saskatchewan had already embarked on similar policies of their own and were able to take quick advantage of the federal assistance that was offered. The position has changed sharply since.

The early emphasis on the use and physical properties of land was reflected in the type of project undertaken initially. According to the ARDA classification employed, an overwhelming majority of projects were classified under the headings of "research", either federal alone or joint federal-provincial, "soil and water", and "alternate land use". Very few projects were undertaken under the heading of "rural development", and some that were might just as appropriately have been classified under other headings.[2]

[1] Descriptions of these are contained in *The ARDA Catalogue, 1962–65* (Ottawa: Department of Forestry of Canada, March 31, 1965). Later years are covered in subsequent catalogues.

[2] In the case of Manitoba, for example, Project no. 7059, approved in June 1964, was classified as Rural Development, but the description reads: "To provide drainage, ditching system, and flood control dam – Fish Lake" Project no. 7058 was of a similar nature and was classified in like manner.

## Table 6:5
### Costs Under the Comprehensive Rural Development Agreement for the Interlake Area of Manitoba

Table 6:5(a), Shared costs ($000)

| | Federal cost | | | | Provincial cost | Total cost |
|---|---|---|---|---|---|---|
| | ARDA | FRED | Manpower | Percentage | | |
| **Education:** | | | | | | |
| Residential technical vocational school | | | 2,250 | 75 | 750 | 3,000 |
| Total education | | | 2,250 | | 750 | 3,000 |
| **Manpower:** | | | | | | |
| General counsellors | | 2,700 | | 90 | 300 | 3,000 |
| Adult education and manpower training centre | | | 750 | 75 | 250 | 1,000 |
| Residential facilities | | 375 | | 75 | 125 | 500* |
| Portable training units | | | 150 | 75 | 50 | 200 |
| Portable teacherages | | | 56 | 75 | 19 | 75 |
| Interlake manpower corps | | 2,700 | | 90 | 300 | 3,000 |
| Community affairs | | 900 | | 75 | 300 | 1,200 |
| Resources management | | 2,550 | | 75 | 850 | 3,400 |
| Training in industry | | 375 | | 75 | 125 | 500 |
| Total manpower | | 9,600 | 956 | | 2,319 | 12,875 |

| | | | | | |
|---|---|---|---|---|---|
| **Development and structural adjustment** | | | | | |
| Agriculture | | | | | |
| Land acquisition | 750 | 3,000 | | 75 | 1,250 | 5,000 |
| Drainage | 750 | 3,450 | | 60 | 2,800 | 7,000 |
| Land development | 750 | 975 | | 75 | 575 | 2,300 |
| Fisheries | | | | | |
| Fisheries adjustment | | 375 | | 75 | 125 | 500 |
| Lake St. Martin Dam | | 375 | | 75 | 125 | 500 |
| Roads | 750 | 5,310 | | 60 | 3,540 | 8,850 |
| Recreation | | 1,020 | | 60 | 1,190 | 2,960 |
| Industrial park | | 200 | | 50 | 200 | 400 |
| Total development and structural adjustment | 3,000† | 14,705 | | | 9,805 | 27,510 |
| General: | | | | | |
| Research | | 168 | | 66.67 | 82 | 250 |
| Administration (including public information) | | 1,333 | | 66.67 | 667 | 2,000 |
| Total general | | 1,501 | | | 749 | 2,250 |
| Total cost | 3,000 | 25,806 + 1,800 | 3,206 | | 13,623 − 1,800 | 45,635 |
| Implementation grant | | | | | | |
| Total, Table 6:5 (a) | 3,000 | 27,606 | 3,206 | 74.9 | 11,823 | 45,635 |

*The capital cost of these facilities is estimated at $1,200,000. The Central Mortgage and Housing Corporation may loan 90% of this capital cost, or $1,080,000, and the province in this case would provide 10%, or $120,000. The Fund for Rural Economic Development could then share in 75% of the operating loss, including the amortization of the loan, which is estimated at $500,000 over the life of the Plan. The total non-recoverable cost for the province over the ten-year life of the Plan is estimated at about $125,000.

†The $3,000,000 represents $1,500,000 from the provincial allotment under the Federal-Provincial Rural Development Agreement (1965-70) and anticipates a further allocation after 1970.

Table 6:5(b), Other costs ($000)

| | Federal Cost | | | | Provincial cost | Total cost |
|---|---|---|---|---|---|---|
| | ARDA | FRED | Manpower | Percentage | | |
| Education: | | | | | | |
| Schools (capital) | | | | | 4,700 | 4,700 |
| Schools (operating) | | | | | 19,000 | 19,000‡ |
| Manpower: | | | | | | |
| Occupational training allowances | | | 12,250 | | | 12,250 |
| Mobility costs | | | 3,500 | | | 3,500 |
| Total, Table 6:5(b) | | | 15,750 | | 23,700 | 39,450 |

‡This cost represents the increase in operating costs expected by the province as a result of the capital investment called for by this plan.

Table 6:5(c), Total costs ($000)

| | Federal cost | Provincial cost | Total cost |
|---|---|---|---|
| Table 6:5(a) | 33,812 | 11,823 | 45,635 |
| Table 6:5(b) | 15,750 | 23,700 | 39,450 |
| Total | 49,562 | 35,523 | 85,085 |

Source: Department of Forestry and Rural Development, *Interlake Area of Manitoba* (Ottawa: Queen's Printer, 1967).

Much of the research pertained to land use, water supplies, or soil capability. Very little expenditure, by comparison, was devoted to the selection of areas that might serve as focal points for development, to education, or to studies of the problems of administrative co-ordination or the factors that inhibit change and mobility in certain communities. A large number of miscellaneous projects were undertaken, but there was nothing to suggest that these were seen as part of a comprehensive development program.

Before the first agreements had run their course, ARDA officials, at least at the federal level, were conscious of the need for a re-orientation of ARDA activities towards a more systematic approach to rural poverty in which various interrelated steps could be taken in the light of more explicitly defined objectives. If an area was not worth developing, then projects of land drainage or the cultivation of new crops had little to recommend them even if they did add to local incomes. Such projects might delay still further a desirable out-migration from the area or inhibit re-orientation of labour towards other types of employment. In other cases, where the area was worth developing, a variety of related projects demanding an integrated approach might be considered desirable.

As indicated above, some federal officials did have misgivings about the wisdom of approving certain projects proposed by provincial governments. At times the underlying studies were inadequate. Indeed much of the early research that was undertaken was indifferent in quality and scattered over a wide variety of miscellaneous topics. It failed, in consequence, to provide the foundations for systematic development.[1]

If one accepts the figure of something like one million people in rural communities who need the sort of assistance that ARDA can provide, the sums involved under the first ARDA agreements appear very modest. In the first three years of its operations, the

---

[1] No attempt to disguise this was made by senior federal officials responsible for the ARDA program. There has been a commendable readiness on their part to recognize inadequacies of the program, and to encourage the discussion of possible solutions.

costs worked out to about twenty dollars a head per year, and that included the provincial as well as the federal contribution. Even admitting that it could have been spent to better advantage, and no one familiar with ARDA operations is likely to question this, the sum could hardly have been expected to make much of a dent in the problem of rural poverty.

The 1965 General Agreements, and the rural development agreements under FRED that followed, mark a turning point. Some of the original emphasis on the qualities of land is still in evidence, but preoccupation with those qualities no longer dominates the scene in the way that it used to. Not only are the over-all expenditures larger, but in conjunction with the expenditures under FRED their allocation has shifted decisively in the direction of education, training, and the provision of employment in non-primary occupations. The new rural development plans reflect a quite different approach from that at the time of ARDA's inception when many of its proponents were thinking in terms of expanding agricultural output. Table 6:5 on the Interlake Area of Manitoba illustrates this change in emphasis. The expenditures on land acquisition, drainage, and land development, totalling $14.3 million, are not much more than a quarter of the amount spent under the headings of Manpower and Education. In the case of the comprehensive rural development scheme for north-east New Brunswick, projected federal expenditures on education and training of almost $23 million over a five-year period are almost double ARDA's total annual expenditure on all programs during the first two years of its operation.

That FRED plans for rural development may lead into the broader field of industrial structure is manifest in the discussions relating to the ARDA plan for Nova Scotia. The basic problem in northern Nova Scotia is thought to be an inefficient and declining industrial sector; without improvements in this sector, action to improve productivity in agriculture, fisheries, and forestry may only aggravate the problem of low incomes and under-employment. The Director of Policy and Planning for ARDA, L. E. Poetschke, recognized this when he stated:

The strategy of planning for this area has not yet been completed. It is our view, however, that the main emphasis must be on the development of manufacturing and service activities. Moreover, we expect that the program cannot be based on further support for the inefficient industries or an expansion of the existing small and regionally market-oriented manufacturing activities which are at present characteristic of the area. The objective must be accomplished through the promotion of developments which take advantage of the area's locational and natural features, and which will entail a change in the total structure of the industrial sector, moving it towards large efficient operations oriented to export markets.[1]

It is obvious that such a course of action impinges upon the functions of the Area Development Agency in the Department of Industry, an agency which – unlike ARDA – started with broad ambitions but now fulfils a very circumscribed role.

With regard to programs under ARDA other than FRED, Table 6:6 indicates the amount of federal expenditures, by province, that have been approved under the various parts of the agreement. Soil and water conservation head the list, followed by land use and farm adjustment, special assistance to certain rural areas, and research, in that order. Remaining items are small. Ontario currently accounts for more than one third of approved expenditures but this is not necessarily indicative of the final distribution.

As shown in Table 6:7, a very large number of projects in Quebec and Alberta have been rejected by ARDA, which suggests a serious difference of opinion as to the type of project that ought to be encouraged. In contrast, Ontario, with an approved program three times that of Quebec, has not experienced a single rejection. The explanation resides in the fact that until recently Quebec and Alberta have attempted to use federal ARDA funds for ongoing programs, many of which had objectives not in line with the agreements as drafted. Ontario, on the other hand, had one large program (land assembly by forest conservation authorities) which fitted well into the concept of taking marginal land out of agriculture. In addition, Ontario has worked towards the develop-

[1] L. E. Poetschke, *op. cit.*, p. 13.

## Table 6:6
### Federal Expenditures Approved Under ARDA, Parts I-V and VII-VIII
### April 1, 1965, to July 31, 1967*

($000)

| | I | II | III | IV | V | VII | VIII | | Total | % of |
| | | Land use and farm adjustment | Rehabilitation of rural people | Rural development staff and training | Special assistance to certain rural areas | Public information services | Soil and water conservation | Multiple or no code | expenditures approved by province | Total expenditures approved |
| | Research | | | | | | | | | |
|---|---|---|---|---|---|---|---|---|---|---|
| Newfoundland | 128 | — | — | 144 | 830 | 19 | 15 | 35 | 1,171 | 2.4 |
| Prince Edward Island | 22 | 179 | — | 38 | 358 | 7 | 420 | — | 1,023 | 2.1 |
| Nova Scotia | 183 | 1,952 | — | 88 | 1,165 | — | 380 | 63 | 3,831 | 7.7 |
| New Brunswick | 143 | 611 | — | 84 | 703 | 12 | 840 | — | 2,392 | 4.8 |
| Quebec | 2,099 | 7 | — | 185 | 1,914 | — | 1,520 | — | 5,720 | 11.6 |
| Ontario | 273 | 5,189 | 30 | 44 | 382 | 9 | 11,208 | 5 | 17,139 | 34.6 |

| | | | | | | | | | |
|---|---|---|---|---|---|---|---|---|---|
| Manitoba | 351 | 38 | — | 234 | 1,050 | 3 | 352 | 143 | 2,171 | 4.4 |
| Saskatchewan | 1,072 | 1,057 | — | 42 | 2,806 | 12 | 775 | 115 | 5,878 | 11.9 |
| Alberta | 891 | 1,500 | — | 427 | 374 | — | 1,218 | 247 | 4,654 | 9.4 |
| British Columbia | 45 | 4 | — | 16 | — | — | 5,442 | — | 5,506 | 11.1 |
| Total† | 5,207 | 10,537 | 30 | 1,302 | 9,582 | 62 | 22,170 | 608 | 49,485 | 100.0 |

Note: Figures do not add to totals in all cases because of rounding.

*Approved expenditures cover periods up to 1972. Some provinces, particularly Ontario, have had programs approved for longer periods than others. Interprovincial comparisons must be made with this in mind.

†Excludes (a) expenditures undertaken by the federal government for its own research, (b) the Canada Land Inventory, and (c) Part VI (FRED). The main approved expenditures have been for soil and water conservation, followed by land use and farm adjustment, and special assistance to certain rural areas, except for those under FRED.

Source: Department of Forestry, "ARDA Project Status Report" (mimeographed).

**Table 6:7**
**Expenditures Under ARDA, Exclusive of Those Under FRED**
**April 1, 1965, to July 31, 1967**

*($000)*

|  | *Approved* | | | | |
| --- | --- | --- | --- | --- | --- |
|  | Federal research | Canada land inventory | Parts I-V and VII-VIII | Rejected | Not yet approved |
| Newfoundland | 127 | 175 | 1,171 | 53 | 208 |
| Prince Edward Island | 233 | 77 | 1,023 | 10 | 432 |
| Nova Scotia | 471 | 182 | 3,831 | 14 | 117 |
| New Brunswick | 155 | 190 | 2,392 | 4 | 15 |
| Quebec | 222 | 1,240 | 5,720 | 561 | 5,081 |
| Ontario | — | 1,398 | 17,139 | — | 2,188 |
| Manitoba | 321 | 1,600 | 2,171 | 5 | 2,412 |
| Saskatchewan | 395 | 546 | 5,878 | 75 | 275 |
| Alberta | — | 660 | 4,654 | 245 | 239 |
| British Columbia | — | 1,561 | 5,506 | — | 70 |
| Total | 1,924 | 7,629 | 49,485 | 967 | 11,037 |

Source: "ARDA Project Status Report" (mimeographed).

ment of such broad new projects as a $7 million farm consolidation program which also accords with ARDA objectives.

On the political side, perhaps the most important factor in an evaluation of ARDA policies has been the evolution of co-operation between the two levels of government. Such co-operation has not been without setbacks, but it has progressed, as is witnessed by the preparation and implementation of FRED plans. To be acceptable and effective, regional planning must be a *joint* effort; traditional shared grants of one sort and another are a poor substitute, apt to impose unwelcome pressures on the provincial governments. The fact that ARDA has been moving in the direction of the joint preparation of plans is a development which augurs well for the future.

# 7. Designated Areas and the Area Development Agency

UNLIKE ARDA, which began with limited objectives and moved into the larger realm of regional economic development, the Area Development Agency has carved for itself a more restricted role than some had foreseen, and those responsible for its administration have shown no inclination to become involved in the complex problems of regional development. The Agency has been the subject of criticism on various counts, and there is a widespread feeling that it has been narrow in interpreting its role and inflexible in its approach. In part, disillusionment with the Agency can be attributed to its title. Whatever the original intent may have been, it has become not an agency for development, in the conventional sense, but rather an agency to relieve local unemployment by influencing industrial location. In other words, the emphasis is not so much on development as on the reduction of local unemployment.

## The Origins of ADA

On June 7, 1963, the Prime Minister moved that the House go into committee to consider the following resolution:

That it is expedient to introduce a measure
(a) to establish a department of industry to be presided over by a minister of industry . . . ;
(b) to provide for the establishment under the direction of the minister of an area development agency and to provide for the appointment of a commissioner and a deputy commissioner for area development . . .[1]

This resolution immediately followed another pertaining to the establishment of the Economic Council, and was related to it in that the point and purpose of the proposed Department of Industry, according to the Prime Minister, was to assist in translating the various ideas and the guidance of the Council into effective action. The Council was to have the task of guiding the public and the government by suggesting how the most might be made of national resources and talents and how the economy might be adapted to changing conditions. The Prime Minister noted that although Canada had a Department of Agriculture concerned with helping farmers, a Department of Fisheries to help fishermen, and a Department of Mines and Technical Surveys for the mining industry, there was no Department of Industry, no department of government especially concerned with the needs and opportunities of the manufacturing industry, and that the main purpose of the resolution was to remedy this deficiency. The Department of Industry was to be for manufacturers what the Department of Agriculture was for farmers; it would be a focal point for the provision of advice and help.[2] In describing more specifically the functions of the new department, the Prime Minister added that it would not be to shelter or shore up weak, pro-

---

[1] Hansard, 1963, Vol. I, p. 801. The bill (C-74) had its first reading June 14, 1963; its second reading thirteen days later; and its third July 5th. Debates on ADA in the Commons took place on June 7, 10, 12, 14, and 28, and July 4th, Hansard, 1963, Vols. I and II.

[2] During the second reading of the bill, the Minister of Defence Production stated: "In so far as the manufacturing industry sector of our total economy is concerned, this new department will be the executive arm of the economic council. In so far as the fisheries end of our whole economy is concerned, the Department of Fisheries would be the executive arm of the economic council of Canada. I could go on with this analogy . . ." (Hansard, 1963, Vol. II, p. 1850). In practice, contrary to what was envisaged at the time, departments have never conceived their role in this way.

tected enterprises but to encourage and build up economic industries and to help them in adapting and, in certain cases, adjusting
themselves to changes that were being made. He felt that he could
hardly over-emphasize the importance which the government
attached to the creation of this new department, observing in this
connection that it was to the manufacturing industries that we
had to look if we were to find employment for the great increases
that were occurring in the size of the labour force (a view which
some have been disposed to question). As for the Area Development Agency, which he had suggested creating some two years
earlier when he was leader of the Opposition and which was to be
an important part of the new department, he described its purposes and functions in these words:

> The areas we are concerned with are those in which unemploy-
> ment is heavy and chronic in its nature, where special govern-
> ment action is therefore called for in order to encourage
> economic development or industrial adjustment. Various
> departments of the federal government can be helpful in dif-
> ferent ways to such areas. The purpose of the proposed area
> development agency is to assist in making sure that this will be
> done. It will create in Ottawa a small group of people whose
> special responsibility, on behalf of the minister of industry, will
> be to make sure that various federal policies are conceived and
> co-ordinated in ways which will be of maximum help to the
> areas of maximum need. Again the point is to make action more
> effective by providing a focus for it. In this sense the area
> development agency will be co-ordinating rather than executive.
> In this way it will not interfere with provincial action to the
> same end. Quite the contrary. If the co-ordination and effective-
> ness of federal action are improved, action by the provinces in
> their areas of responsibility will become easier to take and will
> be made more fruitful.[1]

[1] Hansard, 1963, Vol. I, p. 803. See also the references by the Minister of
Finance to the Area Development Agency in his budget speech of June
13, 1963, in which he stated: "It is important that the new employment we
are seeking to achieve in the Canadian economy, and the new investment
required to produce it, be directed wherever practicable to areas of slower
growth and surplus manpower. To this end the special area development
agency within the department of industry will seek to encourage new
investment in areas where it will do the most good" (Hansard, 1963, Vol.
II, p. 997).

Much of the debate that followed dealt with the new Department of Industry, and questioned the wisdom of establishing it and the functions and relationships it would have with other departments and bodies, rather than with ADA specifically. A number of critics favouring one and not the other would have preferred to see them voted on separately. The government, however, did not desire this, the intention being to relate the activities of the Agency closely with other activities of the Department of Industry. Certain members of parliament who saw potential advantages to their own constituents from federal policies to assist impoverished areas were strongly in favour of some form of federal influence in the matter of location; though a number, some of whom could see a less obvious gain, expressed fears that the proposed Area Development Agency might tread on ground traditionally reserved to the provinces, or induce industry to locate in unsuitable areas. A number of members, particularly from the Province of Quebec, did not wish the new department to interfere with provincial jurisdiction in industrial and economic matters as most provincial governments have departments and bodies of their own concerned with development issues. Although the federal government expressed the desire to work closely with the provinces, it did not choose to make the ADA program a joint one like that of ARDA, or to submit proposals for provincial comment and approval. On balance, this would seem to have been a mistake.

In the debate accompanying the second reading of the bill, the Minister of Defence Production, who was originally responsible for the new department, stated that ADA would develop and implement programs to assist areas with high and chronic unemployment where special action was necessary to promote economic and industrial growth and raise levels of income. He also stated that consideration was being given to the most appropriate criteria for the designation of such areas, the intention being to relate operations to economic rather than political boundaries or areas. Although there had been numerous measures in the past to assist certain areas of the country, this was the first time that the federal government had made provision for a specialized organization to concentrate on area problems in all regions of Canada.

Royal assent was given to the act, which is known as "the Department of Industry Act", on July 22, 1963.[1] Part II, referring to area development, provided for the establishment of an Area Development Agency under the direction of a Commissioner and a Deputy for Area Development appointed by the Governor-in-Council. The Commissioner, the chief executive officer of the Agency, was to be responsible to the Minister.

The Governor-in-Council could designate any district or locality in Canada for special measures to permit economic development or industrial adjustment by reason of the exceptional nature or degree of unemployment in that area. The powers and duties of the Minister included (a) undertaking research and making investigations into the means of increasing employment and income in designated areas; and (b) preparing and carrying out programs and projects to improve the economic development of designated areas which could not suitably be undertaken by other departments, branches, or agencies of the government.

In fact very little appears to have been done in the way of research and investigation. Though the situation is changing somewhat now, ADA is not research-oriented and has a most inadequate staff in this regard; and if the Department of Industry within which ADA functions has collected information contributing to an understanding of the determinants of industrial location and area development, it has not seen fit to publish it. This is a deficiency which hopefully will be remedied. It is very important to know what the implications of technological change and scientific innovation are likely to be for the future of particular industries and their location. One would like to see the Department of Industry participate in such studies to assist in the guidance of those responsible for the framing of longer run regional policies. Some knowledge of inter-industry relationships is also desirable. Lacking information on such issues it is difficult to know what

[1] 12 Elizabeth II, c. 3, pp. 59–63.

developments are to be expected in the future or the types of activity that should be encouraged.

Subject to any existing statutory provision, the Governor-in-Council could authorize and direct departments, branches, and agencies of the Government of Canada to take special measures to facilitate the economic development of any designated area or the adjustment of industry in that area. Again, no such steps appear to have been taken; the Governor-in-Council has not exercised the authority given him.

Contrary to what the Prime Minister envisaged when he described the purposes and functions of the Agency in 1963, it has become an executive rather than a co-ordinating body. Discussions do, of course, take place with various public bodies and departments of government both at the federal and provincial level, but there is little evidence that the Agency fulfils a co-ordinating function or that it provides a focus for effective action. What it does do is administer a program of incentives to secondary manufacturing industries that locate or expand in designated areas.

## Area Designation and the Criteria Employed

Early in September 1963 – some two months after the passing of the legislation – thirty-five areas were designated which were to qualify for special measures of federal assistance for economic or industrial development. The grounds for qualification were chronically high levels of unemployment and slow rates of growth. The ADA program provides for an annual review of the situation, and the list has been changed several times since. In designating areas, ADA used the same boundaries as those which had been set up by the National Employment Service for purposes of local administration. These areas, now called "Canada Manpower Centres", provided information on the local labour force and those seeking employment.

The speed with which the areas were designated left little time for a considered appraisal of the implications of these boundaries, and criticisms were not slow in coming. First, though they have a rationale as labour market areas, they were never drawn up with the objectives of economic development in mind. Second, though there is an obvious administrative convenience in using them, they are not necessarily appropriate if development is to be the prime consideration. The word "if" needs to be stressed, for in practice the criteria used in selecting areas for designation appraised the past growth rate as reflected in changes in the size of the total labour force and not growth potential. The reason for this seems to have been uncertainty about how to identify potentiality for growth and the desire to present an appearance of statistical objectivity in the designation of areas for aid. But what is more important, the ADA program itself has been conceived not as a program for regional development but as one for the reduction of local unemployment. So far as the federal government is concerned this remains the prime objective. A great deal of misunderstanding has arisen on this score.

The federal government laid down four general guidelines, all emphasizing unemployment, for designating the areas which would qualify for industrial incentives under the terms of the Department of Industry Act:

1. Unemployment is very severe;
2. There has been a large and persistent decline in the number of people employed;
3. Unemployment is substantially above the national average and the rate of increase in employment is substantially slower than the national average;
4. Unemployment is reflected in income levels below the national average.

These guidelines have to be interpreted quantitively to permit the making of administrative decisions of an operational nature. If chronically high levels of unemployment are a criterion for the designation of areas which qualify for aid, decisions must be made as to what constitutes "high" and "chronic", and the necessary statistical data must either be already available or be made available.

In the 1965 amendments to the program, the government set

down a fairly complex formula for determining whether an area would qualify for special assistance. According to the six "objective" standards of this formula, Canada Manpower Centres would qualify if they had an unemployment rate for the most recent five years of at least twice the national average (originally the period was eight years), or of one and a half times the national average provided the rate of employment growth was less than half the national average and the average family income was less than the national average; if employment had declined at an annual rate of more than 10 per cent, again over the most recent five years; or if either average family incomes were below a certain figure or 40 per cent of them were below a still lower figure. By including an income qualification, it was possible to take some account of concealed as well as overt unemployment.[1] County or census divisions would also fall within the provisions where family incomes were below a certain minimum if they were contiguous to areas that had already been designated and taken together with those areas constituted "economic regions or districts". A group of Manpower Centres would qualify if they were traditionally recognized as forming a distinct geographic and economic region and satisfied the criteria, considered as a whole. Manpower Centres which had been designated in September 1963 would continue to qualify if the average unemployment ratio in the area, relative to the national average, had not decreased in the past year from its average over the five years preceding. Since the program was designed to provide more opportunities for people where they now resided and not to encourage the opening up of uninhabited territory, the sparsely populated northern regions of the country were excluded from the provisions of the Act.

An examination of the statistical data on which the designation of areas has been based reveals numerous weaknesses. As is well known to those concerned with the administration of the program,

---

[1] The Minister of Industry has made it clear, however, that the purpose of the program is to relieve unemployment, not to raise family income levels. See, for example, his statement in Hansard, 1966, Vol. III, p. 5889. None the less, areas in Manitoba and Saskatchewan were designated on the basis of low income, not unemployment.

the data on which decisions are based are in many cases sparse and of dubious reliability. Labour force estimates for some of the designated areas where there is substantial migration are especially unreliable, and the registration of people seeking work has long been recognized as an inadequate guide to unemployment. Information on income levels also tends to be unreliable since it is often taken from census figures which are only infrequently up to date and refer to census divisions, not to Manpower Centres which are mainly used by ADA for designating areas. While other information on income is now becoming available as a result of the introduction of the Canada Pension Plan, census figures must still be used in some cases. For these and other reasons, some degree of personal judgment has been inevitable at the administrative level. The six "objective" standards developed for the designation of areas to be eligible under the program and referred to by the Minister in a news release on August 5, 1965, suggested a certainty about the process which is, in fact, lacking. With a little juggling of the criteria and the adoption of different but equally valid techniques of statistical calculation, one could present a kaleidoscope of different pictures of which areas should be included and which eliminated. It would change the picture, for example, if the number of years in computing the averages were altered, or if the rapidity and direction of change in employment were considered, or if, in some cases, modal or median incomes were selected as a criterion for designation rather than the arithmetic mean.[1] The combination of all these varied and rough indicators into a formula for designation contributes to the impression that the process is a somewhat hit-or-miss affair, an impression which is reinforced by cases where small changes in boundaries would lead to large changes in the figures.

There is an urgent need for more reliable data on which to base policy, though even the most reliable data have to be tem-

[1] I am greatly indebted to Sheila Y. Isaac for a detailed examination of the statistical data underlying the designation of some areas and the non-designation of others, as well as for much of the statistical work on area development on which I have drawn at various stages of this study.

pered with judgment and seen in the context of the ultimate objectives of the policy being pursued.[1] If there are large numbers of unemployed in an area, there is a case for designation even if the percentage of unemployed falls below 150 per cent of national average. Indeed the designation of such an area might do more to reduce unemployment than the designation of an area with a higher unemployment rate but a smaller number of unemployed. There is also the matter of migration. If out-migration from an area is to be encouraged, there may be little or no merit in designating such an area on the basis of a downward employment trend.

A further observation might be made. The desire to secure the goodwill of the provinces has influenced the formulae which have been selected for designation, though not to the extent that several provinces would like to have seen. Criteria for designation cannot be selected, however, without *some* regard for provincial reaction. Every province seeks to have areas which will qualify.

Fundamental to the whole matter of selecting formulae for designation is the difference of opinion concerning policy and the emphasis to be given to various objectives. Should aid be seen primarily as part of a campaign to reduce extreme poverty and unemployment? If so, it might well be concentrated only in the most needy areas. Or should aid be available to others whose needs are less extreme but whose potential for development is greater? This would tend to diminish the assistance going to the poorest areas, but it might help the larger region of which they form a part to realize its growth potential. Experience in other countries has demonstrated the inadequacies of policies designed to induce industry to establish in small areas where the potentialities for self-sustained development are minimal. Unless designed primarily as a welfare measure, aid is more effectively focused where there are prospects of inducing self-sustained improvement. The decision where to compromise between these two approaches is essentially a political one. The most the economist

[1] The lack of reliable data makes it extremely difficult to evaluate the efficacy of current programs.

can do is to attempt to quantify very roughly the prospective costs and benefits of alternative courses of action.

Since depressed areas vary greatly in the nature and extent of their disadvantages, to treat them as though they were all alike by applying a standard subvention is likely not only to fail in alleviating their distress, but also to prove costlier than it needs to be. Some depressed areas offer prospects for revival and a return on investments in them. Others, especially certain rural areas, as ARDA administrators well know, are not worth reviving. In such instances there is a clear case for channelling most of the aid into measures which will induce out-migration. If areas are to be designated solely because they manifest certain symptoms of chronic distress, attempts to raise incomes and employment in them are bound to be difficult and costly. In so far as the fostering of some activity within their boundaries appears desirable, "make-work" programs might be encouraged, but these are more correctly welfare and not development programs and should be justified as such. The welfare aspect appears to dominate ADA policy, and the ADA program is seen by the Minister of Industry as one which caters to large numbers of people for whom mobility is not regarded as a practical alternative and for whom new industrial jobs are the main hope.

The location of designated areas is also an important consideration. It requires little imagination to see how businessmen will respond to incentives if they have a choice between a small depressed area in southern Ontario and another in north-eastern Quebec. Although incentives may be available in both areas, they will almost certainly assist one more than the other. Equal incentives have not given rise to equal results, nor was it expected that they would. Whatever the intent may be, the most depressed areas are not likely to benefit as much as the less depressed ones. As a result, designated areas in some provinces, among them Ontario and Alberta, have tended to gain more than others. A few have not benefited at all. In practice, therefore, the distinction between welfare and growth is not as clear-cut as discussion might suggest. It is to be expected too that firms will choose the most promising locations *within* the designated areas. To the extent that aid has in fact gone to the more rather than the less promising locations within the designated areas, those who favour a policy that encourages growth have fewer grounds for complaint, though they may argue strongly that policy does not go far enough in this direction.

Those responsible for ADA policies have shown little apparent desire to become involved in controversy concerning the economic implications of the ADA program, and statements of objectives have been couched in general terms emphasizing the limited ambition to reduce local unemployment. The federal government's main argument for stressing unemployment seems to be that regional development is a provincial responsibility while unemployment is a federal one; but such a stand is not entirely convincing. For one thing the Atlantic Development Board, which is a federal agency, is concerned specifically with regional development, and so is ARDA. In this respect ADA is the odd man out. Admittedly the programs under ARDA and the ADB are joint federal-provincial responsibilities whereas ADA is federal only, but there is no compelling reason why this should be the case. Certainly some provincial governments show little enthusiasm for the present arrangement, and a joint program might reduce some of the grounds for complaint.

In any event, there is an equivocal element in some of the ministerial statements on the objectives of the program. On one occasion the Minister of Industry stated: "The functions of the Area Development Agency as a whole relate to industrial development and area development, but the designated area program is limited to being a program related to unemployment."[1] How is such a statement to be interpreted? The only significant action taken by ADA (so far as has been made public) *is* under the designated area program. No other action of any significance appears to have been taken.

What emerges is that any economic development is regarded by the federal government as a consequence of action to alleviate

[1] Hansard, 1966, Vol. VI, p. 5888.

unemployment. It is the relief of unemployment, not economic development, which is its prime concern. This preoccupation with unemployment is criticized by those who feel that regional prosperity calls for major changes in the structure of the economy and who consider unemployment to be only the symptom and not the cause of malaise. There has been little disposition on the part of ADA to concede this point and frame federal policies accordingly, and there is a widespread feeling in consequence that the program is inadequate in scope and misguided in direction. The criticisms are not without substance.

Appearing as a witness before the Standing Committee on Industry Research and Energy Development, the Minister of Industry stated that the establishment of the Department of Industry during the period when unemployment was of critical concern to the government largely determined the character of the Area Development Program as it exists today.[1] The program had grown out of two circumstances: the existence of areas of concentrated unemployment, and the growth and importance of secondary industry. It was clearly anticipated, he added, that any action taken under the Department of Industry Act to alleviate unemployment would be along the lines of economic and industrial development. While noting that decisions on the location of new industries are made essentially by private enterprise, he stated that it was the government's objective to direct some industrial growth to areas where present opportunities for employment and income are inadequate for the people who reside there, and who, for one reason or another, do not wish to move. He welcomed competition among provinces and municipalities in promoting industrial development, providing that it did not lead to economically damaging rivalry in the location of industry, but he added, significantly, that the federal government would carefully avoid

[1] Standing Committee on Industry Research and Energy Development, *Minutes of Proceedings and Evidence*, No. 10, October 18, 1966, p. 263. The Standing Committee was empowered to consider the subject matter of the designated area program and the criteria thereunder. The *Minutes* constitute a most valuable source of information on the functions of the Agency. See in particular nos. 10, 11, 13, 15, 16, and 17 (Ottawa: Queen's Printer, 1966 and 1967).

any element of involvement in this competitive milieu and would have to study and proceed with due caution in any economic program that had regional implications. The program was not one to promote the industrialization of our economy; it was not one that promised new industry for every nook and cranny of our territory; it was but one small part of an over-all policy to ensure an acceptable rate of growth of national output and employment. In short, the ADA program had the relatively limited objective of ensuring that some of that growth took place in areas where there was a long-standing short-fall in opportunities for employment and income for people who lived there.[1] Such a limited objective fell far short of the vigorous policy that some wanted to see in the depressed areas; but even in the fulfilment of this very modest role, the wisdom of selecting criteria for designation which focus so heavily on chronic unemployment is open to question.

Continuing his evidence to the Standing Committee, the Minister of Industry, without giving reasons, stated that he did not consider the ADA program an appropriate response to short-run or cyclical fluctuations in the unemployment rate. What he was concerned with were those areas where the unemployment rate was both chronic and severe. As observed below, however, such an interpretation of responsibilities precludes action to encourage diversification of industries in areas that suffer from chronic instability. Moreover, it is undoubtedly better to take action to minimize unemployment at the first sign of its development than to wait until a serious and prolonged decline in activity has occurred. The same considerations apply at the local level. If there is clear evidence of impending unemployment, action should be taken at once. To delay for five years until a severe and intractable condition of unemployment can be identified involves a serious loss of potential production, and the remedy, when and if it comes, is likely to prove far more costly. Taking impending or probable unemployment into account in the process of designating areas admittedly makes it more a matter of personal judgment and

[1] See Standing Committee on Industry Research and Energy Development, *op. cit.*, No. 10, pp. 263–6.

administrative discretion, since the probability of future unemployment may vary all the way from virtual certainty about the
immediate future to foreseeing a possibility of it some time ahead.
Moreover, statistical criteria that can serve as a guide to decision
are not always available, and when this is the case, administrative
judgments are open to question and suspicion may develop that
aid is arbitrary. There is no easy way out of this dilemma; but
by adopting a cautious attitude, and confining aid to those areas
where the risks of unemployment appear certain, the administrators of the program should avoid making too many mistakes and
acquire a reputation for impartiality. That serious trouble is pend-
ing in certain areas is often obvious enough to people living there
months before unemployment actually occurs, and more flexibility
in the administration of ADA programs might well prevent such
situations from deteriorating further. The attempt to spell out with
complete precision beforehand all the characteristics of the employment situation which may be important in the granting of
aid introduces inflexibilities, though too much administrative discretion could open the door to abuse.

Aggregate figures of unemployment are certainly not enough
in arriving at decisions on what kind of aid should be offered or
whether it should be given at all. In many cases it is the composition of the unemployment which is the relevant consideration.
There is little point, for example, in providing incentives to firms
to move into an area if the types of workers they need are not
those who are unemployed. The distinction between male and
female labour requirements is a case in point. Not infrequently
firms will employ a predominance of one or the other. An over-all
unemployment figure, even where its accuracy is not open to
serious doubt, may be too crude a criterion for aid. The actual
numbers involved as well as the percentage of unemployed may
also be important in assessing the need for aid, and participation
rates may be of further help in making such an assessment. The
stability of employment should also be taken into consideration.
Communities which are heavily dependent on one particular industry or form of activity can lead a precarious existence, so that

even if unemployment does not presently exist there may still be a case for encouraging a more diversified range of employment opportunity. Some industries are especially unstable, and however promising their prospects may appear at the moment, the likelihood of trouble in the future cannot be ignored. Mining industries are a case in point, but there are others, especially those involved in the production of capital goods or military equipment of various kinds. Demand for defence procurements can be very volatile, and some cities and areas are heavily dependent upon industries catering to defence requirements.[1]

Since its inception, ADA has increased the areas of the country which qualify for assistance both in size and in numbers. Changes introduced in 1965 increased the amount of the national labour force covered under the plan to 16 per cent, a figure approximately double that under the former plan. Further areas have been designated since then. Virtually the entire Atlantic region is now covered by the legislation; only two or three areas are excluded, but significantly these are the very ones which the provincial governments consider the most promising for growth. Given the lower incomes and the seriousness of the unemployment prevailing in the Atlantic provinces as a whole, it is hard to see what is to be gained by denying aid to the few areas that do show promise. Assistance to such areas may do little to encourage migration from the poorest localities and may indeed reduce still further the latter's limited prospects of attracting industry, but even so the solution is not necessarily to deny aid to the few promising areas. One alternative would be to expand the ADA program along the lines pioneered by ARDA under the FRED legislation. Given the fact that many provinces have their own plans for area development, there is something to be said for federal-provincial programs in which decisions are taken jointly regarding the areas that will qualify for aid and on the form that aid should take.

No information has been made public on how the increase in the number of designated areas has affected the actual distribu-

---

[1] For a consideration of the spatial and other implications of defence expenditure on the Canadian economy, see Gideon Rosenbluth, *The Canadian Economy and Disarmament* (Toronto: Macmillan, 1967).

tion of assistance, but presumably it has benefited the relatively more promising areas at the expense of the poorest and least promising ones.

## Locational Incentives

The thirty-five areas designated in September 1963 were located in seven provinces. Some were dependent primarily upon the development of natural resources and others on manufacturing industries. A three-part tax incentive program designed to attract industry to these areas was instituted in the same year.

As described in the budget speech of June 13, new manufacturing and processing enterprises located in designated areas of slower growth were exempted from income taxes for the first three years. In addition, such enterprises were entitled to write off new machinery and equipment for two years thereafter, and the cost of new buildings at the rate of 20 per cent per annum straight line. The Minister of Finance then went on to say: "If these proposals do not stimulate very marked activity in the Atlantic provinces and in other areas of slowed economic progress, I do not know what will. These are major incentives to new industry locating in these areas."[1]

The incentives in 1963 took the form of tax concessions. Grants were not offered. Critics, however, pointed out that contrary to the expectations of the Minister of Finance such tax concessions were not of great value to firms during their first years of operation since their profits at such a time were likely to be quite nominal. Under the originating legislation, provision had been made for the annual review of the Area Development Program, and in 1965, as noted above, significant changes were introduced.[2] These changes broadened the incentives to include

[1] Hansard, 1963, Vol. II, p. 1004.

[2] The revised provisions are contained in the Area Development Incentives Act (14 Elizabeth II, c. 12, pp. 47–54), to which assent was given June 30, 1965. The Area Incentives regulations will be found in the *Canada Gazette*, Part II, Vol. 99, No. 16 (August 25, 1965), SOR/65 365. These were subsequently amended on July 13, 1966 (SOR/66 291). Changes are made to the list of designated areas from time to time, new ones as they qualify under the criteria for designation being added and others that no longer qualify being dropped. In June 1967 they numbered 95.

capital grants, increased the number of designated Manpower Centres to sixty-five, designated sixteen counties and census divisions, and included certain manpower measures. It was also decided to terminate the tax incentives in 1967 and to replace these with either cash grants or, if preferred by the applicant, credits of an amount equivalent to the grant as a deduction from income tax liabilities.[1]

Under the 1965 legislation, manufacturers and processors who locate or expand their operations in designated areas qualify for two main forms of aid under the Area Development Program. These forms of aid consist of development grants as well as accelerated capital cost allowances. Grants are on a sliding scale amounting to one third of the first $250,000 spent on new machinery, equipment, and buildings, one quarter of the next $750,000, and one fifth of the remainder to a maximum of $5 million. The amount of the grant for an expansion facility is based on the same rates except that the rates are applied to the cost of the expansion in excess of $10,000 or 10 per cent of the value of the existing facility, whichever is the greater.

The investment costs to which the grants may be applied include company expenditures for facilities such as water supplies, sewage disposal, electric power, and wharves and docks where these are company owned. The grants are not regarded as income for tax purposes, nor are they deducted from the capital sum against which capital cost allowances may be claimed. The grant can take the form of either an actual payment or a credit against tax payable, at the choice of the company.

The accelerated capital cost allowances permit a depreciation rate of up to 50 per cent per annum straight line on most new industrial machinery and equipment, instead of the normal 20 per cent per annum on a diminishing balance, and a depreciation rate

---

[1] It was thought that some firms might be sensitive about receiving outright grants from the government but would not be adverse to claiming income tax deductions. The tax exemptions originally offered under the ADA program terminated March 31, 1967. Though not under the ADA program, tax incentives had been offered to firms manufacturing new products or establishing in labour-surplus areas since 1961. The incentives took the form of double depreciation, permitting a faster write-off of assets.

of up to 20 per cent per annum straight line for new buildings or significant extensions instead of the normal 5 or 10 per cent per annum on a diminishing balance. Such allowances can be a valuable incentive constituting in effect an interest-free loan over several years.

These incentives, it should be noted, apply only to manufactures and processes as they are defined in the regulations pertaining to ADA.[1] The wisdom of this restriction is open to question. There is no manifest reason why aid should be confined to manufacturing and processing, for these may be the least advantageous of the various forms of development that could be fostered in a particular area. If an area has very limited potential for secondary manufacturing or processing but does have potential for other types of development, be it primary production, the establishment of certain commercial or government activities, or tourism, then these are the types of development which ought to be encouraged rather than secondary industries.[2] The government might well arrange for some of its departments and agencies to be located elsewhere than in Ottawa if there is no clear need for them to be in the capital. There are parts of eastern Ontario that are designated areas in which they might operate equally well. The type of activity which offers the greatest potential for development is the one that most merits encouragement. It is difficult to see why those depressed areas whose potential for development does not lie in secondary manufacturing or processing should be placed at a relative disadvantage to others.

Not only are all depressed areas not alike, the inducements necessary to attract industry into them vary with the nature of the industry. An increased supply of trained labour may be the critical element in one case, improved communications in a second, better local government services in a third, and so on. More thought needs to be given to the types and combinations of industry which

[1] *Ibid.*
[2] Some preliminary studies of the tourist industry have been made by ADA, but there is no evidence to suggest that ADA wishes to see an expansion of its operations to include major service industries, whether or not such industries might constitute a potential source of "exports" from the area.

are to be encouraged and to their specific potentials and needs.

In this last regard it is sometimes recommended that more encouragement be given to labour-intensive industries to establish in designated areas, a recommendation that could be accomplished by gearing aid directly to the employment created rather than to capital investment. On the face of it, such a recommendation would seem to be eminently sensible, but closer examination raises a number of doubts. For one thing, direct contributions to the wage bill may lead to increased wage demands, and for another, labour-intensive industries are apt to be among the lower paying industries unless they provide highly skilled and professional services, and these are more likely to be found in large and prosperous urban centres. Linking aid with investment may thus be more rewarding in the long run, though its initial impact on employment may be less.

The proposal, however, that the amount of aid might be related at least to some extent to the numbers employed is not without merit, and there may well be situations where it would make more sense to allocate aid in this way.[1] In some cases, for example in the development of Alberta's oil and petro-chemical industry, very heavy capital investment may be required but the number of local employees likely to benefit directly or indirectly by such expenditure may be negligible. Even if it is agreed that the substitution of labour for capital is not the way to reduce unemployment, subsidies to increase capital formation are not necessarily the most appropriate solution.

According to the former Minister of Industry, the development grants payable under the Area Development Program were instituted to overcome possible cost disadvantages, thus making it possible for firms to establish "economic" (*sic*) operations in a

---

[1] In September 1967, the government of the United Kingdom introduced a regional employment premium amounting to 7½ per cent of labour costs for a period of at least seven years to all manufacturing employees in the development areas. It was considered that this sort of incentive was preferable to increasing grants to new investment, public or private, or to permitting regional variations in income tax. The hope was that the measure would reduce regional unemployment differentials by one half within a few years.

designated area in competition with manufacturing elsewhere.[1] Such a statement, considered in conjunction with ADA's emphasis on the reduction of unemployment and its explicit lack of any intention to provide for a comprehensive program of regional development, contributes to the view that it is less an area development agency in the sense in which such an organization is apt to be understood than an industrial location agency with limited social welfare objectives.

## Co-ordination with Other Plans and Policies

Spokesmen for some of the provincial governments have pointed to the dangers of channelling inappropriate types of aid to depressed areas of a province and have been disturbed at the failure of the federal government to provide the kind of assistance that is required and to concentrate it where it can achieve its greatest impact. In spite of assertions on the complementarity of federal and provincial programs made by the Minister of Industry in his testimony before the Standing Committee on Industry Research and Energy Development, the fact is that a number of provincial governments do not regard the ADA program as complementary to their own but as one that is apt to work at cross-purposes.[2] ADA may make it more, not less, difficult to achieve the types of development or out-migration regarded as most appropriate for specific areas. Some of the more promising areas for development within a generally depressed province do not qualify for federal assistance, and provincial attempts to attract firms to them are weakened when federal incentives are offered only to the less promising ones. In general, the criticism that federal policies are being mechanically applied on a narrow front without regard for their potential impact on long-run growth forms a strong undercurrent. ADA policies in this respect have left much to be desired

[1] "Address by Hon. C. M. Drury, Minister of Industry, to the Georgian Bay Economic Development Conference, September 19, 1966", a news release (Ottawa: Department of Industry), p. 8.
[2] Officials of the Atlantic Provinces Economic Council have drawn attention to this repeatedly. See, for example, *First Annual Review: The Atlantic Economy* (Halifax: APEC, 1967).

and are in sharp contrast to those developed by ARDA under the FRED legislation. Originally some of the official literature suggested that ADA would undertake a thorough economic appreciation of assigned areas, including natural resources, primary and secondary industry, the business and financial community, services, transportation, labour resources, and so on, and then proceed to the preparation of an over-all development plan for each area, enlisting the assistance of local and provincial authorities and other specialists.[1] In fact, such ambitious notions were promptly scuttled, and there is some doubt now as to whether they were ever seriously contemplated. But whether they were or not, they at least contained an implicit awareness that the problem of depressed areas called for something more than blanket financial incentives to secondary manufacturing.

In spite of official references to co-operation with other federal departments and branches, such as Manpower and ARDA, there is little to suggest a common purpose. ARDA, for example, cannot proceed effectively with rural plans under FRED without the full support of ADA and the Department of Industry, but ADA shows no inclination either to hand over responsibilities for industrial development in rural areas to ARDA or to participate in the planning itself. What is lacking is a sense of unified direction and drive.

With regard to the broader manpower objectives mentioned at the time other changes were made in 1965, the hope was expressed that close co-operation would be achieved between the firms receiving financial incentives, provincial authorities, and the Canada Manpower Service, so that there would be effective planning to meet the long-term manpower needs of the new industries as well as their immediate requirements. To some extent, this has begun. The Department of Manpower now conducts joint surveys with provincial and local authorities to assess training needs and facilities, and assists in the development of new training methods

[1] See T. N. Brewis, "The Problem of Regional Disparities", in *Areas of Economic Stress in Canada*, eds. W. D. Wood and R. S. Thoman (Kingston: Queen's University Industrial Relations Centre, 1965), pp. 109–10.

through joint pilot training programs. The provinces are also being assisted to expand their activities under the Technical and Vocational Training Assistance Act in order to develop training for the under-employed as well as the unemployed.

Although consultations do take place between ADA and the Department of Manpower, there is very little integration of policy. Each body pursues its own ends with little regard for the action of the other. The Department of Manpower has long been aware of the shifts in demand for various classes of workers and of the problems arising out of technological change that confront some regions of the country more than others. For example, the decline in the numbers employed in the primary industries has been of particular importance in the Atlantic provinces where the comparative absence of alternative employment has contributed not only to unemployment specifically, but to lower labour force participation rates and under-employment. While measures have been taken under the Manpower Mobility Program introduced in 1965 to encourage the relocation of workers from labour surplus to labour deficient areas, it is too early yet to assess the impact of this program. It has certainly shown promise; but if it is to have any significant effect on the depressed areas, it will have to accomplish very much more than was accomplished under earlier policies with similar intent. Originally, the National Employment Service (now called the Canada Manpower Service) was empowered to pay for the transportation costs of moving workers, their dependents, and their household effects from "labour surplus areas" designated from time to time by the Minister of Labour. These expenses were authorized when the worker was unemployed, had a job to go to, and was unable to pay the costs himself. At the outset the policy was a mere gesture. In the two years from 1961 to 1963, only 157 workers and their families were assisted in this way. Far more is being and will have to be done if federally assisted labour mobility is to be effective.

So far as interprovincial mobility is concerned, one difficulty is the sensitivity of provincial governments to federal action that is likely to lead to a reduction in their populations. Losses of population are regarded with serious misgiving, and in view of this, some consideration might be given to federal policies for reducing such concern. Federal grants might be made to provinces which have had a net out-migration, for example. The net receiving provinces, such as Ontario and British Columbia, would receive nothing. Those losing population, such as the Atlantic provinces, would be compensated for the costs they have incurred in educating their youth only to lose them during their most productive years. One merit of such a procedure would be that the provinces that have benefited from the inflow of productive workers, would, in effect, share the expense of their education with the provinces that have lost them.

## The ADA *Program: An Appraisal*

In comparison with ARDA, which has devoted a substantial part of its resources to various studies and research projects designed to guide policy and provide a foundation for it, ADA has done little in the way of investigating regional economic problems and only one or two studies have been made public. In the legislation, the powers and duties of the Minister were to include undertaking research and making investigations respecting the means of increasing employment and income in designated areas, but whatever knowledge the Agency itself may have on the subject, it releases only the barest details that would permit any appraisal of its operations.[1]

The apparent lack of comprehensive and continued study of regional economic problems by the Agency may have other explanations, but in part it seems to reflect the circumscribed role that the Agency has chosen or been called upon to play and

[1] Doubtless information about individual firms must be kept confidential, but it is hard to believe that this is the only explanation for silence. Though it has been slow in starting, the Agency is now beginning to strengthen its research activities. The cost of certain feasibility studies is being shared with individual provinces, but the initiative for such studies has to come from the provinces. Pilot studies have been undertaken of possible ways of delineating area boundaries and efforts are being made to study the impact of the incentives in certain areas, as well as the effects of certain forward and backward linkages between particular industries.

the restricted approach that it takes to the problems of the designated areas. The Agency maintains liaison with the line branches of the Department of Industry and obtains some information from them, but the latter have no regional orientation and little concern with the special problems of the designated areas. They see their main responsibility as one of providing various types of information to industry rather than of fostering specific development objectives.

In appraising the role of ADA, of course, it is necessary to see it in the context of the entire program of area development, including the operations of other federal departments and bodies – among them the Department of Manpower and the Atlantic Development Board. ADA is not operating alone, and those responsible for its policies may reasonably claim that not all the deficiencies in regional policies should be laid at its door. None the less, the fact that the Agency has explicitly down-played the role of development makes it one of the weaker links in the chain.

The following tables cast some light on the operations of the Agency.

These tables indicate that between December 1963 and December 1967 almost 50,000 jobs resulted from the program, though this figure is only an estimate derived from the stated expectations of employers at the time of submitting applications for aid. Some of the employment would have resulted even without the incentives, and to this extent the gain would not be net, but additional employment would result from the multiplier effect.

Fixed assets investments under the program for the same period, 1963 to 1967, totalled $1,846 million, working out at close to $37,000 per job created. How much of this sum was actually contributed by the federal government is not known, but given the schedule of government grants, presumably the figure works out at somewhere between one fifth and one third. If we assume it to be one quarter, then the federal contribution per job created was over $9,000, though it varied greatly from province to province. In Alberta the federal contribution was apparently not far short of $30,000 (one quarter of $118,000), a consequence of

## Table 7:1
## Job Opportunities, Investment, and Value of Incentives Under ADA
## December 1963 to December 1967*

| | Job opportunities under ADA | | | Investment | | | | Value of incentives under ADA | | |
|---|---|---|---|---|---|---|---|---|---|---|
| | Total (number) | Per 1,000 of labour force in designated areas (number) | Per 1,000 of labour force in province or region (number) | Under ADA in fixed assets in designated areas (a) ($000,000) | Private and public, in province or region (b) ($000,000) | (a) as % of (b) | Total ($000,000) | Total ($000,000) | Per 1,000 of labour force in designated areas ($) | Per 1,000 of labour force in province or region ($) |
| Newfoundland | 3,912 | 28 | 26 | 220.7 | 1,471 | 15.0 | 26.6 | | 191 | 187 |
| Prince Edward Island | 767 | 21 | 21 | 7.2 | 284 | 2.5 | 1.7 | | 47 | 47 |
| Nova Scotia | 6,674 | 39 | 26 | 243.3 | 1,916 | 12.7 | 39.4 | | 233 | 159 |
| New Brunswick | 4,955 | 34 | 24 | 204.4 | 1,743 | 11.7 | 38.3 | | 267 | 187 |
| Atlantic provinces | 16,308 | 33 | 25 | 675.7 | 5,414 | 12.5 | 106.1 | | 217 | 168 |
| Quebec | 10,538 | 16 | 4 | 480.8 | 16,673 | 2.9 | 90.3 | | 138 | 42 |
| Ontario | 18,164 | 48 | 6 | 435.9 | 24,525 | 1.8 | 126.5 | | 335 | 46 |

| | | | | | | | | |
|---|---|---|---|---|---|---|---|---|
| Manitoba | 1,325 | 10 | 3 | 50.5 | 3,270 | *1.6* | 12.4 | 100 | 34 |
| Saskatchewan | 1,071 | 9 | 3 | 67.6 | 4,200 | *1.6* | 7.2 | 61 | 21 |
| Alberta | 714 | 14 | 1 | 84.2 | 6,920 | *1.2* | 14.1 | 293 | 25 |
| Prairie provinces | 3,110 | 10 | 2 | 202.3 | 14,390 | *1.4* | 33.7 | 116 | 26 |
| British Columbia | 1,744 | 39 | 2 | 49.6 | 8,924 | *0.6* | 13.1 | 298 | 18 |
| Undecided | 93 | | | 1.8 | | | 0.4 | | |
| CANADA | 49,957 | 26 | 6 | 1,846.0 | 69,926 | *2.6* | 370.4 | 200 | 49 |

Note: Figures do not add to totals in all cases because of rounding.

*Statistics relating to the ADA program are based upon active applications received by the agency during the given period; they exclude applications that have been rejected, reserved, or withdrawn. Value of Incentives includes both financial grants and tax holiday incentives, and refers to the total amount of incentives in which benefits are normally allocated over a three-year period.

Sources: Statistics relating to private and public investment are based on D.B.S. and Department of Trade and Commerce, *Private and Public Investment in Canada*, (61-205), various years; the balance have been provided by the Program Co-ordination Division, Area Development Agency (unpublished data).

**Table 7:2**
**Investments Per Head of the Labour Force and Per Job**
**Created Under ADA**
**December 1963 to December 1967**

($)

| | Investment under program per head of labour force in designated area | Investment under program per head of labour force in province or region | Investment under program per job created |
|---|---|---|---|
| Newfoundland | 1,588 | 1,554 | 56,434 |
| Prince Edward Island | 200 | 200 | 9,408 |
| Nova Scotia | 1,439 | 981 | 36,460 |
| New Brunswick | 1,429 | 1,001 | 41,252 |
| Atlantic provinces | 1,387 | 1,072 | 41,435 |
| Quebec | 737 | 227 | 45,633 |
| Ontario | 1,156 | 158 | 23,999 |
| Manitoba | 407 | 140 | 38,132 |
| Saskatchewan | 572 | 197 | 63,121 |
| Alberta | 1,755 | 149 | 117,995 |
| Prairie provinces | 695 | 159 | 65,072 |
| British Columbia | 1,128 | 70 | 28,482 |
| CANADA | 997 | 247 | 36,959 |

Source: Program Co-ordination Division, Area Development Agency (unpublished data).

very heavy investments by one or two firms in the oil and chemical industry.[1] It is difficult to see how the extremely heavy subsidies of close to $30,000 per job could possibly be justified. The benefits must accrue overwhelmingly to the companies financing the investment rather than to the unemployed. Admittedly Alberta is an exceptional case, but even apart from Alberta there is a striking variation between the provinces, a variation which would repay study.

How many of the additional jobs assumed to have been created resulted in a reduction of local unemployment cannot be stated with certainty, for to some extent workers would be recruited from outside the boundaries, and in some instances the numbers involved might be large. In other cases the gains in employment in the designated areas would be at the expense of employment elsewhere, but there is no way of quantifying this. Changes in the definition of unemployment complicate the matter further.

The Agency does make on-site inspections to check up on the experience of firms that have received aid, but it appears that, by and large, recipients have fulfilled expectations in the matter of employment creation. This is not just the result of chance. Applications for aid are examined critically and a large number – approximately one third – are rejected, notwithstanding protests from applicants, supported in some cases by their member of parliament. The efficacy of this initial scrutiny is indicated by the complete absence of any failure up to the end of 1967 among firms that have been assisted. In this respect, at least, the federal government has been more successful than certain provincial governments which have provided aid to industry.

A rough indication of the success of the program in terms of reducing unemployment might be gained by comparing the unemployment rates in designated areas with those in non-designated areas. Information is available on the areas that have improved

---

[1] In 1964, before northern Alberta was designated, Blairmore was the only area designated in that province and it had a labour force of less than 4,000. As a result, investment under the program in that one area came to over $19,000 per head of the labour force, a figure far in excess of that in other provinces.

sufficiently to result in their being deleted from the designated list. Approximately a dozen were deleted by the end of 1967 and the impact of new investment has still to work itself out in a number of other cases. Some of the areas removed from the list were borderline in the first place, however, and other forces have also been at work.

What is clear is that the Atlantic provinces have shown very little improvement, if any, in employment rates relative to the rest of the country. If one accepts the official figures at their face value, employment created by the program has been greater in Ontario than in the Atlantic provinces, this in spite of the fact that the labour force in designated areas in the Atlantic provinces was over three times that of Ontario. Moreover, the better performance in Ontario was achieved with a much smaller level of investment under the program.

There is a great deal of dissatisfaction with the ADA program in the Atlantic provinces, not only because of its limited efficacy in reducing the high levels of unemployment which prevail there, but also because of the desire of many to see industry concentrated in those areas where its potential for growth offers the greatest promise.

In spite of the absence of data, some qualitative summary comments can be made about the basic approach to policy. As noted above, no effort is made to analyse the causes of distress or to provide assistance within the framework of some coherent program of development worked out in conjunction with provincial governments. The designated areas are not selected with a view to encouraging economic growth but are convenient administrative units which happen to display certain characteristics of distress, notably chronic unemployment. Since the emphasis is on chronic unemployment, steps to forestall impending distress are not taken. Incentives, concentrated as they are on manufacturing and processing activities, are applied without regard to the particular circumstances of individual areas; this is likely to lead to a certain misallocation of resources and, though it is no part of the intent of the program, to benefit certain areas much more than others.

What would seem to be desirable is a complete revamping of the program to bring it more into line with the objectives pursued by ARDA under the FRED legislation and into harmony with other provincial and federal policies, including those of the Atlantic Development Board. The special problems of the Atlantic provinces and the functions of the ADB are the subject of the following chapter.

It has been argued, and quite rightly, that if the program concentrated more on growth and deliberately focused aid on the more promising of the distressed areas, the least promising areas would be even more neglected and their plight would deteriorate still further. The answer for the areas that lack growth potential, however, does not lie in the present Area Development Program which does very little for them anyway, but in the development of other policies combining welfare, special assistance to migration, and temporary subsidies to permit a phasing out of unprofitable operations, thereby reducing abrupt and unacceptable dislocation. In some instances industries as well as workers might be given assistance to relocate elsewhere. As for the specific types of incentive offered, the Agency has been making enquiries among business firms to ascertain their reactions and to discover whether different forms of incentive might not be more effective in inducing decisions to locate in the designated areas.

A relationship must exist between various amounts of subsidy and the employment created, though what that relationship is may be very difficult to determine. Beyond a certain point subventions of one sort and another are bound to seem excessive, even in the limited context of employment creation, and before that stage is reached serious reservations can be expected as to whether resources are being allocated efficiently. The higher the subsidies needed to encourage firms to locate in designated areas, the stronger is the likelihood that the location will be an inappropriate one from the standpoint of the firm and that the wisdom of such a policy will be placed in doubt. Inevitably, moreover, criticisms from the non-designated areas increase when local efforts to attract industry are frustrated by substantial federal incentives to induce industry to locate elsewhere. There is no easy way out of this dilemma. If the incentives are modest enough to have little impact on the location of industry, they fail in their purpose. If they are large enough to be effective, they will be a source of criticism.[1]

Occasionally firms already established in an area will complain that assistance is being given to new competitors, but by and large such aid does not appear to trouble the great majority of them. If they care to expand they too can take advantage of assistance under the program.

The limitations of the ADA program are well known in government circles and a phasing out of the Agency's operations is to be expected. Within the compass of the restricted objectives set for it the Agency may have operated as well as could be expected but a new approach to regional problems is needed with the emphasis on a long-term restructuring of the poorer regions.

[1] Parliamentary debates bring this out very clearly: see, for example, the debates of June 2 and 3 (Hansard, 1966, Vol. III).

*8. The Atlantic Provinces and the Atlantic Development Board*

OF THE VARIOUS REGIONS in Canada that have experienced prolonged periods of unemployment and low incomes, the Atlantic provinces come most readily to mind. There have been exceptional periods – the war years are a case in point – when economic activity there has increased sharply, but for several decades the region has not participated fully in the prosperity that other parts of the country have enjoyed.

As Table 8:1 shows, there was a very marked decline in male employment in particular industries between 1951 and 1961. Agriculture had the most outstanding drop – almost 50 per cent – with an absolute decline of over 32,000 in the male labour force. The decline has continued since then, and at a more rapid rate than for the country as a whole. As elsewhere, farms are becoming larger and fewer. Fishing and trapping accounted for another 12,000 to 13,000 drop in employment, and forestry and logging for 8,000. In all the above cases the percentage drop was very large. Transport and communications, trade, finance, and government services, on the other hand, accounted for increases in employment, though the total increases were not sufficient to

165

## Table 8:1(a)
## Structure of the Labour Force in the Atlantic Provinces by Sex
## 1951 and 1961

| | 1951 | | 1961 | | Change: 1951-61 | | | |
| --- | --- | --- | --- | --- | --- | --- | --- | --- |
| | Males | Females | Males | Females | Males | Females | Males | Females |
| | (thousands) | | (thousands) | | (thousands) | | % | |
| **GROUP 1** | | | | | | | | |
| Agriculture | 65.3 | | 33.3 | | − 32.0 | | − 49.0 | |
| Forestry and logging | 32.6 | | 24.6 | | − 8.0 | | − 24.5 | |
| Fishing and trapping | 34.1 | | 21.5 | | − 12.6 | | − 37.0 | |
| Mining and quarrying | 20.3 | | 15.8 | | − 4.5 | | − 22.2 | |
| Construction | 35.3 | | 37.6 | | + 2.3 | | + 6.5 | |
| Total, Group 1 | 187.6 | 2.0 | 132.8 | 3.2 | − 54.8 | + 1.2 | − 29.2 | + 60.0 |
| **GROUP 2** | | | | | | | | |
| Transport and communication | 43.2 | 3.7 | 52.8 | 6.4 | + 9.6 | + 2.7 | + 22.2 | + 73.0 |
| Trade | 53.1 | 21.8 | 61.9 | 30.8 | + 8.8 | + 9.0 | + 16.6 | + 41.2 |
| Finance | 4.1 | 3.1 | 6.3 | 5.3 | + 2.2 | + 2.2 | + 53.7 | + 71.0 |

| | | | | | | | | |
|---|---|---|---|---|---|---|---|---|
| Government service (excluding armed forces) | 23.3 | 6.1 | 33.2 | 8.0 | + 9.9 | + 1.9 | + 42.5 | + 31.1 |
| Other services | 23.1 | 49.5 | 34.4 | 68.5 | + 11.3 | + 19.0 | + 48.9 | + 38.4 |
| Electricity, gas, and water | 4.9 | 0.3 | 5.0 | 0.4 | + 0.1 | + 0.1 | + 2.0 | — |
| Manufacturing | 70.2 | 11.5 | 65.2 | 12.5 | − 5.0 | + 1.0 | − 7.1 | + 8.7 |
| − Fast-growth industries | 3.7 | 0.4 | 9.4 | 1.1 | + 5.7 | + 0.7 | +154.1 | — |
| − Slow-growth industries | 52.2 | 9.1 | 44.4 | 8.7 | − 7.8 | − 0.4 | − 14.9 | − 4.4 |
| − Other industries | 14.3 | 2.0 | 11.4 | 2.7 | − 2.9 | + 0.7 | − 20.3 | + 35.0 |
| Total, Group 2 | 221.9 | 96.0 | 258.8 | 131.9 | + 36.9 | + 35.9 | + 16.6 | + 37.4 |
| All industries (excluding armed forces) | 416.8 | 99.9 | 397.7 | 135.2 | − 19.1 | + 35.3 | − 4.6 | + 35.3 |
| Armed forces | 14.0 | — | 28.2 | 0.6 | + 14.2 | + 0.6 | +101.4 | — |
| Total, all industries | 430.8 | 99.9 | 425.9 | 135.8 | − 4.9 | + 35.9 | + 1.1 | + 35.9 |

**Table 8:1(b)**
**Structure of the Male Labour Force in the Atlantic Provinces**
**by Education**
**1951**

| | (a) Total | (b) Less than 5 years education | (b) as % of (a) |
|---|---|---|---|
| | | (thousands) | |
| **GROUP 1** | | | |
| Agriculture | 65.3 | 10.8 | 16.5 |
| Forestry and logging | 32.6 | 11.6 | 35.6 |
| Fishing and trapping | 34.1 | 11.2 | 32.8 |
| Mining and quarrying | 20.3 | 3.4 | 16.7 |
| Construction | 35.3 | 5.5 | 15.6 |
| Total, Group 1 | 187.6 | 42.5 | 22.7 |
| **GROUP 2** | | | |
| Transport and Communication | 43.2 | 4.4 | 10.2 |
| Trade | 53.1 | 3.8 | 7.2 |
| Finance | 4.1 | 0.1 | — |
| Government service (excluding armed forces) | 23.3 | 1.6 | 6.9 |
| Other services | 23.1 | 1.6 | 6.9 |
| Electricity, gas, and water | 4.9 | 0.5 | 10.2 |
| Manufacturing | 70.2 | 10.1 | 14.4 |
| Total, Group 2 | 221.9 | 22.1 | 10.0 |
| All industries (excluding armed forces) | 416.8 | 65.9 | 15.8 |
| Armed forces | 14.0 | 0.1 | — |
| Total, all industries | 430.8 | 66.0 | 15.3* |

Note: Figures do not add to the totals for "All industries (excluding armed forces)" because of rounding and the inclusion of "no stated industry".

*The corresponding figure for females is 4.3%. The figures are too small to show by industry breakdown.

Sources: D.B.S., *1951 Census of Canada*, Vol. IV, Table 11 and Table 19, and *1961 Census of Canada*, Vol. III (94-503) and (94-518).

offset the declines. If, moreover, armed forces are excluded from the calculations, the total decline amounted to between 4 and 5 per cent. What is also notable in the light of some development plans stressing manufacture is that manufacturing alone in the second group showed a decline. Though an upward trend in this sector has occurred since, its rate of growth still lags behind the over-all rate of growth of the regional economy.[1]

In striking contrast to male employment, female employment rose from 100,000 to almost 136,000, and in 1961 constituted almost a quarter of the labour force, whereas it amounted to less than a fifth in 1951.

The data relating to education are also very revealing. Those industries characterized by low educational levels are the ones that have declined most rapidly. This is true of agriculture, forestry and logging, and fishing and trapping, as well as of manufacturing.

Although the Atlantic provinces are alike in important respects, they differ widely in some ways. As Table 8:2 shows, the occupational structure is far from uniform. Primary occupations including construction account for a much larger proportion of the labour force in Newfoundland and Prince Edward Island than in Nova Scotia or New Brunswick, where manufacturing is concentrated. Among the primary occupations there is heavy concentration on agriculture in Prince Edward Island and virtually no agriculture at all in Newfoundland. Government services figure prominently in Nova Scotia but are much less important in the other Atlantic provinces. Given the diversity which exists, policies need to be reviewed in the light of their probable variation in impact, and tailored to meet individual requirements. Uniform incentives will not affect all provinces alike.

Of particular importance is the need for government policies to phase out obsolete industries and foster the growth of more promising ones. In practice, a number of policies have operated in precisely the opposite way and have tended to perpetuate

[1] The reader is reminded, however, of the dangers in attempting to assess trends on the basis of relatively short time periods (see Chapter 4). Depending on the years selected, the picture can and does change substantially.

**Table 8:2**
**Distribution of the Labour Force in the Atlantic Provinces**
**1951 and 1961**

(thousands)

| | Newfoundland | | | | Prince Edward Island | | | |
| | 1951 | | 1961 | | 1951 | | 1961 | |
| | *Males* | *Females* | *Males* | *Females* | *Males* | *Females* | *Males* | *Females* |
|---|---|---|---|---|---|---|---|---|
| GROUP 1 | | | | | | | | |
| Agriculture | 3.4 | | 1.5 | | 12.7 | | 8.5 | |
| Forestry and logging | 10.5 | | 6.9 | | 0.3 | | 0.1 | |
| Fishing and trapping | 18.4 | | 8.4 | | 1.6 | | 2.1 | |
| Mining and quarrying | 3.6 | | 4.2 | | — | | — | |
| Construction | 7.2 | | 9.4 | | 1.9 | | 2.2 | |
| Total, Group 1 | 43.2 | 0.3 | 30.4 | 0.3 | 16.5 | 0.3 | 12.9 | 0.7 |
| GROUP 2 | | | | | | | | |
| Transport and communication | 9.5 | 0.5 | 13.1 | 1.1 | 1.9 | 0.2 | 2.3 | 0.3 |
| Trade | 10.3 | 4.4 | 12.8 | 6.1 | 3.2 | 1.1 | 3.5 | 1.3 |
| Finance | 0.4 | 0.2 | 0.8 | 0.6 | 0.2 | 0.2 | 0.3 | 0.3 |
| Government service | 7.9 | 1.6 | 10.8 | 1.8 | 2.0 | 0.3 | 2.6 | 0.4 |
| Other service | 3.8 | 8.2 | 6.3 | 11.5 | 1.3 | 3.1 | 1.7 | 4.0 |
| Electricity, gas, and water | 0.6 | — | 0.9 | 0.1 | 0.3 | — | 0.2 | — |
| Manufacturing | 12.6 | 1.6 | 10.8 | 1.3 | 2.5 | 0.7 | 2.2 | 0.9 |
| Total, Group 2 | 45.0 | 16.7 | 55.5 | 22.6 | 11.3 | 5.6 | 12.7 | 7.1 |
| Total, all industries | 89.5 | 17.1 | 88.7 | 23.6 | 28.2 | 6.0 | 26.1 | 8.1 |

| | Nova Scotia | | | | New Brunswick | | | |
| | 1951 | | 1961 | | 1951 | | 1961 | |
| | Males | Females | Males | Females | Males | Females | Males | Females |
|---|---|---|---|---|---|---|---|---|
| **GROUP 1** | | | | | | | | |
| Agriculture | 22.8 | | 11.5 | | 26.4 | | 11.8 | |
| Forestry and logging | 5.8 | | 4.2 | | 16.0 | | 10.4 | |
| Fishing and trapping | 9.7 | | 7.4 | | 4.4 | | 3.6 | |
| Mining and quarrying | 15.5 | | 10.0 | | 1.2 | | 1.6 | |
| Construction | 16.2 | | 15.2 | | 10.0 | | 10.8 | |
| Total, Group 1 | 70.0 | 0.9 | 48.4 | 1.1 | 58.0 | 0.7 | 38.2 | 1.0 |
| **GROUP 2** | | | | | | | | |
| Transport and communication | 16.5 | 1.7 | 19.7 | 2.8 | 15.3 | 1.4 | 17.7 | 2.3 |
| Trade | 22.8 | 9.2 | 25.4 | 11.4 | 16.8 | 7.0 | 20.2 | 9.0 |
| Finance | 2.0 | 1.5 | 3.1 | 2.6 | 1.5 | 1.2 | 2.1 | 1.8 |
| Government service | 20.2 | 2.7 | 32.9 | 4.0 | 7.2 | 1.5 | 15.1 | 2.4 |
| Other service | 10.4 | 21.6 | 15.1 | 29.8 | 7.6 | 16.6 | 11.3 | 23.2 |
| Electricity, gas, and water | 2.4 | 0.2 | 2.2 | 0.2 | 1.6 | 0.1 | 1.7 | 0.1 |
| Manufacturing | 30.6 | 4.4 | 28.7 | 5.4 | 24.7 | 4.9 | 23.5 | 5.0 |
| Total, Group 2 | 105.0 | 41.2 | 127.2 | 56.1 | 74.6 | 32.8 | 91.6 | 43.7 |
| Total, all industries | 178.1 | 42.7 | 178.6 | 58.3 | 135.0 | 34.1 | 132.5 | 45.8 |

Note: Figures do not add to totals in all cases because of rounding and inclusion of "no stated industry" in the totals for "all industries".

Source: D.B.S., *1951 Census of Canada*, Vol. IV (Table 11 and Table 19); *1961 Census of Canada*, Vol. III (94-503 and 94-518).

inefficient industries and uneconomic resource allocation. The most notorious example of this is the coal industry in Nova Scotia. In one year alone, 1965, federal subsidies to the coal industry amounted to $22 million. Some four million tons of coal were marketed that year, and 7,500 persons employed, which meant the subsidy was close to $3,000 a year per worker.[1] The extremely heavy subvention of this industry, whose economic situation has deteriorated over the years and continues to do so, is only one aspect of misallocated resources. Another is that the perpetuation of this industry has retarded the implementation of structural shifts in the economy, which are required if the economy is to attain approximate per capita income parity. The same complaint can be levelled at the policy extending unemployment insurance to inshore fishermen, a policy that has encouraged a labour force to remain in that occupation far in excess of what can be justified. A list of such policies could readily be drawn up.

So long as the average income of the labour force in the Atlantic provinces remains significantly lower than elsewhere over a prolonged period of time, there can be little doubt that resources are being misallocated, for there is no reason to suppose that the intrinsic quality of the labour force in the Atlantic provinces, taken as a whole, is inferior. One element in that misallocation are the policies described above which tend to perpetuate an inappropriate industrial mix through the propping up of unprofitable industries and the encouragement of industries in which there are lengthy periods of unemployment.

## *The Origins of the* ADB

The causes contributing to the slow economic growth of the Atlantic provinces have been the subject of numerous enquiries, submissions to federal authorities, and royal commissions, and various measures have been introduced at one time and another

[1] The industry, which is now deliberately being cut back, has been the subject of many reports over the years. Among the more recent, mention might be made of J. R. Donald, *Report on the Cape Breton Coal Problem* (Ottawa: Queen's Printer, 1966). The subject is discussed further in Chapter 10.

designed to improve the situation. Indeed so much has been written on the subject that there is a risk of being overwhelmed by it. As might be expected, the quality of the various studies is not uniform, and the data and reasons for the differing conclusions that have been drawn need to be appraised. This in itself is a formidable undertaking.[1]

In *An Analysis of Interregional Differences in Manpower Utilization and Earnings*, Frank T. Denton contrasts the Atlantic region with other regions in Canada and points out that it suffers from a particularly unfavourable set of characteristics: "The effect of relatively low basic rates of earnings," he observes, "is reinforced by very high unemployment rates, an unfavourable age structure, and low labour force participation rates. Seasonal fluctuations are severe, the general educational level of the population is lower than in other regions, and a large proportion of the population live in rural, non-farm areas which tend to have low income levels."[2] To the above might be added the great geographic dispersion of industry within the region and the lower levels of investment per capita.

Among the more extensive enquiries was one undertaken in the mid 1950s by the Royal Commission on Canada's Economic Prospects (The Gordon Commission).[3] It was the view of the Commissioners that the Atlantic economy required considerable expenditures on the development of basic public facilities and resources, among them the transportation system and sources of power. They also expressed the opinion that a better knowledge

---

[1] The task has, however, been lightened by the publication of *Evaluation of Economic Research Relating to the Atlantic Region,* a report to the Atlantic Provinces Research Board prepared by Louis J. Walinsky (Fredericton: Atlantic Provinces Research Board, June 1967). The terms of reference were: to review the results of economic research which had been conducted over the last decade; to point out areas of agreement and disagreement; to indicate areas where further economic research needed to be undertaken; and to indicate the economic policies suggested by the research findings on which there was general agreement.

[2] Frank T. Denton, *op. cit.,* p. 14.

[3] Royal Commission on Canada's Economic Prospects, *Final Report* (Ottawa: Queen's Printer, 1957). See also the excellent study prepared for the Commission by R. D. Howland, *Some Regional Aspects of Canada's Economic Development* (Ottawa: Queen's Printer, 1957).

of the resources of the region and better land use were needed. Significantly, the Commissioners felt that it was desirable to fit the various measures into a comprehensive economic framework in order to achieve a fuller and more efficient use of resources, and that in pursuing this objective it might be desirable for part of the labour force to switch occupations and relocate not only elsewhere within the region but also in some instances outside of the region. The reference to possible migration out of the region triggered off an outburst of criticism, much of it more emotional than thoughtful, and certain major suggestions of the Commission received less attention at the time than they merited. Among those suggestions was one that federal funds be provided to assist in the economic development of the Atlantic provinces and that these be supervised by an appropriate federal agency in accordance with an over-all co-ordinated plan to strengthen as much as possible the basic economic structure of the region.

At the regional level a number of officials, notably those associated with APEC,[1] had also suggested that there was a need for a federal authority which could serve as a focal point for all matters pertaining to the economy of the Atlantic region. Such an authority, recognizing the many changes occurring in the structure of the region, could recommend the lines along which development might take place.

In the throne speech of 1962, some five years after the appearance of the Gordon Report, the government expressed its intention to establish a development board to advise on measures and projects that would promote the economic development of Canada's Atlantic region. A resolution to that effect was introduced in the Commons on December 4th of that year, and was given its first reading. It read as follows:

> That it is expedient to introduce a measure to establish an Atlantic development board and to define the duties thereof, to provide for the appointment of the chairman and other

---

[1] APEC is a non-profit, non-political organization, formed in 1954, to promote and encourage the economic and social development of the whole Atlantic region. Its publications have contributed greatly to informed discussion of policies. Notable among these has been an annual review, the first of which appeared in October 1967.

members of the board and for the payment of certain expenses of the members thereof, to provide for the appointment of an executive director of the board and for the payment of his remuneration, to provide further that the board may engage the services of such advisers and staff as may be necessary to enable it to carry out its duties and to provide further for other related and incidental matters.

In introducing the resolution, the Minister of National Revenue said that the proposed legislation to set up the board was the most forward step ever taken in his lifetime for the benefit of the Atlantic provinces and that it had tremendous possibilities which should increase the level of income and ultimately contribute to greatly increased employment in the region; he went on to say that the program might very properly be considered to be partly the development of the national economy, with special reference to the difficulties peculiar to the Atlantic region.[1] He pointed to the grave disparity between the average standards of the Atlantic region and those of the rest of Canada, a disparity that could be measured by average incomes, which were lower in the Atlantic provinces by more than a third; by capital investment per head, which was half that in the other provinces; or by the lack of opportunity which, measured by employment available, was much greater.

Much of the discussion that followed was devoted to reciting the benefits which each of the parties claimed to have provided to the Atlantic provinces and to rebutting of the claims of others. Few points of substance were made, but there was a general feeling that to be effective the Board would require more than just advisory powers. It was decided that powers of an operational nature were necessary, and that there should be a corresponding provision for these in the budget. As originally envisaged, the Board had no funds with which to initiate projects.[2] There was

[1] Hansard, 1962–3, Vol. III, p. 2291.

[2] Much was made of the absence of any funds and of the fact that the chairman of the board was to receive a salary of $3,000 a year, a figure, it was suggested, that reflected a lack of serious intent on the part of the government. The bill was given its second reading on December 5, and the debate continued intermittently until the 11th. The third reading followed the next day, December 12, 1962.

also a view, however, which was not given the attention it merited, that capital projects were but a minor part of what was needed for the development of the region.

The act to provide for the establishment of an Atlantic development board, cited as "the Atlantic Development Board Act", received royal assent on December 20, 1962. Under its provisions, the "Atlantic region" comprised the provinces of New Brunswick, Nova Scotia, Prince Edward Island, and Newfoundland. (In the debate on the bill there was a suggestion by a member from Quebec that parts of Quebec might also be included, but this was not pursued.) The Board originally consisted of five members appointed by the Governor-in-Council. Later, in July 1963, to change the political complexion of the Board, the number was increased to eleven. In the original legislation the Board had advisory powers only, but this too was changed, and a special fund of $100 million was put at its disposal. Still further changes were made on July 11, 1966, in an act to amend the Atlantic Development Board Act.[1] One was to increase the fund to $150 million.

There have been advantages in providing the Board with a fund of this nature, but there have also been certain disadvantages. The Board has shown a disposition to focus its attention on various projects and to concentrate less on the more fundamental task of deciding the lines along which basic changes in the economy might best be effected.[2] It seems to be a global characteristic to associate development with heavy expenditures on infra-structure. It is difficult to be sure, however, that the Board would have served its purpose better had it been just an advisory body. Such bodies also have their weaknesses: lacking operational powers, they run the risk of becoming ineffectual.

As stated in section 9 of the legislation, the objectives of the Board are to inquire into measures and projects for fostering the

[1] Original legislation 11 Elizabeth II, c. 10, Dec. 20, 1962. Amended legislation 12 Elizabeth II, c. 5, July 31, 1963. Amended legislation 14-15 Elizabeth II, c. 31, July 11, 1966.

[2] See, for example, the views of F. T. Walton, "Atlantic Development – An Appraisal", *The Business Quarterly* (London: University of Western Ontario, School of Business Administration, Summer 1968. Vol. 33, No. 2, pp. 61–71).

economic growth and development of the Atlantic region and report on them to the Minister, whether or not such measures require the use of the fund. In contrast to ADA and ARDA, the Board is solely concerned with the Atlantic provinces. In furthering its objectives, the Board may prepare on a systematic and comprehensive basis an assessment of factors relevant to economic growth in the Atlantic region, keep under constant review appropriate methods of encouraging sound economic development, introduce new programs and projects, and remove or mitigate factors that appear to inhibit such development. It may also prepare, in consultation with the Economic Council of Canada, an over-all co-ordinated plan for the promotion of the economic growth of the region. Subject to approval by the Governor-in-Council, the Board is empowered to enter into agreements with provinces in the Atlantic region or with persons for undertaking projects or programs which in the opinion of the Board will contribute to the growth and development of the economy of the region and for which satisfactory financing arrangements are not otherwise available. The last qualification draws attention to the fact that the role of the Board is in some respects a "gap-filling" one. In the fulfilment of its objectives the Board is required to consult and co-operate with the Economic Council and with those departments and agencies of the federal government having duties and objectives related to those of the Board. The main agencies and departments concerned would be ARDA, ADA, and the departments of Fisheries, Manpower, Energy, Mines and Resources, and Public Works. The provincial governments are consulted before action is taken on specific projects, whether or not they contribute to the cost, and Treasury Board or Cabinet approval is required for all expenditures.[1]

[1] The relationship between the Board and the Minister of Transport, to whom the Chairman reports, doubtless varies with the individuals involved, but there is a feeling among some in the Atlantic provinces that the Board is an arm of the federal government rather than of the Atlantic provinces. Disliking this, certain people would like to see the Board established in the Atlantic region rather than in Ottawa. Such an arrangement, however, would make the Board's task of co-ordinating the actions of various federal departments extremely difficult.

Contrary to what is commonly believed, the legislation made no specific mention of narrowing the income gap between the Atlantic provinces and the rest of the country or of reducing the comparatively high levels of unemployment in the region. The focus is on growth and development, not on the reduction of disparities. The reduction of such disparities, however, appears to have been implicit in the fact that such legislation has been enacted. As observed in Chapter 1, the difference between incomes in the Atlantic region and the rest of Canada has remained fairly constant over several decades, and were its perpetuation acceptable it is difficult to see the grounds for establishing the Board at all. Certainly many in the Atlantic provinces believe a policy objective should be a contraction of the income gap, though there are no doubt differences of opinion as to the amount of contraction that is desirable and the time period required for its accomplishment. Federal policies to redistribute wealth across the country are a common and accepted practice, but there is considerable uneasiness over policies designed to achieve specific rates of regional growth in either absolute or comparative terms, since the accomplishment of such rates may prove both difficult and costly. It seems highly unlikely, however, that a federal government which expresses satisfaction with the fulfilment of the same percentage rate of growth in the Atlantic provinces as elsewhere will win much support from that region.[1]

## *The Operation of the* ADB

It was considered important in the early days of the Board that some prompt action should be taken. While it was not denied that further investigation might be needed, it was considered that such investigation should accompany and not be a substitute for action in those directions where the case for it had already been established or at least been made reasonably clear. A long period of

---

[1] See, for example, the comments of the President of APEC, Gilbert Finn, at the Atlantic Conference held in Halifax in October 1967 and reported in the *APEC Newsletter*, II, no. 7 (December 1967), 1–2.

gestation while the Board made up its mind on the sort of role it might best perform and the steps it might take would have invited strong criticism. Accordingly, in its initial operations the Board relied heavily on a number of studies that had already been completed on certain basic needs of the Atlantic provinces.

As a preliminary step, it was decided to classify those sectors of the economy which were important for development under the following headings: power; transportation; primary industries, including processing; secondary manufacturing industries; and miscellaneous, including research and tourism. This classification made it easier to scan the subject matter and consider priorities. In the light of a recently completed study in the Atlantic provinces, which projected energy requirements up to the year 1980 on the assumption of certain growth rates in the economy,[1] the Board decided to give high priority to a considerable expansion in the power supply, having in mind especially the development requirements of the mineral and forest resources of the region.

But some sort of over-all view was essential to provide a framework for the operations of the Board, and a heading on economic planning was added. The Department of Finance was not happy with an arrangement whereby large sums would be spent without a clear sense of direction and recognition of the way in which the various projects would be interrelated. This apart, the opinion of officials on the Board has been that the development of the Atlantic region calls for quite basic changes in the economy, not merely for minor adjustments, and without some plan of over-all development, it is difficult to make informed decisions regarding priorities or to ensure a desired integration of different projects. With the passage of time, therefore, increasing emphasis has been placed on this aspect of the Board's work.

In point of fact, the plan is still in the course of preparation and project expenditures of one sort and another proceed without it, though discussions do take place between the operational and

[1] D. M. Nowlan, *The Demand for Energy in the Atlantic Provinces 1950–1980* (Ottawa: Queen's Printer, 1962).

planning staffs. In the course of evaluating particular projects, the Board may form impressions of their likely impact on the economy of the region, but especially in the early years of its operations discussions on planning and discussions on specific projects tended to go their separate ways. As in all planning that involves more than listing of desirable projects and steps, some quite basic questions have to be asked regarding the specific lines along which development should be encouraged and the interrelationship of various projects. The input-output table prepared for the region will help to throw light on the latter, but it has not yet been made public.

Over the past couple of decades considerable experience has been accumulated in various countries on the requirements of good planning and the pitfalls to be avoided. Since opposition to the view that the government should try to influence the direction of the economy has now diminished, the ADB plan could make a valuable contribution to resolving the difficulties of the Atlantic provinces. As stated in the Board's 1965-6 annual report, the work of the Board represents the federal government's first major commitment to broad and systematic regional planning.

In its early years the Board strongly emphasized the provision and improvement of infra-structure, perhaps excessively so, given the limitations of the ADA program and the choice of designated areas under it. As noted in Chapter 4, in the discussion of the determinants of regional growth, the provision of infra-structure may be a pre-condition of growth but it is unlikely to be a sufficient condition. Here again, however, it is a question of deciding which body shall be responsible for doing what. There is no reason why the Board should not contribute to the costs of certain types of infra-structure and concentrate on this, so long as other agencies and departments are performing other essential functions. The Board itself made it clear in its annual report for 1963-4 that the provision of basic service facilities such as power and transportation might not suffice to encourage the location of secondary manufacturing industries in the Atlantic region, and pointed to the need for additional incentives to achieve this end.[1] Cause for concern arises when gaps occur, functions overlap, or various bodies are at cross-purposes.

In the earlier years especially the Board was under pressure to approve various projects having a strong political appeal but of less obvious economic merit, and these pressures were not easy to resist. Since the four Atlantic provinces have varying needs it is considered essential to tailor aid according to individual circumstances but at the same time the Board has had to avoid appearing to favour one province more than another and a rule-of-thumb formula has been adopted for the allocation of aid between the individual provinces.

Although the Board does not depend upon formal provincial co-operation in the way that the ARDA program does, little headway would be made were co-operation lacking. In practice it is not always easy to attain. For one thing inter-provincial rivalries are seldom far below the surface. A decision to aid a province in one way is apt to lead to demands for comparable aid by another but to meet such demands could result in a needless duplication of facilities. To mention an obvious illustration, the provision of a deep-water harbour in one province should not be made the justification for building a second or third one in the other provinces.

What the Board has attempted to do is ensure that the merits and demerits of particular projects are given due weight from an economic point of view, and the appraising of various proposals is one of its most important tasks.

According to its annual report for 1964–5, "The Board incorporates three essential principles in regional economic development: joint and closely co-ordinated development of programs with the governments of the Atlantic provinces; a concern with the over-all basic structure of the regional economy and with the

---

[1] The functions and operations of the Board are described in its annual reports and in testimony before a standing committee of the Senate. See The Senate of Canada, *Proceedings of the Standing Committee on Finance*, No. 10 (Ottawa: Queen's Printer, June 16, 1966).

causes of the current problems rather than their symptoms; and federal financial assistance for essential development projects for which satisfactory financial arrangements are not otherwise available."[1]

Among its activities, the Board stated in this report, special emphasis was being given to the establishment of the organization necessary to carry out the economic planning function, and approval had been sought for the establishment of a planning division within the staff of the Board. As for specific projects, it was the Board's view that priority should be given to those intended to achieve long-term improvement in the basic facilities or infra-structure of the region, the adequacy of which differed greatly among the four provinces. Improvements in the power supply were given a high priority, but attention was also being directed to improving the water supply, investigating the development of certain resources, and assisting the creation of industrial parks. As far as research and planning were concerned, particularly notable was the ADB's support of the major input-output study of the region initiated by the Atlantic Provinces Research Board.[2] Some assistance was also being given to the creation of capital facilities for applied research, details of which are given below in the statistical survey of the Board's activities.

In providing assistance for particular projects, the Board usually shares costs with the provinces. Agreement between the Board and the province concerned on the nature and details of the project as well as on the manner in which the costs are to be shared is thus necessary. The formula for cost-sharing is not completely inflexible, and it is possible to modify the amount of aid according to the needs of the recipient. Only grants are made, not loans, and the Board generally finances some particular aspect of the work.

Projects for development originate in various ways – in some cases with the Board itself, but more often with the individual

[1] Atlantic Development Board, *Annual Report: 1964–65* (Ottawa: Queen's Printer, 1965), p. 11.
[2] A body established by the four provincial premiers and answerable to them.

provinces or with private businesses. Unlike the provisions governing ADA, assistance is not made available automatically to any projects falling within a certain classification. The Board has a degree of discretion, which makes its task more demanding but also potentially much more fruitful. It can recommend whether or not to go ahead with a particular project, but it does not have the final decision. Generally its recommendations are made through the President of the Treasury Board, which takes the final decision, but on occasion proposals are submitted directly to the Cabinet, though there is invariably prior consultation with other government departments where their interests are involved.

The underlying problem remains, however, of trying to determine the merits of individual projects without knowing enough about over-all intentions regarding growth paths and the relationship which one project will bear to another. To a degree it is possible to tie in certain social capital expenditures with the needs of specific industries, as in the case of water supply and the needs of fish-processing plants, but when sectors such as transportation are involved, it is essential to have some idea of projected population distribution and industrial location. There is no point, for example, in improving roads to communities which seem destined to disappear or in assisting industries which have become obsolete – an improvement in communications is not an end in itself. The currently scattered population in the Atlantic provinces is frequently cited as a major obstacle to development, costs being high and services poor, and its consolidation is considered to be highly desirable. A transport policy cannot be fashioned without regard for industrial and population distribution.[1] Recognition of this may explain why the Board's transportation improvement program has consisted mainly of small contributions towards the cost of bringing provincial trunk highways up to all-season, all-freight standards rather than of measures designed to modify the routes themselves.

The 1965–6 annual report reflected a broadening of the Board's

---

[1] A further major transportation study has recently been authorized by the Minister of Transport under whose over-all direction the Board operates.

concern. The developmental strategy in which all agencies, public and private, might be expected to participate was summarized as follows:

> (i) major investment in infrastructure – water, power and transportation;
> (ii) assisting present industry to achieve higher productivity;
> (iii) intensifying the investigation and utilization of resources;
> (iv) up-grading of labour force skill;
> (v) encouraging, by a variety of incentives, the growth of secondary industry.[1]

Prior to this the Board had concentrated on infra-structure; henceforth it hoped to achieve a greater degree of comprehensiveness and provide a framework within which decisions by various agencies might be made mutually consistent. It was suggested not that the Board itself should undertake all these functions but that it should serve as a co-ordinating agency.

The 1966–7 annual report covered many of the same themes, and affirmed once again that the preparation of an over-all co-ordinated plan for the promotion of the economic growth of the Atlantic region was one of the Board's major objectives. It was hoped that by the end of 1967 the first draft of a development plan would be completed – a hope which will not now be fulfilled until the end of 1968. Meanwhile, given the breadth of the Board's interests, it is expected that the task of co-ordinating various departmental programs will be an important and continuing aspect of the Board's functions.

Though the Board cannot be expected to foresee many of the changes which will take place in the future, the recognition of certain trends might serve as a guide to policy. Among these are urbanization, the increasing demand for skills in the labour force, the continued decline of some industries and the probable expansion of others. The studies undertaken by the planning section of the Atlantic Development Board will presumably throw some light on which avenues of development suggest promise and

[1] Atlantic Development Board, *Annual Report: 1965–66* (Ottawa: Queen's Printer, 1966), p. 11.

which do not.

It is hoped that the Board will follow the practice of the Economic Council and encourage the publication of significant studies relating to the region so that other interested bodies can be kept informed of the issues which bear on policy. Open discussion of many of the problems, uncertainties, and recommendations contained in such studies could do much to dispel illusions and create a climate in which sensible political decisions can be made.[1]

## *Expenditures by the* ADB

The following table shows the expenditures of the Board in the individual provinces. Approved expenditures totalled $188 million up to May 29, 1968, of which little more than half had actually been spent. It will be noted that power supply accounted for almost a third of the total expenditure. As mentioned in the preceding section, a number of studies had indicated the need for substantial increases in the power supply. It was the view of the Board that assistance should be given in this direction not by paying the full cost of any large power project but by increasing the scale of production, thereby making technical economies possible which would be reflected in lower costs of supply. The sharing of the capital costs would also reduce financing costs.[2]

The contribution towards highway development was seen as a start towards the achievement of all-weather standards on certain trunk highways in areas not covered by the trans-Canada high-

[1] On the above subject, particular mention might be made once again of the staff study prepared for the Economic Council by Frank T. Denton (*op. cit.*). It appeared to him that one could not go far in accounting for differences in levels of earnings between different regions in terms of mere statistical differences in industrial and occupational distributions, age composition, hours and weeks of work, average levels of education, and rural-urban distributions, and he stressed in this regard that the contributions of the various factors taken one at a time cannot be added together without considerable double-counting because of their interdependence. The conclusion he reached was a negative one: "even at the level of mere statistical distributions, the factors examined do not account for much of the observable variation in earnings; something more basic must be sought" (p. 13).

[2] See The Senate of Canada, *Proceedings of the Standing Committee on Finance*, No. 10.

**Table 8:3**
**Expenditures Approved and Funds Disbursed by the ADB**
**to May 29, 1968**

($000,000)

| | Power | | Highway development | | Water supply and sewage systems | |
|---|---|---|---|---|---|---|
| | Approved | Spent | Approved | Spent | Approved | Spent |
| Newfoundland | 24.0 | 23.8 | 4.0 | 3.3 | 9.6 | 3.6 |
| Prince Edward Island | 4.3 | 0.1 | 1.7 | 1.6 | 0.3 | — |
| Nova Scotia | 12.1 | 2.6 | 3.0 | 2.6 | 4.8 | 1.2 |
| New Brunswick | 20.0 | 20.0 | 3.0 | 3.0 | 5.2 | 0.5 |
| Atlantic provinces | 60.4 | 46.5 | 11.7 | 10.5 | 19.9 | 5.3 |

| | Industrial parks* | | Other basic services† | | Research and research facilities‡ | |
|---|---|---|---|---|---|---|
| | Approved | Spent | Approved | Spent | Approved | Spent |
| Newfoundland | — | — | 0.2 | 0.1 | 3.6 | — |
| Prince Edward Island | 0.1 | 0.1 | 1.0 | 1.0 | 1.0 | — |
| Nova Scotia | 5.8 | 2.3 | 8.8 | 3.6 | 5.5 | 0.9 |
| New Brunswick | 3.1 | 1.9 | 0.5 | 0.1 | 4.9 | 1.5 |
| Atlantic provinces | 9.0 | 4.3 | 10.5 | 4.8 | 17.0** | 2.4 |

| | Total by province | | Trunk highway program | | Over-all total | |
|---|---|---|---|---|---|---|
| | Approved | Spent | Approved | Spent | Approved | Spent |
| Newfoundland | 41.4 | 30.8 | 16.5 | 8.4 | 57.9 | 39.2 |
| Prince Edward Island | 9.1§ | 3.0§ | 5.5 | 2.8 | 14.6 | 5.8 |
| Nova Scotia | 40.1 | 13.1 | 16.5 | 6.6 | 56.6 | 19.7 |
| New Brunswick | 36.7 | 27.0 | 16.5 | 12.1 | 53.2 | 39.1 |
| Atlantic provinces | 129.2 | 73.9 | 55.0 | 29.9 | 187.9†† | 106.1†† |

Note: Figures do not add to totals in all cases because of rounding and inclusion of other figures not allocable by province or category in them.
*Includes all basic services (water, etc.) for industrial parks.
†Includes some highway development and water supply where these figures are not separated.
‡Includes mapping and land registration.
§Includes $0.6 million approved and $0.3 million spent for the Fathers of Confederation Citizens Memorial Foundation.
**Includes items not allocable by province.
††Includes $2.0 million approved and spent, Dosco operating expenses, and $1.8 million approved and $0.3 million spent, special assistance to Bell Island.
Source: Atlantic Development Board (unpublished data).

way program. The provincial governments also contributed to the costs of the work involved.[1]

Expenditures on water supply were related in large measure to the requirements of fish and vegetable processing plants, especially those in Newfoundland which lacked adequate supplies of pure fresh water. Concern with pollution problems, among them those of the St. John River and Mactaquac Dam, will entail further expenditures, as will programs of recreational development, which will be imperilled if anti-pollution measures are not taken. It should be noted in the matter of water supply and pollution that the Board is concerned with the requirements of industry and not with the provision of municipal water and sewerage works as such. But since it would make no sense to cater solely to the needs of industry without regard for other municipal requirements, the two aspects are dealt with jointly in the arrangements that are made in the smaller communities.

The assistance given to industrial parks reflects the view that to promote industry in the Atlantic region it is desirable that certain centres be in a position to offer serviced land at reasonable prices. One difficulty is deciding where they should be sited; differences of opinion on this are inevitable, but agreement has been reached with the provincial governments. Contributions by the Board vary according to assessment of the need for aid, though the full cost is never paid.

In the matter of research, the final heading mentioned in the table, efforts have been made by the Board to improve the facilities for applied research, making them available to smaller industries in particular. As an aspect of this program various laboratories have been created and expanded.

## *The* ADB: *An Appraisal*

Attempts to evaluate the operations of the Board (with the exception of planning, which is the subject of Chapter 10) present numerous difficulties. Many of the expenditures are likely to be

[1] A supplementary sum of $30 million was also voted by the federal government, but this did not fall within the administration of the ADB.

productive only over a period of several decades. Admittedly, it is possible to look at individual expenditures and form some qualitative impressions, and this is in fact what the Executive Director of the Board did in his evidence to the Senate Standing Committee on Finance.[1] But the weakness in this procedure is that individual projects cannot adequately be assessed in isolation. An impression has to be formed of the general lines along which growth is to progress and the intersectoral relationships before the efficacy of individual projects can be appraised. It is necessary to know how the various types of investment are interrelated with each other in the light of specific objectives. In the absence of such a framework it is impossible to say whether very heavy emphasis on particular projects, such as the production of power, can be justified. The trouble with the project by project type of approach to development is that funds tend to be dissipated either in too many unrelated projects of minor importance, or, as may be the case with the ADB, in a few unduly large ones.[2]

More generally, an impression of the joint impact of ARDA, the ADA, and the ADB in the Atlantic provinces over the past four or five years might be formed by looking at income, investment, and employment figures for the period, and noting any change in trends. The period is too short to permit conclusions to be drawn, but the figures might at least serve to dispel a few misconceptions. Some of the basic data were presented in Chapters 1 and 4 which reviewed certain salient features of the economy and the determinants of growth.

So far as personal income is concerned, there is evidence that since 1950 there has been some improvement in Newfoundland and Prince Edward Island relative to the rest of the country, but

[1] He pointed out, for example, that a number of paper companies had expanded their operations in Newfoundland, influenced by the promise of increased and cheaper power, and that several new industries had indicated their intention of establishing in Newfoundland, with power being a fundamental factor in their decision. The smelter and lead–zinc complex in northern New Brunswick was influenced in its timing by the Mactaquac operation, and industrial parks elsewhere have attracted a number of firms.

[2] Cost benefit studies are made of particular projects for the use of the Treasury Board, but these are not made public.

### Table 8:4
### Unemployment in the Atlantic Provinces*
### 1960 to 1966

| | *1960* | *1961* | *1962* | *1963* | *1964* | *1965* | *1966* |
|---|---|---|---|---|---|---|---|
| *(%)* | | | | | | | |
| Newfoundland | 17.1 | 16.7 | 16.4 | 16.0 | 15.7 | 13.3 | 11.8 |
| Prince Edward Island | 14.9 | 13.7 | 13.5 | 13.2 | 12.2 | 11.2 | 10.5 |
| Nova Scotia | 12.2 | 12.6 | 11.2 | 10.8 | 10.1 | 8.7 | 8.3 |
| New Brunswick | 15.1 | 14.7 | 13.5 | 13.4 | 12.1 | 10.8 | 10.2 |
| Rest of Canada | 10.7 | 10.0 | 8.7 | 8.6 | 7.6 | 6.6 | 6.1 |
| *(as % of rest of Canada)* | | | | | | | |
| Newfoundland | 160 | 167 | 189 | 186 | 207 | 202 | 193 |
| Prince Edward Island | 139 | 137 | 155 | 153 | 161 | 170 | 172 |
| Nova Scotia | 114 | 126 | 129 | 126 | 133 | 132 | 136 |
| New Brunswick | 141 | 147 | 155 | 156 | 159 | 164 | 167 |

*Based on average registrations of Canada Manpower Service offices and estimates of paid workers. These figures are not comparable with the unemployment figures shown in Chapter 2.

Source: Department of Manpower and Immigration (unpublished data).

Nova Scotia and New Brunswick have shown no relative gains. Unemployment rates, as seen in Table 8:4, appear to have displayed no secular fall in comparison with national ones.

In regard to capital and repair expenditures, however, these have shown a marked upward trend in the Atlantic provinces since the mid 1950s (see Table 8:5). Individually as well as collectively these provinces have more than held their own. Between 1964 and 1966, capital and repair expenditures for the region as a whole amounted to $640 per capita, compared with $363 between 1955 and 1957. The corresponding figures for the rest of Canada were $882 and $657. As a result, expenditures in the Atlantic provinces rose from 55 per cent of the rest of Canada to 73 per cent. In dollar terms, the per capita expenditure in the Atlantic region increased by $277, compared with a $225 increase for the remainder of the country, with Newfoundland and Prince

## Table 8:5
### Capital and Repair Expenditures in the Atlantic Provinces
### 1955-1957 and 1964-1966

|  | Average 1955-7 | Average 1964-6 | Increase | |
|---|---|---|---|---|
|  | ($ per capita) | ($ per capita) | ($ per capita) | (% change) |
| Newfoundland | 301 | 696 | +395 | +131 |
| Prince Edward Island | 315 | 632 | +317 | +101 |
| Nova Scotia | 359 | 584 | +225 | + 63 |
| New Brunswick | 423 | 664 | +241 | + 57 |
| Atlantic provinces | 363 | 640 | +277 | + 76 |
| Rest of Canada | 657 | 882 | +225 | + 34 |
| Atlantic provinces as % of rest of Canada | 55 | 73 | | |

Source: Based on Table 4:1.

Edward Island showing exceptionally large increases. This gives residents in the Atlantic provinces some ground for hoping that their income disparities may tend to diminish.

Education is a field in which the ADB has not participated. This aspect of activity has been left to ARDA and to the Department of Manpower as part of the latter's training program. ARDA, however, is only concerned with education in rural areas and then only in specific cases.

Table 8:6, which follows, shows that between 1951 and 1961 educational levels in Newfoundland, as reflected in years of schooling, have been increasing more rapidly than in the country as a whole, but educational levels in New Brunswick and Prince Edward Island have shown no net gain, and unlike those in Nova Scotia remain far below those of the rest of the country.

If basic education is as important in the stimulation of economic growth as is generally believed, the efforts to improve the school system currently being made by the New Brunswick government

## Table 8:6
## Population in the Atlantic Provinces Ten Years of Age and Over, not Attending School, with no Secondary Education*
## 1951 and 1961

|  | (%) Age Groups | | | | | | |
| --- | --- | --- | --- | --- | --- | --- | --- |
|  | 15-19 | 20-24 | 25-34 | 35-44 | 45-64 | 65+ | Total |
| **Newfoundland** |  |  |  |  |  |  |  |
| 1951 | 66.3 | 61.7 | 66.4 | 68.7 | 76.1 | 85.6 | 71.0 |
| 1961 | 44.3 | 35.1 | 48.3 | 61.7 | 68.0 | 83.7 | 58.5 |
| Change | 22.0 | 26.6 | 18.1 | 7.0 | 8.1 | 1.9 | 12.5 |
| **Prince Edward Island** |  |  |  |  |  |  |  |
| 1951 | 55.3 | 46.5 | 46.7 | 52.6 | 58.5 | 68.1 | 55.2 |
| 1961 | 45.9 | 31.9 | 40.3 | 43.6 | 52.9 | 61.4 | 48.7 |
| Change | 9.4 | 14.6 | 6.4 | 9.0 | 5.6 | 6.7 | 6.5 |
| **Nova Scotia** |  |  |  |  |  |  |  |
| 1951 | 52.3 | 41.5 | 40.6 | 47.7 | 55.5 | 65.5 | 50.4 |
| 1961 | 42.6 | 28.4 | 33.7 | 37.0 | 47.4 | 60.5 | 42.5 |
| Change | 9.7 | 13.1 | 6.9 | 10.7 | 8.1 | 5.0 | 7.9 |
| **New Brunswick** |  |  |  |  |  |  |  |
| 1951 | 62.1 | 55.4 | 57.4 | 61.4 | 65.8 | 73.2 | 62.8 |
| 1961 | 54.9 | 38.1 | 47.3 | 54.9 | 63.1 | 73.8 | 56.8 |
| Change | 7.2 | 17.3 | 10.1 | 6.5 | 2.7 | +0.6 | 6.0 |
| **Canada** |  |  |  |  |  |  |  |
| 1951 | 54.7 | 44.1 | 44.4 | 52.6 | 61.1 | 69.4 | 54.1 |
| 1961 | 41.4 | 31.0 | 37.0 | 42.2 | 54.7 | 68.5 | 47.0 |
| Change | 13.3 | 13.1 | 7.4 | 10.4 | 6.4 | 0.9 | 7.1 |

*1951 – % with 8 or fewer years of education.

Source: D.B.S., *1951 Census of Canada*, Vol. II, Tables 27, 28, and *1961 Census of Canada*, Vol. I (92-557).

merit strong support. Unlike the situation in Quebec where federal aid to education is a very sensitive political issue, the government of New Brunswick appears to welcome such assistance. In some areas of that province, as in eastern Quebec, educational standards have been abysmally low, however, and it may well take a couple of decades before such areas draw close to the national average. As a result, much educational expenditure has to be seen as a very long term investment.

While not decrying the value of many of the individual projects which the ADB has assisted, it is difficult to avoid the conclusion that the Board has had to rely thus far on an interim strategy of development.[1] The fostering of economic growth and the development of the Atlantic region calls for clearly articulated lines of action over a broad front and agreement with the provinces on both ends and means. Such lines of action have yet to be determined. Not only is there a tendency for several different bodies to pursue isolated objectives, in some cases at variance with each other, but during its first five years of operation the Board has done little but focus on an expansion of infra-structure. In the opinion of some the basic weakness lies in the lack of a long-term comprehensive development plan for the whole region, a plan jointly approved by the provinces and the federal government and in which the efforts of numerous government departments would be integrated.

[1] The extreme difficulty in recruiting an adequate planning staff has been a major handicap in this regard.

*9. Planning for Development*

### The Concept and Growth of Planning

ONE OF THE notable features of the post-war economic scene has been the widespread adoption of economic plans. Before the Second World War the Soviet Union was almost alone in the world in the planning of its economy, but the scene has now changed to such an extent that countries which do not have some kind of a program as a framework for development may well be in the minority. Admittedly, the nature and extent of planning differ widely from one country to another. The Soviet methods of planning have little in common with those of, say, France. None the less, the disposition of countries to prepare economic plans of one form or another is not only widespread but seemingly increasing.

At an early stage in the operation of the World Bank, it became apparent that if aid to the less developed countries was to be effective, it would need to be integrated with various government policies to form a coherent framework; since then, the Bank has assisted a great many countries to prepare comprehensive development programs. The experience gained by the Bank in working with underdeveloped countries is not without relevance to a discussion of the development of depressed areas in the wealthier countries. In both the less and the more developed countries the

193

provision of individual assistance on a project by project basis is open to criticism. To achieve maximum results, projects have to be related to each other and formulated in the context of other institutional developments.

In preparing a plan, the desirable lines of development are clarified, and the very act of preparing one is a useful exercise in itself, for it focuses attention on the objectives and problems to be overcome, the information required, and the prerequisites for fulfilment. It is the purpose of planning to ensure coherence and co-ordination. Failing these, waste and dislocation are likely to result. Though development planning is primarily concerned with the economic sphere, it is likely to affect political, social, and administrative spheres as well, for these are all interrelated. In some cases social attitudes may be one of the greatest impediments to economic change.

In Canada the subject of planning has been brought to the fore not only as a result of rural development under the FRED legislation and through the functions of the Atlantic Development Board but also, as noted in the following chapter, through the planning operations of certain provincial governments. However, it was not until the 1960s that regional planning evoked any significant interest in Canada, and considerable doubt remains in many quarters as to its nature, purpose, and wisdom.

It is the intention of this chapter to touch very briefly on the planning process which is of increasing concern to some of the provinces. The term "planning" conveys different things to different people. In common usage it covers a wide spectrum from the detailed and comprehensive direction of an entire economy by a government to the lesser efforts of public or private agencies to co-ordinate various aspects of economic policy. In the view of one writer on the subject, economic planning is a "comprehensive and co-ordinated social action to guide the future course of the economy".[1] The Atlantic Development Board for its part regards

---

[1] H. E. English, "The Nature of Democratic Economic Planning", *Canadian Public Administration*, VIII, no. 2 (June 1965), 125. This volume of the journal and Vol. IX, no. 2 (June 1966) contain a number of contributions on the subject of planning, including regional planning. See also T. N.

planning as the formulation of a comprehensive set of mutually consistent policy proposals, arranged in order of priority, scheduled over a period of time, and directed toward the attainment of given objectives. In the present context, regional economic planning is understood to mean the establishment of specific regional economic objectives couched in operational terms and the selection and implementation of measures to achieve them.

Planning for regional development has much in common with planning for development at the national level, but there are various issues which, at least in Canada, can largely be disregarded in planning at the regional level. Among these are the international balance of payments and its impact on national price levels and credit conditions. On the other hand, interregional flows of labour, goods, and capital are of particular importance in regional planning. A reduction in unemployment in the Atlantic provinces may influence levels of migration materially, and the increased incomes that result may lead to a rise in "imports" from other parts of the country, with repercussions on the interregional flow of funds. At the moment very little is known about these interregional relationships in Canada, but discussion and experience in other countries leaves little doubt of their importance. We know, for instance, that the movement of workers to and from Northern Ireland is greatly influenced by the relative availability of jobs in England. Improved conditions in Northern Ireland lead to a reduction in the exodus of workers and to some extent there is a reverse flow, so that unemployment diminishes less than would otherwise be the case. Similarly, when the labour market is very tight in England, English firms tend to expand their operations in Northern Ireland; then when the pressures slacken they tend to

Brewis and Gilles Paquet, "Regional Development and Planning in Canada: an Exploratory Essay", a paper presented to the annual meeting of the Canadian Political Science Association in Ottawa, June 1967 (*Canadian Public Administration*, Summer 1968, XI, no. 2, pp. 123–62). Several enlightening papers on the subject of planning in Canada have been prepared by the Policy and Planning Directorate of ARDA, containing observations arising out of experience. See for example, ARDA *and Poverty: Lessons in Developmental Planning* by Leonard E. Poetschke, a mimeographed paper prepared for presentation at the Canadian Agricultural Economic Society Annual Meeting in Hamilton, Ontario, June 25, 1968.

reduce them. The same kind of pattern may well operate in the Atlantic provinces.

The size of the region selected for planning is itself a matter of crucial importance – the smaller the area selected, the more important the flows into and out of the area are likely to be. Thus a major investment in a small area may lead to a heavy influx of workers from outside so that there is virtually no change in the employment situation of workers who are long-time residents of the area.

A distinction needs to be drawn between the plan itself and the process involved in its preparation. The plan is the end product. Unless the information on which it is based has been adequately prepared, it is unlikely to be of much use and may indeed prove detrimental to development. Since the information that ideally one might wish to have is never likely to be complete, at some stage enquiry has to give way to decisions. The enquiry stage can be so prolonged that the plan itself is unduly delayed. This appears to have been the case with the Atlantic Development Board. Detailed studies extending over several years have still to find their expression in a plan for the Atlantic region. Several factors have accounted for the delay, among them an earlier lack of interest at the political level.

Before continuing with a discussion of the actual process of planning, it may be helpful to note the meaning of certain expressions commonly used in planning terminology. A "comprehensive rural development" is, to quote from the FRED legislation, "a program, consisting of several development projects, that is designed to promote the social and economic development of a special rural development area and to increase income and employment opportunities and raise living standards in the area, and that makes provision for participation by residents of the area in the carrying out of the program".[1] The Agreement Covering a Comprehensive Rural Development Plan for the Interlake Area of Manitoba[2] defines "development strategy" as the means by which the objectives of the Agreement will be promoted in the Special Rural Develop-

---

[1] Bill c. 151, p. 2, para. 5(a).
[2] Department of Forestry and Rural Development, *op. cit.*, p. 8.

ment Area; "plan" as the over-all design for implementing the rural development strategy; "program" as a definite course of intended proceedings for a major operation within the plan; and "project" as an undertaking with specific objectives that forms a self-contained unit within a program.

## The Process of Planning

Action has to be taken on several fronts in the preparation of a plan. One of these is the collection of information which will serve as the basis for establishing clearly defined objectives. Such information will include data on resources; on the labour force, its size, composition, rate of growth, and skills; on the economic structure of the region; on the various types of economic activity, primary, secondary, and tertiary, and the changes that are occurring therein; and especially on potentialities for growth. Much of this information is unlikely to be available and will have to be collected.[1]

Typically, the planning process begins with the furnishing of certain estimates at the macro level, and this is accompanied by more detailed projections for individual industries and sectors. Thus, assuming the objective is to provide employment for the expected growth in the labour force of the region over a specified period of time, required output can be calculated in aggregative terms, using a national accounts type of framework. The probable deficiency in output needed to achieve the requisite level of employment can then be ascertained on the basis of past and current growth trends and productivity. The magnitude of the gap will suggest an objective in aggregative terms and alternative ways of closing it can be examined. Along with this, the potentiality of specific industries can be explored in detail, and in the light of

[1] There have been many works in recent years on the subject of planning, a number of which are listed in the bibliography at the end of this volume. A good brief introduction to the subject is Jan Tinbergen's *The Design of Development* (a publication of the Economic Development Institute, International Bank for Reconstruction and Development [Baltimore, Md.: Johns Hopkins Press, 1958]). A more technical study is J. R. Boudeville's *Problems of Regional Economic Planning* (Edinburgh University Press, 1966). See also W. Arthur Lewis, *Development Planning: The Essentials of Economic Policy* (London: Allen & Unwin, 1966).

the projections estimates can be made of future total output and employment. Here there is often a temptation to review the potential largely from the standpoint of supply and to give insufficient thought to possible changes in demand which are equally deserving of attention. But even granting this qualification, the summing of the sectoral data will still not be an adequate exercise in itself, for the sectors are interrelated, and the assumptions regarding potential output in one will have implications for others. Adjustments must be made on this account, and upon their completion the detailed industry estimates will permit a refining of the estimates made at the macro level.

The determination of general goals, such as the reduction of income disparities and unemployment, may be taken at an early stage; but without a clear awareness of the potentialities of the region it is unwise to be too specific, for the costs of attaining such goals may prove to be excessive. There is no point in establishing targets without regard for the costs of their attainment. For example, it may appear possible to raise per capita incomes in the employed labour force by increased investment, but increases in labour productivity and wages associated with larger capital inputs may lead to a reduction in the number of workers required. To increase local employment substantially at the same time as incomes are raised nearer national levels might thus involve extensive intervention on the part of the federal government, more perhaps than is considered justifiable or politically feasible. Objectives, in short, should not be spelled out in detail until their implications are clear; but until they are spelled out they cannot form an adequate basis for a plan. As an illustration, a general goal to reduce income disparities between the Atlantic region and the rest of the country, without stating the amount by which they are to be reduced or the time period involved is not sufficient, though it can serve as a starting point.

The time period over which the plan is to be fulfilled must also be decided. There is something to be said for setting up both a long-run plan, which will make it easier to maintain a sense of direction, and a short-run plan, which will indicate the immediate steps to be undertaken. Ideally, the short-run plan should be tied in with the preparation of the annual budgets at the provincial level to ensure effective implementation and avoid conflict.

Inevitably there will be developments that were not foreseen or correctly appraised at the outset, and for this reason some flexibility has to be maintained. To allow for these, the plan should be kept under constant review and modified in accordance with the need for change. A static plan will quickly become obsolete. A compromise must be struck, however, between excessive change on the one hand and undue inflexibility on the other.

Target rates for the growth of the more important sectors of the economy, based on past trends and an evaluation of future possibilities should be established. There will undoubtedly be differences of opinion as to what constitutes a feasible rate of growth for various sectors of the economy, and an indication of the range of opinion is desirable. The estimates can then be reviewed at the over-all planning stage, and the interrelationship of the various sectors can be examined with a view to avoiding inconsistencies between them. For example, if a recommended rate of development of a particular industry calls for a certain input of skilled labour, the supply must be adequate. This may in turn have implications for the construction of technical schools and the training of instructors.

For certain purposes and for larger regions, it would be helpful to have an input-output table prepared, so that the implications of expansion in one industry can be traced through to every other, but the construction of such tables is a demanding undertaking and the manpower available for such a task is in very limited supply.[1] Such tables, moreover, need to be kept up to date. This

[1] Input-output analysis is a powerful analytical tool in the study of economic development, showing in detail how changes in one or more sectors of the economy will affect the total economy. For an excellent introduction to the subject see William H. Miernyk, *The Elements of Input-Output Analysis* (New York: Random House, 1965). In Canada quantitive data on the economic relationship between regions in the form of input-output tables have only recently become available. They are the subject of discussion in the Statistical Appendix. The input-output study of the Atlantic provinces, which was completed under the direction of Kari Levitt, extended over several years and was completed only a short time ago. It has yet to be made public.

is of increasing importance when significant changes are contemplated in the structure of a region that will result in new relationships between industries. An industry might continue to draw upon local supplies until it reaches a certain size, then turn to outside suppliers. Alternatively, an industry might attract new sources of local supply as it grows, decreasing its dependence on imports from outside. Once the market reaches a certain size, new plants may be attracted which would formerly have found it unprofitable to operate there. The more rapidly a region grows, the more likely are inter-industry relationships to shift. A mere projection of past relationships may thus prove seriously misleading.

Account should also be taken of changes in consumption patterns, which are to be expected as incomes rise. In some cases these will lead to an expansion in local purchases, in other cases to the opposite, as where consumers turn to larger urban centres which offer a wider range of choice of superior goods. There are, in short, non-linearities in production and consumption.

Having something in common with input-output analysis is industrial-complex analysis. The limitations of input-output studies have encouraged a related but quite distinct approach to the subject of inter-industry relationships, and it has important implications for those engaged in regional planning. As observed in Chapter 4, specific inter-industry connections may be essential to profitable production, and important external economies may emerge as development takes place. Although it has features in common with the input-output matrix, industrial-complex analysis has certain advantages from the standpoint of those engaged in efforts to encourage regional growth. This kind of analysis outlines in more detail than is possible in an input-output table the relationships existing within a relatively narrow range of activities, and it does not have to depend on the historical evidence of past inter-industry coefficients. What it loses in breadth, it gains in depth and flexibility.[1]

[1] An analysis along these lines is currently being undertaken for the government of New Brunswick.

## The Strategy of Development

As mentioned above, one of the major functions of the planning process is to make as clear as possible the relative advantages and disadvantages of alternative courses of action, so that the strategy of development can be decided upon. To achieve economies of scale, it may seem wise to encourage the re-structuring of certain industries and the re-grouping of population in new urban centres. Various ways of accomplishing this are likely to present themselves and a choice between them will need to be made. But it is necessary not only to decide where the main thrusts of policy are to be directed and the form they should take but also to ensure that the machinery for implementation is adequate. This last is of particular importance. The administrative machinery for the fulfilment of development plans is often weak. Development planning is a new art and traditional practices have to be designed and refashioned to accomplish it.

Given the limitations of staff and data as well as the need to obtain public understanding and support, there is likely to be merit in keeping the plan fairly simple, concentrating on those areas where agreement can most easily be reached and where the powers to implement change are likely to be most readily available. This will frequently be in the area of public investment, and a useful first step is often the co-ordination of various public investment expenditures. It is not uncommon to find expenditures are being undertaken by a number of bodies with different objectives. Changes in the private sector are likely to be less amenable to public influence, but much will depend on how closely the government and the private sector have co-operated in arriving at decisions on how to develop a region. There are occasions when sanctions may be necessary, but as a general rule it is preferable to avoid these and create conditions which ensure that the incentives offered by the private sector harmonize with the public interest. In a democratic society public support for the plan is indispensable. Without it the whole process is likely to be in vain.

# 10. The Role of the Provinces in Planning and Development

CHAPTERS 6, 7, AND 8 concentrated on the federal scene. This chapter draws attention to some of the plans and programs that are under the auspices of the provinces. Provincial governments play an important and in some cases a decisive role in the formulation of regional development policies in Canada, but though all provinces want substantial autonomy, the poorer ones see the advantages in a strong central government which has power to transfer resources to them and encourage industrial development within their borders.[1]

The powers and responsibilities of the various levels of government, their interrelationships and associations with other organizations concerned with regional development, present a complex and changing picture. Although description of provincial actions and policies is possible, virtually nothing is known about their net impact. We have no measure of the extent to which the actions of

[1] Quite apart from any deliberate policies that the individual provinces might pursue to influence locational patterns of industry, the very fact that provincial boundaries do exist has some impact on traffic flow, as has been shown in Ontario and Quebec. See Peter Haggett, *op. cit.*, p. 45.

one province cancel out the actions of another or of whether specific policies justify the sums spent on them.[1]

## Provincial Programs

In the past decade an awareness of the need for some kind of regional planning has spread, and a number of groups in various parts of the country have now taken the initial steps in setting up plans for their region. In Nova Scotia the government decided late in 1961 that it would be helpful to draw up a comprehensive plan for economic development in the province, and in 1963 it introduced the Voluntary Planning Act.[2] In Manitoba, also in the early sixties, the government invited a committee of forty-two citizens to look into the growth potential of the province and to recommend programs for creating the jobs that would be required in the future. The committee published its report in 1963.[3] In Quebec a non-profit company, the Eastern Quebec Planning Board (BAEQ),[4] was founded in 1963, and in 1966 it published a ten volume report on its development plan. The document, in the words of its authors, "provides the governing bodies and the people of the pilot region with a development, which in the opinion of the Planning Board, when implemented, should ensure a local standard of living comparable to that in the Province of Quebec without necessitating a massive redistribution of wealth in the form of government transfers". In Prince Edward Island, ARDA, in addition to its planning operations mentioned in Chapter 6, commissioned an extensive study of development planning which was completed in 1967. Neither in Nova Scotia nor in Prince Edward Island have the plans been prepared in conjunction with the Atlantic Development Board, though discussions between ARDA

---

[1] It should be noted, however, that the Canadian Trade Committee has embarked on a major study of some of these issues, which is urgently needed.

[2] A report on progress towards the preparation of the first plan for the economic development of Nova Scotia was made by the Voluntary Planning Board in February 1965.

[3] *Manitoba 1962–1975: Report of the Committee on Manitoba's Economic Future* (Winnipeg: Committee on Manitoba's Economic Future, 1963).

[4] Bureau d'Aménagement de l'Est du Québec.

and the ADB have taken place. The ADB, as noted earlier, is collecting information for a plan of its own, but how far its objectives will conform with those currently being pursued by other agencies and by the provinces concerned remains to be seen. The possibility that conflicts will emerge cannot be overlooked.

Some provincial governments in the Atlantic region, as elsewhere, show little interest in or enthusiasm for development plans, and this attitude is shared by a number of ministers at the federal level. Had there been a strong and widespread desire among politicians to see an integrated development plan for the Atlantic provinces, it is hard to believe that there would not have been greater progress. Two to three years elapsed before an attempt was even made to establish a planning division in the ADB, and the Atlantic provinces have tended to go their separate ways. Close and effective co-operation with the ADB at the technical and higher planning levels remains inadequate. It is not a plan for the entire region that interests provincial premiers so much as the sums that will be made available by the ADB for the implementation of particular projects within their own political jurisdiction. The operations of the ADB reflect this attitude. There has been no disposition on the part of its members to make the provision of funds *conditional* upon the formulation of an agreed plan, and in the absence of such a condition, it is most unlikely that the present dichotomy between expenditures and plans will be closed. The planning operations of the ADB will continue to constitute little more than a sort of appendix to its main function of distributing funds for what appear to be desirable ends. Such an arrangement leaves a great deal to be desired; it opens the door to conflicts of objectives and to pressures to undertake assorted *ad hoc* projects.

If there is to be an over-all plan for the whole region rather than separate plans for the individual provinces, and that would certainly appear to be desirable, interprovincial co-operation will be that much more important. The choice of common goals is rendered difficult because of interprovincial rivalries, but the alternative choice of separate plans falls short of what is needed. Ideally there should be an integration of ADA, ARDA, and ADB policies with all the provincial plans. As it stands, there is a collection of miscellaneous and largely unrelated measures.

Even at the federal level there is no common purpose. The Economic Council drew attention to this in 1966 when it referred to "the importance of developing a deliberate and consistent focus upon the regional problem within the area of federal government operations in themselves", and raised the issue "of attempting to assess the total potential impact of numerous separate programmes upon a particular region, and of bringing them together in the most consistent, efficient manner".[1]

At the outset, agreement needs to be reached on over-all objectives. These objectives are still vague, and there is a conflict of opinion not only on which ones should be emphasized, but also on how they can best be achieved. For example, it is contended in some quarters that migration out of a region should be encouraged as a means to raise the per capita incomes of those who remain, and in others that migration will retard growth and reduce the employment and income of those who stay behind. The subject of migration is indeed a thorny one, not only politically but also from the standpoint of theory. At the risk of sounding trite, it should perhaps be pointed out that generalizations regarding the advantages or disadvantages of migration can be misleading. There are areas where there is little doubt that migration is the only feasible solution to the distress in which people find themselves, areas with meagre resources far removed from the main stream of activity. There are others from which migration, especially of the younger and more able members of the community, is likely to destroy the prospects of viable growth, growth that would probably be attainable with a measure of additional help at the outset. Misguided policies will result from treating both as if they were alike. Policies have to be tailored in the light of particular circumstances.[2]

There appears to be a general consensus that unemployment

[1] Economic Council of Canada, *Third Annual Review: Prices, Productivity and Employment* (Ottawa: Queen's Printer, 1966), pp. 264–5.
[2] APEC, in its *First Annual Review*, came out strongly against the view that migration is the answer to the problems of the region.

rates and income levels in the Atlantic provinces should be brought closer to the national average. Little, however, has been said about the extent to which incomes and employment opportunity should be equalized as a matter of federal policy, and the federal government has avoided clear commitments. Some argue, moreover, that equalizing income and employment should not be ends in themselves so much as a consequence of policies designed to stimulate the economic growth of the region so that it makes a maximum contribution to *national* output. Regional policies, in their view, should not be seen in isolation but as an aspect of national policies designed to maximize output in the country as a whole. Those who subscribe to this view argue that no investment should be encouraged in the Atlantic provinces which does not offer the same or higher returns than investment elsewhere in the country, and though they are ready to recognize formally the distinction between private and social costs, they are inclined to discount the latter. Regional development policies, in other words, should concentrate on raising aggregate output, and only to the extent that they accomplish this end should they be considered justified.

Impatience with the view that the Atlantic provinces are poor relations who ought to be supported by the rest of the country as an act of grace is not confined to critics from outside the region. There is an understandable impatience with such a view in the Atlantic provinces as well. What is needed, they urge, is policies that contribute to strong and sustainable growth, not ones that bolster up various forms of weak industry in the interests of reducing unemployment and raising per capita incomes. Those who see the problem in this light place the main emphasis on raising productivity and making associated changes in the structure of the economy.

In a report of the Nova Scotia Voluntary Planning Board[1] it is stated that "The Voluntary Planning Board has opted for pro-

[1] *Voluntary Economic Planning for the New Nova Scotia, Report on Progress: Overall Plan, Nova Scotia to 1968* (Halifax: Voluntary Planning Board, 1965), p. 248.

moting the achievement of the most efficient economic structure possible. In other words, for encouraging the growth of competitive and self-supporting activities in all sectors of the provincial economy . . . A corollary to this approach is that planning must encourage the ultimate termination of economic activities which are obsolete or not competitive." How this corollary would affect the express goal of maintaining the highest possible level of employment was not examined, though the point was made that "due to the substitution of capital for labour, no substantial increase in primary manufacturing employment should be expected during the 1965–68 period".

A brief review of some of the aspects of planning in Nova Scotia and Quebec furnishes an illustration of the way in which a number of the issues raised in the foregoing discussion have been dealt with in practice. In Nova Scotia it was decided that the general planning objective should be to achieve the maximum rate of economic growth by making the best use of provincial resources and opportunities without regimentation or compulsion. The success of the plan would thus depend on voluntary co-operation.[1] The economy was divided into main sectors and subsectors. In each, a committee was made responsible for drawing up a sector plan containing a statement of resources, past experience, potential for growth and obstacles in the way of realizing that potential, a statement of the annual target for the next four years as a percentage of annual growth, and the policies which should be pursued to attain the targets. The committees submit their sector plans to the Nova Scotia Voluntary Planning Board, consisting of twenty-eight members representing industrial sectors, labour, and government. Independent advisory councils also submit reports. The Board has the task of co-ordinating the sector plans and drawing up an over-all plan for the province on the basis of the submissions it has received. This plan is passed on to the provincial government and, subject to such changes as may be required and agreed upon, the government approves it. Though

[1] J. R. Mills, "Voluntary Economic Planning in Nova Scotia", *Canadian Public Administration*, VIII, no. 2 (June 1965), 160–5.

the Board considers all sectors important, it attaches the highest priority to the expansion of employment in secondary manufacturing.

Such an outline introduces numerous questions, among them the criteria to be used in deciding the best use of provincial resources and opportunities. The decision to emphasize manufacturing has been questioned by some observers, who express considerable doubt that such an emphasis can be justified in view of the poor growth performance of manufacturing in the past and the increasing importance of service industries. The sector targets have also been criticized for lack of consistency – the lack of correlation between investment and employment targets being a case in point (though as it happens, investment targets have apparently had no impact on actual investment decisions). The mechanism both for reconciling objectives and implementing them has been considered inadequate, and the evaluation of particular projects has been deficient and biased by special interests.[1]

The plan prepared by the Eastern Quebec Planning Board was a much fuller and in many ways a more sophisticated one, but it is doubtful whether it will be any more successful than the Nova Scotia plan in influencing the actual course of events. The broad objective of the BAEQ plan was to provide eastern Quebec with a standard of living equal to that of Quebec as a whole, an ambition entailing the virtual elimination of disparities in employment, productivity, and income. Per capita income in the area was little more than half the Quebec average in 1961, and approximately one third of the wage earners were unemployed for six months in the year. Four primary development objectives were put forward: "professional and geographical mobility of the labour force; the establishment of an institutional framework for planning and participation; the creation of a regional enthusiasm and the rational organizing of the area".[2]

Modernization of the traditional primary sectors – agriculture,

---

1 These views are drawn from an unpublished paper, "Economic Planning in Nova Scotia", by Paul B. Huber of Dalhousie University, Halifax, N.S.
2 *Development Plan, Pilot Region: Lower St. Lawrence, Gaspé and Iles-de-la-Madeleine* (BAEQ, pre-publication copy, June 30, 1966), I, 19.

fishing, and forestry – the encouragement of mining, and the expansion of relatively new, dynamic, foot-loose industries were to constitute important elements in the plan. Since the region currently does not provide conditions likely to attract the new, dynamic types of industry, the establishment of two industrialization centres which would have the requisite appeal was to be given priority. The plan proposed radical changes in the whole social and economic set-up of the region, including a complete reorganization of the scattered municipal government structure, a regrouping and reduction of the two-hundred-odd existing municipalities to twenty-five, and an acceleration of the process of urbanization. The intention was to concentrate the population so that public and private investment would be more effective and economical. A corollary was to close down those areas where there is almost no development potential. The employment objective hinged on keeping the population at a stable level until 1982; out-migration of such a magnitude as to occasion an absolute fall in population was not desired.

Among the difficulties confronting those who framed the plan was the lack of a development plan for the whole province with which the regional plan could be integrated. This lack necessitated their making certain assumptions about a larger development framework into which the smaller region would fit.

Whatever reservations may be felt about certain of the proposals and procedures described in the plan, there is no denying that extensive effort and thought have gone into its preparation. From a pedagogical standpoint it is an excellent case study. Its influence on the economy of the region, however, has been disappointing. Local political forces have resisted many of the fundamental changes that the plan proposed and have accepted only piecemeal modifications. Some of the changes recommended in the plan were indeed drastic – the reduction of 12,000 farms to 4,000 was one – but it is difficult to escape the conclusion that the deep poverty of the area does, in fact, call for drastic solutions. The excessive expectations for improvement that were engendered among the local population became a source of embarrassment to the provincial government, and this seems to have been an additional reason for the lack of political endorsement. A substantial part of the Eastern Quebec Planning Board's staff has been disbanded (its relations with the ten-member board of directors were often strained), and to a large extent the plan as originally conceived is a dead letter.[1]

Experience in both Nova Scotia and Quebec serves as a salutary reminder, if such is necessary, that it is one thing to approve the concept of planning and quite another to develop coherent and feasible plans that will command political support and achieve the objectives in mind.

This raises the question as to how far individual provincial governments are, in fact, capable of producing effective plans for regional development. From the technical point of view, provincial governments vary greatly in capacity. Some, such as the Quebec government, are well able to undertake the task; others are much less so and if they favour planning will probably have to rely heavily, at least at the outset, on the technical resources of the federal government and its agencies, though even at the federal level competent manpower is limited. The Atlantic provinces and the Prairie provinces might well be encouraged to develop plans for multi-province regions into which provincial programs can be fitted. This may sound unrealistic at the moment, but it could prove the shape of things to come, for individual provinces are to some extent incapable of solving problems of development in isolation. Moreover, given the close economic interrelationships between provinces, individual plans run the risk of incompatibility. It would make much more sense to have one plan embracing all the Atlantic provinces than four plans that cannot be reconciled with one another.

---

[1] The course of events has taken a new turn since the above was written. On May 26, 1968 the federal government entered into a five-year agreement with the government of Quebec to provide a sum of over $200 million for the implementation of a comprehensive rural development plan for the lower St. Lawrence and the Gaspé. This is the most ambitious agreement so far under the FRED legislation. Although a number of recommendations in the BAEQ plan will be implemented, the new plan differs in both direction and content.

Attempts by provincial governments to influence provincial and sub-provincial growth rates are not, of course, confined to planning. Indeed some of the provinces which show singularly little interest in formal plans of one sort or another are very active in implementing measures to influence industrial location and development. Such measures appear to be increasing in number and magnitude, and some of their implications for the regional economic scene in Canada are considered in the paragraphs that follow.

Before leaving the subject, however, one final observation should be made. No matter how carefully a plan is constructed to ensure coherence and acceptability, it will still fall short of expectations if individual projects are themselves poorly selected. The relative costs and benefits of individual projects need to be studied with care. Experience in many countries suggests that the success or failure of a plan often stands or falls on the selection of sound projects.

The government of Ontario has also been active of late in the pursuit of policies designed to encourage the expansion of economic activity in some of its poorer areas. Ontario, according to a classification made some years ago, is divided into ten regions, each consisting of several counties or districts. Interested local groups and municipal governments who wish to participate in the selection and pursuit of certain goals can establish a regional development council, which is an individual corporation with elected directors, except for one who is appointed by the provincial government. Initiative for action rests with the regional council, though the provincial government offers its co-operation.[1] Financing is provided by participating municipalities which contribute on a per capita basis, the rate being determined by the Board of Directors; modest additional support is provided by the provincial government. The regions are generally subdivided into three or four smaller zones and sectors, each of which has its own chairman

[1] The Eastern Ontario Regional Development Council, established in 1954, was the first of these. At that time its title was the Eastern Ontario Development Association. It has been very active in pressuring the provincial government to take greater measures to assist the poorer areas.

and executive and elects directors to the regional council. The zone organizations meet several times a year and submit projects and ideas for consideration and action to the Board of Directors. The situation is a fluid one, however, and administrative changes are made from time to time.

In announcing new regional development policies in 1966, the Ontario premier stated that he wanted to see the development of an effective two-way system of communication between the province and the municipal governments and regional organizations. It was not the intention of the provincial government to embark on plans contrary to the wishes of a majority of the local councils, but rather to foster their initiative. At the same time, assurance was given that the regional development councils would not become a new form of government.

Recently the Ontario government undertook an extensive and detailed inventory of data in each of the ten regions, which is to serve as a basis for the determination of the most promising courses of future action but while this economic inventory was still in progress, a provincial committee on taxation whose task it was to look into the tax structure of the province came forth with a recommendation for a new system of regional government set up on an entirely different geographical basis, a recommendation which, if accepted, will require a radical change in the boundaries of the currently defined economic regions.[1]

Another government body concerned with regional development is the Ontario Development Corporation, which was established in 1966 and makes grants for buildings and machinery to new or expanding industries in approved areas. In eastern and northern Ontario the grant consists of one third of the cost up to the first quarter of a million dollars expended, and one quarter of the balance up to a maximum of half a million dollars. Grants are lower in the rest of the province. A condition is that the recipient must have an equivalent equity in the venture, and areas already

---

[1] There appears to have been a complete lack of liaison between those concerned with regional development and those concerned with taxation and regional government boundaries.

qualifying under the federal ADA program are excluded. It seems likely that most of the fifty municipalities in eastern Ontario will be eligible to offer these grants as an incentive to prospective industries, since eastern Ontario, like northern Ontario, is one of the poorer regions of the province.

Although the assistance is designed to encourage secondary manufacturing, the Ontario grants, unlike the federal ones, are not restricted to secondary manufacturing, and any firm or industry than can make a substantial contribution to the improvement of a municipality can qualify. Tourism, for example, is one of the industries qualifying for aid.[1] Moreover, each application is considered on its merits; there is no rigid formula applying to either companies or municipalities. In this respect, too, the provincial scheme is an improvement on the federal one. The Corporation will also supplement the grants with conventional loans and provide technical assistance where it is needed.

Early in 1968 the Ontario government announced an Equalization of Industrial Opportunity program whose main objective is to expand industry and employment in areas of slow growth in order to provide jobs for young people in smaller centres of population and a wider base of industrial assessment for smaller municipalities.

Whatever the details of the assistance it provides, the very fact that the government of Ontario and its agencies makes assistance available within its own borders can be expected to have repercussions on regional programs elsewhere, and to affect the impact of federal programs. In so far as provincial governments are competing for industry – and there is no doubt that they are – some are in a much more favourable position than others. Were the government of Ontario to see fit to outbid other provinces in the incentives that it offers to new industry, it would be difficult to

---

[1] Tourism, it may be noted, figures prominently among development programs in many of the provinces, and it is difficult to avoid the impression that its potential is often overrated. Not only do the requirements of the industry frequently entail substantial imports from outside the region, local costs and expenditures for facilities may be high too, particularly in areas where road and other communications are poorly developed.

challenge it effectively. It has financial resources far in excess of those in the poorest provinces, and the poorer regions of Ontario are not subject to such severe disadvantages as are some elsewhere. Eastern Ontario is, for example, much less remote from the large centres of population than is eastern Quebec or Newfoundland, and its prospects of undertaking profitable secondary manufacturing are, as a result, generally much greater. As for federal programs, they can be undermined by independent provincial action.

It is difficult to know what can be done about competitive provincial incentives, but it is important that they be curbed. Many provincial governments feel that they should have the prime responsibility for area development (a view to which some in Ottawa also subscribe), and so long as this is the case there are limits to what the federal government can do to establish *national* objectives. Unlike the situation in the United Kingdom, where Whitehall has overriding powers to influence industrial location in the country as a whole, Ottawa has to reckon with the provinces. Its powers over the provincial governments are limited, and if they decide they want to play their cards in a certain way, there may not be much the federal government can do about it, whether it wants to or not. Unless the provincial governments co-operate, it will prove very difficult to implement regional policies of development in line with what are conceived to be national interests, but great effort should be made by Ottawa to achieve as much consensus as possible.

Concern with regional development has not been confined to the eastern and central provinces. Manitoba, for example, established a regional development branch in 1959 to assist in the promotion and furtherance of economic expansion throughout the rural parts of the province. Its principal objectives include working with municipalities and local development agencies to achieve orderly community growth and encouraging the development of industry and business within rural communities. The regional development branch has carried out extensive surveys in certain parts of the province to determine the most promising lines along which growth might be fostered, and it works closely with the industrial development branch, which is responsible for encouraging industrialization in the province as a whole. The Committee on Manitoba's Economic Future, reporting in 1963, outlined further programs to accelerate the economic development of the province,[1] and in 1968 the Commission for Targets for Economic Development[2] was appointed to re-assess the situation, set targets, and influence economic trends up to 1980.

Every province has taken some kind of action on regional development. Most provinces have set up development funds, and all have established departments and agencies to foster economic growth within their boundaries. Several also offer direct tax concessions to new industry, some offer advisory services, and a few have bought stock in particular companies and make or guarantee operating loans. The government of Alberta does not offer tax concessions but is spending heavily on railroad construction to open up its natural resources.[3]

The nature and extent of co-operation between the different levels of government varies with the type of area development program. The Cape Breton Development Corporation, unlike most provincial development corporations, is a hybrid. Legislation establishing the Corporation was passed by the federal government on July 7, 1967.[4] Its functions and the circumstances which led to its establishment are worth noting.

In 1966, in his study of coal production in Cape Breton Island, J. R. Donald[5] had pointed to the steadily increasing amount in federal subsidies required to support uneconomic mines and stressed the urgency of adopting and implementing new policies. In essence, the Donald Report recommended that during the next fifteen years the subsidies supporting uneconomic coal production

[1] See *Manitoba 1962–1975: Report of the Committee on Manitoba's Economic Future.*

[2] Known as "TED".

[3] The implications of these practices and others are currently being examined by the Private Planning Association of Canada.

[4] 16 Elizabeth II, c. 6, "An Act to establish the Cape Breton Development Corporation".

[5] J. R. Donald, *op. cit.*

be made available to support other forms of industrial development and economic activity in the region – forms which offered
greater promise. The federal government concurred in these
views, and the Prime Minister expressed willingness "to assist,
on a massive scale, the transition of the area from dependence on
a declining natural resource to a sound economic base".[1] With
the participation of the Nova Scotia government, the federal government established the Cape Breton Development Corporation
(known as Devco), giving it the responsibility to acquire, reor-
ganize, and manage the coal mining interests of the Dominion
Steel and Coal Corporation and to help promote and finance the
development of modern industry on the island within the context
of a comprehensive economic development plan covering both the
Cape Breton area and eastern Nova Scotia. The Corporation thus
has two main divisions, a Coal Division and an Industrial Development Division.[2] The main financial burden is carried by the
federal government, but the government of Nova Scotia has contributed and will continue to contribute to certain costs. Devco
differs from development corporations in other provinces in that
it is required to co-operate with both the federal and the provincial government.

In implementing the switch of resources it is intended to phase
out mine output as new industries are brought in, thereby reducing
the dislocation of the labour force, which in any event is likely to
be considerable. An annual statement must be submitted to the
Nova Scotia and federal governments indicating the relationship
between industrial development and the phasing out of uneconomic mines. The establishment of Devco offers hope that more
rational measures will be taken in the future with regard to the
coal industry than have been taken in the past; but the problems
it faces are very great. They were accentuated at the outset by the
decision of the Dominion Steel and Coal Corporation (Dosco)

[1] From "Press Release Policy Statement by the Prime Minister, Cape
Breton Coal", December 29, 1966.

[2] The objects and powers of the Industrial Development Division of the
Development Corporation are listed in sections 22 and 23 of the legislation.

to close its steel mill in Sydney, a city whose population of 34,000 depends almost entirely on its two main industries, coal and steel, both of which Dosco owned. The mill had been incurring losses for many years and was not only technologically obsolete but very poorly situated in relation to North American markets. Faced with a crisis situation involving steel as well as coal, the government of Nova Scotia decided to underwrite the continued operation of the steel mill for a transitional period and to seek federal help. As matters stand, steel production in Cape Breton has become largely a provincial responsibility, but the situation is a fluid one.

## Industrial Parks

In addition to grants and loans to new industry that are along the same lines as those adopted by the government of Ontario, a number of provincial governments have established industrial parks (or "estates", as they are sometimes called) as a lure to industry.[1] Ontario is pursuing this avenue of development too, and a large park has been established at a former military base some twenty-five miles north of London. Industrial parks have a long history dating back, in the case of the United Kingdom, to the last century. The British government has made extensive use of them in its own regional development policies, but their numbers have also been growing rapidly in Canada and elsewhere in recent years. Though industrial parks are by no means confined to depressed areas, they have become an important instrument in the attraction of industry to such areas.

Industrial parks can take several forms. They frequently offer a variety of inducements to would-be occupants in addition to the serviced site itself. Apart from basic infra-structure and utilities

---

[1] For a discussion of the subject, see *Establishment of Industrial Estates in Under-developed Countries* (New York: United Nations, Department of Economic and Social Affairs, 1961). (The title is misleading in that the publication also gives extensive coverage to the United States, the United Kingdom, and other developed industrial countries, though the study is addressed primarily to authorities in charge of industrial development in under-developed countries.)

such as communications, water, and power, they may also offer a number of additional facilities such as maintenance services, banks, restaurants, playing fields, and other types of activities and amenities that might be a convenience to firms establishing there. Inducements to attract firms include ready-built factories for rent which can be quickly adapted to meet individual needs, and various forms of aid to firms to establish themselves initially. A network of readily available services can be a strong magnet, and as occupants increase in number, external economies of operation can result, making the site increasingly attractive.

In a number of cases industries can gain the advantages of an urban site without the disadvantages often associated with urban life such as air pollution, noise, and traffic congestion. At best, industrial parks can make possible strong growth in localities which would otherwise experience considerable difficulty in attracting industry. There is, however, no guarantee of success; and those situated fairly close to large urban centres will usually do better than others. If they are geographically isolated and unsupported by other measures to foster growth in the area, they are unlikely to live up to expectations.

The Atlantic Development Board has encouraged the establishment of two or three parks in the Atlantic region, and this experience will be worth watching. Hopefully, the ADB will make public sufficient data on their operations to permit an evaluation, though this cannot be counted upon.

In Nova Scotia, Industrial Estates Limited (I.E.L.), a Crown corporation established by the government of that province in 1957, makes virtually no information available that would permit an assessment of its operation, though it would appear that substantial subsidies have been paid to individual firms.[1] Unlike the conventional industrial park, the Corporation was created to promote the establishment and expansion of secondary manufacturing throughout the province. For secondary manufacturers locat-

[1] See Albert Breton, *Discriminatory Government Policies in Federal Countries* (Montreal: Canadian Trade Committee, Private Planning Association of Canada, 1967), pp. 32–3.

ing or expanding in Nova Scotia it will finance 100 per cent of the cost of land and buildings anywhere in the province, and not just at specific sites. The buildings may be constructed to the manufacturer's specifications on a site of his own choosing. In addition I.E.L. will finance 60 per cent of the installed cost of new machinery. Existing tax agreements with most municipalities limit municipal taxes on corporation-assisted industries for a ten year period. Working capital has been increased from a $12 million limit in 1957 to $60 million in 1966, and lending terms to manufacturers are very favourable, often granting an interest holiday over the first three years. The exact terms, however, are not made public, partly because it increases the flexibility of individual arrangements by avoiding inter-firm comparisons and partly because of the desire of business itself to keep the information confidential. The General Manager has stated that I.E.L. operates as a business and in a business atmosphere, and those people who want to see details published do not know how business works.[1]

Up to a point such a stand seems reasonable, but the provincial government has also become very heavily involved not only with finance for the corporation but also with a number of financial deals supplementing the corporation. The heavy water plant, Deuterium of Canada Ltd., has had to be baled out of difficulty, and the province and I.E.L. now seem to have a combined stake in it of some $80 million. Expenditures of such a magnitude raise serious questions about their wisdom not only from a provincial standpoint but from the national standpoint as well.

Whether or not government subventions in individual cases are justified depends on the circumstances and the judgment of the observer. Certainly in some instances such subventions may be regarded as desirable because of their catalytic effect on other expansion. But there is another aspect of the matter that has been causing concern. There is a feeling in some quarters that it is essential to concentrate industry in certain areas of the province to

[1] According to "How I.E.L. Explains its Success", a feature report on the Maritimes in the *Financial Post* (June 24, 1967). There is no justification, however, for keeping matters secret indefinitely. Like other government agencies, I.E.L. has backed losers as well as winners.

promote rapid expansion for the least cost in terms of public expenditure. Those who subscribe to this view feel that I.E.L. should concentrate its aid more rather than disperse it in the way that it is doing. I.E.L., which makes aid available anywhere within the province, as a result finds itself in conflict with those who want to see it concentrated in specific growth areas. A consensus on policy has yet to be reached.

## Municipal Responsibilities and Budgeting

Many municipal boundaries were established when the economy was largely rural and communities were much more self-sufficient than they are today. A sense of local identity facilitated the task of demarcation. However, with the urbanization of the economy, the growing interdependence of communities, and the spiralling expenditures on roads, education, health, and welfare, old boundaries have lost their rationale and local governments have found themselves increasingly incapable of fulfilling their responsibilities. Those municipalities whose needs for a program of development are greatest are frequently those whose capacity to undertake the work and bear the expense is least. The poorer the municipality, the poorer its services are likely to be and the weaker its chances of fostering the new development it requires to improve its economic situation.

As a result, there is a need for a substantial redistribution of governmental powers and financing. The economies of agglomeration are pulling firms towards the larger centres. Small, isolated communities lacking rich primary resources are in many cases faced with extinction. In an effort to make more uniform the quality of services provided by various municipalities, provincial governments have subsidized the financially weaker municipalities, and the federal government for its part has assisted the weaker provinces.

In 1966, the government of New Brunswick decided to take over virtually the entire financial and policy-making responsibility for education, thereby greatly reducing the powers and responsibilities of local governments. Local governments, especially in rural areas (though this is not peculiar to New Brunswick), are finding themselves with less and less to do. Pursuing more strongly a trend which has become well established in other provinces, New Brunswick is reducing school districts from 422 to 34 in an effort to obtain the efficiencies of scale that can be characteristic of education as well as of many other services. Equal pay for teachers with equal qualifications is to be provided throughout the province, and the province will decide what schools are to be built and where. The provincial government is also empowered to determine municipal boundaries and to direct annexations and amalgamations where they appear to be in the best interests of the province and the people concerned. The objective of the program, to be accompanied by sweeping financial changes, is to allow for the transfer of powers and responsibilities to the unit of government best able to do the job and the transfer of costs to those best able to pay.

The allocation of financial powers and responsibilities, and the preparation of budgets is a crucial issue in regional development programs. In this connection Eric Beecroft makes some highly relevant observations.[1] Having referred to the lack of communication between those who are developing regional science and those who manage the processes of financial planning and financial decision-making, Eric Beecroft points out that if we are interested in action-oriented regional analysis, the process of budget-making is a vital matter requiring examination and that there is an urgent need in each area of development for an integrated public finance program related to the entire range of services required for economic, physical, and social development. Unhappily, he notes, we do not start with a clean slate. We are handicapped by conventional habits of mind "that have been developed in a fragmented system of local government and in provincial and federal departmental machinery that is also ill-adapted to the concept of regional planning and development". "Budget-making," he concludes, "far from being a secondary

[1] Eric Beecroft, "Financial Planning in Regional Development", *Canadian Public Administration*, IX, no. 2 (June 1966), 194–200.

function, is possibly the most crucial exercise – the indispensable catalytic operation – in all our efforts to make regional planning successful."

The importance of the budgetary process and the need to anticipate the implications of various development measures has encouraged the view that all levels of government should set up their budgets within the framework of a period longer than just one year to give an indication of probable long-run trends in revenue and expenditure.[1] The effects of an expanded industry in a particular locality may lead not only to increased direct needs for services by the industry itself but also to the need for a multiplicity of additional expenditures on social capital for the expanded labour force. Rational policies cannot be designed within the framework of one year budgets alone. Municipal and local governments which offer incentives to attract new industry need to reflect on the long-run financial implications of such programs.

## The Allocation of Responsibilities for Regional Aid

The situation in Cape Breton illustrates the basic problem of delimiting the respective roles of different levels of government in the pursuit of area development objectives. Where, it might be asked, should federal responsibility begin and where should it end? Clearly there are many considerations involved. What, for example, is to be the relation between Devco and the various development bodies concerned with related aspects of the Nova Scotian economy, among them the ADB, Industrial Estates Limited, the provincial departments of Trade and Industry and of Manpower, ADA, and ARDA? Difficulties inevitably arise with so many cooks in the kitchen. It is common knowledge that rivalries exist among a number of them and that important differences of opinion and emphasis occur.

A partial solution would be for the federal government to abandon responsibility for area development in the wealthier provinces.

[1] See, for example, Jacques Parizeau, "The Five-Year Budget", *ibid.*, 201–10.

The latter are well able, if they are so disposed, to assist poorer areas within their boundaries. Given the fact that they consider regional development to be their responsibility rather than that of the federal government and that their views on what is desirable or which areas should be assisted do not always coincide with those of the federal government, it would not seem unreasonable for the federal government to leave the problem in their laps.

In the case of the poorer provinces the situation is different, in that their need for remedial action is greater and their capacity to undertake it alone is less. What is suggested in their case is that provincial governments prepare development programs for federal support. Programs under the FRED legislation could serve as a pattern, but attention should not be confined to rural areas. In this way the federal government would be able to maintain the national perspective, which is essential, and guide provincial measures to accord with it. The automatic subventions of ADA would disappear, and provincial governments would be obliged to clarify their objectives and strategies for development, and harmonize them with those of the national government. When accepted by the federal government, they would serve as a guide to participating government departments at both the federal and provincial level and contribute to a greater uniformity of action than there is at the present time. The federal government for its part needs to clarify its own objectives and establish some branch with responsibility for ensuring that those objectives are pursued by the various departments involved. This indeed is what the government is now in the process of doing. Responsibility for regional policy at the moment is scattered among several departments and boards which are not answerable to each other. A consequence of this is that it is difficult to form a composite picture of policy or to arrive at a consensus among those responsible for its implementation.

*11. The Canadian North*

ALTHOUGH THE AREA lying north of the sixtieth parallel of latitude, comprising the Yukon and the Northwest Territories, constitutes 40 per cent of the entire area of Canada, it accounts for only one quarter of one per cent of the national population. The responsibility for administering this area is shared between the federal government and the territorial government concerned, with the Yukon having a greater measure of independence and local authority than have the Territories. The ADA and ARDA legislation does not cover the North, where problems differ in degree and to some extent in kind from those in other parts of the country.

*Population and Labour Force*

Table 11:1 shows that since 1931 the Indian and Eskimo population has dropped significantly as a percentage of the population living in the North. By 1961, it accounted for less than 16 per cent of the total population in the Yukon and 60 per cent in the Territories. The balance of the population, constituting "Others" in the table, is concentrated in a few communities. Approximately a quarter of the labour force consists of government employees, most of whom return to southern Canada on completion of their tours of duty.

## Table 11:1
## Population of the Yukon and Northwest Territories
## Decennial Census Years 1921 to 1961

|  | 1921 | 1931 | 1941 | 1951 | 1961 |
|---|---|---|---|---|---|
| YUKON |  |  |  |  |  |
| Indian | 1,390 | 1,543 | 1,701 | 1,533 | 2,207 |
| Eskimo | — | 85 | 41 | 30 |  |
| Others | 2,767 | 2,602 | 3,172 | 7,533 | 12,421 |
| Total | 4,127 | 4,230 | 4,914 | 9,096 | 14,628 |
| Others as % of "Total Yukon" | 66.5 | 61.5 | 64.6 | 82.8 | 84.9 |
| NORTHWEST TERRITORIES |  |  |  |  |  |
| Indian | 3,873 | 3,689 | 4,334 | 3,838 | 13,233 |
| Eskimo | 3,242 | 4,623 | 5,404 | 6,822 |  |
| Others | 1,028 | 1,004 | 2,290 | 5,344 | 9,765 |
| Total | 8,143 | 9,316 | 12,028 | 16,004 | 22,998 |
| Others as % of "Total Northwest Territories" | 12.6 | 10.8 | 19.0 | 33.4 | 42.5 |

Note: In the North, as elsewhere, there is a trend towards urbanization that extends to the indigenous population. Approximately one-third of the population in the Yukon lives in the town of Whitehorse and two-thirds of the population in the Northwest Territories lives in the Mackenzie District. In the Arctic area above the tree line, the population is very small and predominantly Eskimo, whereas the white population lives mostly in mining towns and administrative centres.

Source: 1921-51: R. D. Howland, *Some Regional Aspects of Canada's Economic Development*; 1961: D.B.S., *1961 Census of Canada*, Vol. I (92-545).

## Table 11:2
## Distribution of the Labour Force in the Yukon and
## Northwest Territories
## 1961

|  | Yukon | | Northwest Territories | |
| --- | --- | --- | --- | --- |
|  | *Males* | *Females* | *Males* | *Females* |
| Agriculture | 33 | 1 | 23 | — |
| Forestry | 42 | — | 40 | 1 |
| Fishing and trapping | 71 | 6 | 1,589 | 21 |
| Mining | 968 | 42 | 966 | 26 |
| Manufacturing | 73 | 22 | 113 | 33 |
| Construction | 433 | 14 | 272 | 8 |
| Transport and communications | 1,055 | 173 | 572 | 71 |
| Trade | 342 | 201 | 263 | 86 |
| Finance, insurance, and real estate | 36 | 29 | 14 | 15 |
| Service industries | 463 | 690 | 608 | 642 |
| Public administration and defence | 1,159 | 159 | 1,770 | 129 |
| Unspecified | 161 | 69 | 158 | 32 |
| All industries | 4,836 | 1,406 | 6,388 | 1,064 |

Source: D.B.S., *1961 Census of Canada*, Vol. III (94-518).

As far as the industrial classification of the labour force is concerned, Table 11:2 shows that in the two territories the largest group is employed in public administration and defence.[1] Mining also accounts for a great deal of employment in both, as does

[1] Among the most useful sources of information on the changing northern scene and the federal role therein are the annual reports of the Advisory Committee on Northern Development, made available by the Department of Indian Affairs and Northern Development and entitled "Government Activities in the North". The 1966 Report covers the work of the branches and divisions of twenty-nine federal departments and agencies active in the North. See also *The Northwest Territories Today*, a reference paper for the Advisory Commission on the Development of Government in the Northwest Territories (Ottawa: Queen's Printer, 1965).

transport. The two territories differ in a number of instances, however. In the Yukon many more are employed in transport in both relative and absolute terms, while in the Northwest Territories fishing and trapping account for the largest occupational group after public administration and defence.

Workers from the south of Canada who seek temporary employment in the North do not generally spend the bulk of their earnings there. Many seek to accumulate savings rapidly which can provide the means to relocate elsewhere, or they make extensive expenditures and transfers of funds outside the area. The local multiplier effect of incomes earned in the North is thus significantly less than that in the more developed areas of the South.[1]

## Natural Resources and Potential for Development

There is general agreement that while there are limited possibilities in other directions, major economic development in the North can only be effected through the exploitation of non-renewable natural resources. Geological, climatic, and other factors vary greatly from one part of the North to another, however, and sub-classifications by region may be essential in the formulation of specific development policies.

There is scope for limited agricultural and forestry expansion in the Yukon and many parts of the Mackenzie District, where local timber can be utilized for local needs, but in other regions such possibilities are lacking completely. The pulp industry may develop in time, but even in the best areas the tree cover is thin, distance to markets is great, and operating costs are likely to be high. As for agricultural production, while some expansion is possible in one or two localities, the growing season is very short and, unlike Siberia, glacial action has left only small areas of soil coverage. Fishing and trapping are equally unpromising sources of substantial growth, and it seems unlikely that they will provide more than a marginal livelihood for a small number, notwith-

[1] An attempt to estimate the multiplier effect of mining expenditures in the North is currently being undertaken by S. J. May of Carleton University, Ottawa.

standing the technical assistance that the federal government can and does give in this direction. A market for arctic char is developing, but trapping provides a precarious livelihood since the catch and fur prices vary greatly from year to year and there is an increasing threat of competition from synthetics. Attempts to encourage the herding of reindeer have met with virtually no success.

Tourism has a modest potential; fishing and hunting camps off the beaten track are growing in popularity, and for those whose tastes run that way, the Arctic has a certain appeal. With the growth of communications, tourism seems likely to expand as a source of income, though a highly seasonal one. In contrast, net value added by manufacturing is likely to remain very small. In 1964, it totalled less than $2 million.[1]

Water resources may also become important; they are certainly extensive. Indeed, much of the North is covered by fresh water. The Yukon contains some of the largest hydro power sites in the world and has vast water storage potential. Oil and gas production shows promise of expansion as well. There are over 600,000 square miles of sedimentary rocks, and some of the geological formations give ground for hope that they will prove rich producers. Extensive exploration is being undertaken, though major finds have still to be made.[2]

The hard-rock mining industry still leads the field by far in terms of production, and is the most rapid growth sector. To mention one aspect, the Precambrian area is three times as large as that of Ontario and seems comparable in nature. Since Ontario produces over a billion dollars worth of minerals a year, production in the North might eventually approach such a figure. Geological surveys in various areas have encouraged a certain optimism, though there can be no doubt that inaccessibility and the harshness of the climate will discourage the pace and extent of

[1] In 1967, the Yukon territorial government and the Department of Indian Affairs and Northern Development commissioned an extensive economic study of the Yukon Territory to examine the potential for growth and measures to stimulate it. It constitutes one of a series of area economic surveys carried out by the Industrial Division of the Department.

[2] In this regard, see G. David Quirin, *The Economics of Oil and Gas Development in Northern Canada* (Ottawa: Queen's Printer, 1962).

exploitation. In spite of the handicaps of distance and climate, mineral production in the Yukon rose from $1 million to $14 million between 1944 and 1964, and in the Northwest Territories from $1 million to $18 million, but substantial variations occurred from year to year. More recently, production has risen dramatically. The hundred million dollar mark has been passed, and annual shipments from the two territories may reach a quarter billion dollars by 1970.[1] Major mining developments include lead and zinc, iron ore, asbestos, gold, and silver. Associated with the above, processing and refining offer prospects for expansion although subventions will probably continue to be needed.

To the extent that resources are exploited, benefits will accrue to the local population, though it may gain less than those from outside the region who provide the requisite financing and professional and managerial skills. Because of this, pressure on the federal government to spur the development of the North is as likely to come from non-residents as from the indigenous population.

## *The Rationale for Federal Policies*

As might be expected, the cost of creating and maintaining various services in the North and of keeping open communications with the rest of the country is extremely high. Given the smallness of the population resident in the North and the fact that a substantial proportion even of this is only temporary, one may be disposed to question the justification for federal expenditures there on a substantial scale. Some indication of the extent of these expenditures can be gained from the following table.

A number of difficulties are encountered in attempting to analyse government expenditures in the North and compare them with similar expenditures in the South. Departments do not code their expenditures on a geographic basis, and allocations cannot

---

[1] There is no doubt that some ventures have proved extremely profitable to their backers. Pine Point Mines is often cited in illustration. In the first twenty months of operation, profits of $55 million were made on sales of $69 million. The profits were tax free, and the company repaid its entire capital debt and acquired a working capital of some $12 million.

## Table 11:3
## Main Government Activities in the Yukon and Northwest Territories
### 1961-1966

($000)

| | 1961-2 | | 1962-3 | | 1963-4 | | 1964-5 | | 1965-6 | |
|---|---|---|---|---|---|---|---|---|---|---|
| | Revenue | Expenditure | Revenue | Expenditure | Revenue | Expenditure | Revenue | Expenditure | Revenue | Expenditure |
| Agriculture | 9 | 208 | 11 | 228 | 19 | 271 | 10 | 221 | 5 | 188 |
| Indian affairs | — | 1,348 | — | 1,371 | 21 | 1,797 | — | 1,847 | — | 2,467 |
| Finance | — | 2,503 | — | 3,735 | — | 4,728 | — | 8,181 | — | 9,262 |
| Fisheries | 23 | 226 | 22 | 217 | 21 | 238 | 17 | 192 | 18 | 288 |
| Justice | 28 | 365 | 386 | 417 | 34 | 327 | 92 | 386 | 45 | 376 |
| Labour | — | 65 | — | 661 | — | 233 | — | 284 | — | 446 |
| Mines and technical surveys* | 3 | 447 | 3 | 850 | 3 | 1,084 | 3 | 1,151 | 5 | 1,064 |
| National defence† | — | 8,268 | — | 9,402 | — | 7,986 | — | 3,563 | — | 3,896 |
| Health and welfare‡ | 1,138 | 6,970 | 1,226 | 7,922 | 1,207 | 8,248 | 1,330 | 8,219 | 1,264 | 8,851 |
| Northern affairs and natural resources‡ | 3,526 | 22,228 | 2,389 | 31,741 | 2,883 | 24,437 | 3,797 | 27,028 | 9,279 | 30,509 |
| Power commission§ | 3,442 | 1,768 | 3,721 | 3,002 | 4,083 | 5,579 | 4,550 | 9,394 | 4,838 | 7,134 |
| Post office | 270 | 1,359 | 285 | 1,438 | 297 | 1,608 | 300 | 1,940 | 318 | 2,094 |
| Public works | 535 | 1,600 | 621 | 1,394 | 235 | 2,224 | 610 | 10,637 | 849 | 9,963 |
| R.C.M.P. | 185 | 2,236 | 174 | 2,149 | 1,041 | 2,221 | 855 | 2,382 | 700 | 2,507 |

| | | | | | | | | | | |
|---|---|---|---|---|---|---|---|---|---|---|
| Transport | 711 | 12,371 | 671 | 8,989 | 817 | 8,604 | 872 | 10,857 | 1,204 | 11,084 |
| National revenue | 3,349 | 188 | 3,314 | 216 | 3,433 | 211 | 2,427 | 218 | 906 | 252 |
| Total of above | 13,219 | 62,150 | 12,823 | 73,732 | 14,094 | 69,796 | 14,863 | 86,500 | 19,431 | 90,381 |
| Over-all total (including items not listed above) | 13,220 | 62,289 | 12,827 | 73,904 | 14,096 | 69,936 | 14,867 | 86,618 | 19,434 | 90,548 |

*New classification: Energy, Mines, and Resources.
†New classification: National Health and Welfare.
‡New classification: Northern Development.
§New classification: Northern Canada Power.

Source: Advisory Committee on Northern Development, "Government Activities in the North" (mimeographed), various years.

be determined with any degree of certainty. Considerable work may be undertaken in Ottawa which applies mainly to the North, but other areas may benefit from it too. Some expenditures for defence purposes cannot be meaningfully allocated, and weather stations in the North do not serve the territories exclusively. Adjustments also need to be made for the fact that in the North educational expenditures are borne entirely by the federal government, whereas elsewhere they are a provincial responsibility and are financed out of provincial taxation.

The interpretation of data on the North is further complicated by the forms of classification employed. Expenditures are apt to be collated in ways having an administrative rationale but having little or no relevance from the standpoint of those concerned with the direction and appraisal of policies designed to stimulate economic growth.

Taking the figures as they stand, however, expenditures in the North in 1965–6 amounted in round figures to $90 million and revenues to $20 million, making a net expenditure of $70 million. Since the population totalled around 40,000, this represents some $1,750 per head, though there is no way of knowing how much of this actually benefits local residents. The figures certainly suggest a much higher degree of federal subvention in the North than in other parts of the country. What then are the grounds for justifying it?

Three main reasons are commonly advanced for federal subventions and other kinds of assistance to the North. First, a sense of moral obligation to the indigenous population, a feeling that their welfare is a national responsibility; second, a desire to establish unequivocally a national claim to the territory extending to the north; and third, a belief that the potential mineral riches of the area are very substantial and efforts should be made to encourage their exploration and exploitation.

The living standards of the indigenous population fall well below the national average. Their housing is extremely primitive and their educational standards are inadequate to meet the demand for skilled employment. Following many years of neglect, it is considered urgent to improve both. Inevitably, the costs involved in undertaking this have been heavy, but in time the improvements in education will show returns in terms of increased earning power, although for a number of years the gains are almost certain to be small.

The scattered population adds to the increased cost of providing adequate educational, health, and housing services, and because of this efforts are being made to concentrate inhabitants in centres where employment can also be found. Certain firms show a marked reluctance to engage local labour, however, and the government is anxious to change this. In some cases, as one of the conditions of receiving government assistance, private firms have been required to make a greater effort to employ such labour. Working conditions and demands in industry admittedly involve difficult adjustments for those whose education and way of life has not equipped them for the new environment but once such adjustments are made, many may not wish to remain in the North. The fact that people do not leave in greater numbers at the present time may be indicative less of choice than of their present lack of ability to find profitable employment south of the sixtieth parallel.

As for the development of natural resources in the North, the third reason for federal assistance, the Minister of Indian Affairs and Northern Development has stated that the government is willing and anxious to play a role, and programs of assistance are both flexible and wide ranging. Government policy, as he outlined it, is designed "to reduce the risk and make the North as attractive to the developer today as many other regions in Canada or even in the world. What is lacking, perhaps, is an awareness by the potential investor of both the prizes that may be won in the North and the willingness of the Canadian government to assume a reasonable part of the risk." But he added, "the traditional roles between the private and public sectors of the company are maintained in the North with the government recovering its share of the risk where success is achieved through the normal processes of royalty and taxation."[1]

[1] From a speech to the New York Society of Security Analysts, "Investment Possibilities in Northern Canada", April 26, 1967. The word "company" was presumably intended to read "country".

It is difficult to know how much weight to attach to the statement that it is government policy "to reduce the risk and make the North as attractive to the developer today as many other regions in Canada or even in the world". Depending on how it is interpreted, it could entail expenditures on a scale that would dwarf all the other expenditures on ARDA, ADA, and the ADB taken together. It is hard to believe that this is what was intended; but how much development expenditure is justified in the North? If potential returns are greater elsewhere in Canada, it is hard to see the case for increasing aid to the North; such justification as there is has to be sought less on economic grounds than on grounds of social welfare and sovereignty.[1]

## Manpower and Educational Policies

Since neither the ARDA nor the ADA program applies to the North, northern development is the subject of a separate array of federal policies. The economist who concerns himself with the problems of northern development, particularly as they bear on the integration of the indigenous population into an industrial type of economic system, soon finds himself out of his depth. The sociologist and the social anthropologist remind him of his limitations. Basic assumptions on what constitutes likely behaviour patterns have to be revised. Regular industrial employment is not the ambition of many Indians and Eskimos of the older generation; their attitudes towards life and work differ from those of other Canadians in some significant respects. These differences are also manifest among the Indians who have preferred to stay on reservations in the various provinces and have not welcomed absorption into conventional Canadian society. There are ten times as many Indians on the reservations as there are in the North.[2]

[1] While the case for improving social welfare is conceded, it is none the less worth recalling that the indigenous population of the North is extremely small. Each of the provinces could probably count more people in its most impoverished areas.

[2] Although those provinces that desire it may include Indian lands and Indian people within the purview of the ARDA program, the assumption that middle-class values and aspirations are shared by Indians — or for that

The indigenous population of the North has suffered as well as benefited from the incursions of southern enterprise. The traditional mode of life of Indian and Eskimo inhabitants has been disrupted, and for many no satisfactory alternative has been found. It is important, however, that the differences which undoubtedly exist between the conventions and aspirations of the Indians and Eskimos on one hand and the white population on the other should not be exaggerated, and the desire of some well-intentioned people to preserve cultural diversity needs to be weighed against the major economic changes that are occurring and should be encouraged. Looked at over the next quarter of a century, there is no reason to expect that the traditional way of life will survive for the great majority of Indians and Eskimos. Their only hope would seem to lie in integration with the industrial world.

A survey of federal policies, both past and present, reveals that a variety of measures to improve the economic lot of the North's indigenous population have been taken, measures which have a parallel in many of the less developed countries of the world.

As elsewhere in Canada, education could contribute to the creation of employment opportunities, but its pursuit is expensive and presents unusual difficulties in the North. Education costs tend to be much higher there. Heavy construction costs, higher salaries for teachers, the small size of schools, and the need for hostels to board students all contribute to this situation. Neither Eskimo nor Indian parents, who are themselves illiterate, attach much importance to the formal education of their children. Those children who do attend schools frequently leave after two or three years with only the most rudimentary knowledge, lacking the preparation on which future industrial skills usually depend. The nomadic habits of some parents add to the difficulties of providing schooling; teachers recruited from the South are unfamiliar with local attitudes and needs; and in many cases the children lack an adequate knowledge of English, in which instruction is given. Not infrequently, indeed, the children speak only Eskimo

---

matter many other people – is a questionable one. This may be the rock on which many development programs will founder.

or some other language that has nothing in common with English.[1] The frustrations of teaching children whose progress by conventional standards is extremely slow discourages many teachers and, added to other disadvantages of life in the North, results in a rapid turnover of staff, a factor which further impedes progress. Most teachers only stay a year or two.

Attempts are made to provide boarding schools in which instruction can press forward more quickly – by exposing the children to longer periods of English for one thing – but separation from families creates its own problems. The more completely the child becomes adjusted to a different world, the more alienated he becomes from his former cultural group. But if the indigenous population is to participate in a rapidly evolving industrial economy, sooner or later such a break has to come. The new generation has to adjust to a different social and economic environment, and adapt to new values. The most that can be done is to smooth the process of transition; but it cannot be stopped, and it cannot be reversed without destroying virtually all hope of economic improvement in the future. Attempts to retain in modified form traditional ways of life seem likely to prove of only temporary value and may retard more fundamental changes which ultimately will have to come. In this connection, the development of handicrafts has supplemented the incomes of a few, but it is hard to believe that it can be relied upon to make a major contribution to over-all economic development.

Given the limited prospects in other directions, there is a strong case for the federal government's pressing ahead with its plans to encourage the exploration and development of mineral, oil, and gas reserves, and to equip the local population to acquire the attitudes and skills needed to participate in this area as well as in administrative services and tasks associated with the broad functions of government.

[1] Of 1,826 pupils enrolled in schools in the Northwest Territories Arctic District in 1966, only fifteen were in high school grades. Four had reached Grade 10, a grade which for many employers constitutes a minimum basic education. Admittedly this situation reflects not only a high drop-out rate but the fact that schooling for the great majority of pupils did not begin until the middle 1950s. If expectations are fulfilled, the members in high school will increase sharply during the 1970s.

While figures are lacking for the North as a whole, family allowances and welfare payments of one sort and another constitute the largest part of the current cash income of the inhabitants in certain areas, as they do in a few of the more depressed localities in southern Canada. For the time being, there may be no alternative method of dealing with the situation, but reliance upon such payments as a major source of income over a prolonged period is indicative of the inadequacy of other policies.

## Assistance to Mining

With regard to mineral resource exploitation, important contributions are being made by the federal government in the form of geological surveys and mapping. Mining and petroleum industries throughout Canada can take advantage of special concessions granted under the Income Tax Act. Among these is the tax exemption on the income from the first three years of operating a new mine. Moreover, since the taxpayer may defer deduction of any capital cost allowance or development costs until after this period of exemption, income tax is unlikely to be paid for several years. This situation has led to a prolonged debate over the various concessions granted to the mining and petroleum industries, some arguing that the concessions are warranted because of the special risks associated with mineral and petroleum extraction and others that they have led to the opening of uneconomic mines with resultant waste of capital and manpower. There is no gainsaying that they have been expensive, and the Royal Commission on Taxation has put the cost of the three year exemption and the depletion allowance at over $150 million a year to government, with most of the benefits from the concessions accruing to a few large and wealthy companies.[1] But whether the concessions are warranted or not, the fact that such concessions are made in the

[1] The subject is discussed in *The Report of the Royal Commission on Taxation* (Ottawa: Queen's Printer, 1967), IV, Chapter 23. While the Commissioners consider that the concessions probably brought about an increase in the allocation of capital and labour to mineral and petroleum extraction, they doubt that it had a beneficial effect on the economic well-being of Canadians generally. Even if such benefits did result, the concessions were considered an unnecessarily costly method of achieving them.

North as elsewhere in Canada has had a bearing on northern development for, as already noted, that development depends in large measure on mining operations.

Regulations governing mineral exploration grants under the Northern Mineral Grant Program announced in 1966 permit up to 40 per cent of the cost of an approved exploration program in search of minerals or oil to be provided by the Department of Northern Affairs (now the Department of Indian Affairs and Northern Development). If the program is successful, the grant is repayable over a ten year period, commencing when production starts. If it is unsuccessful, the grant will be regarded as a contribution to the northern exploration effort and is not repayable. The purpose of this incentive is to increase the pace of northern exploration and development. The Prospectors' Assistance Program, designed to assist small-scale individual prospectors has the same general objective.

Another way in which northern mining has received preferential treatment is in federal assistance for road construction. Transportation is a key element in northern development and substantial assistance has been given to it. The Northern Roads Network Program, announced in 1965, calls for an average expenditure of $10 million a year, double the annual roads investment of the previous ten year period. Low standard roads (tote trails) designed to provide access to a resource project in the exploration or development stage are financed by the territorial governments, but more expensive roads, where the prospects seem to warrant it, are financed in part by the federal government. These may be either initial access roads or permanent access roads, the federal contribution for the latter being up to two thirds of the cost of construction or $40,000 per mile, whichever is less. In general, the government subscribes to the view that the first industry to move into an area should not be asked to pay for all the transportation and communication facilities that the community as a whole will ultimately require. Industries engaged in the development and extraction of resources such as hard-rock minerals, petroleum, and natural gas are the main beneficiaries, but sawmills, tourist lodges, canneries, or any other industry which will add to the growth and development of the area may be eligible for federal road-building assistance.

The construction of airfields, like the construction of roads, constitutes another form of aid in which resource exploration and exploitation is encouraged. While the Department of Transport has the primary jurisdiction in the matter of airport construction, the Department of Indian Affairs and Northern Development also has an interest and will pay half the cost of an individual exploratory airport up to a maximum federal expenditure of $20,000. The federal expenditure for this is expected to total about $160,000 a year. Federal cost-sharing may be with a mining or other natural resource company, a private recreational enterprise, or any established air carrier.

From an economic standpoint, the construction of road and rail communication and other forms of assistance to exploration are bound to be something of a gamble; the stakes are considerable but so also are the potential rewards, and the question arises as to how they should be shared between the federal government and private industry. If, in addition to granting tax concessions, the government is to undertake heavy expenditures on mapping, exploration, and communications, it would not seem unreasonable that it should also share in the rewards of subsequent exploitation, royalty payments and income tax notwithstanding. This view has now received a certain recognition.

Under the provisions of the Northern Grants Program, a new Canadian consortium, Panarctic Oils Ltd., will invest not less than $20 million on a three year oil-exploration program in the Arctic islands and the federal government has joined it. The participating companies will invest $11 million and the government $9 million over a three year period. In return for this participation the government will hold 45 per cent of the common shares and 45 per cent of the preference shares issued by the company. If the program is extended, the government retains the option of extending its interest *pro rata*. The government also has the power to control the transfer of shares and thereby the degree of Canadian ownership and control. This kind of participation by the government is to be welcomed; otherwise heavy public expenditures are incurred, and any benefits would accrue almost exclusively to a few individuals and companies. Control would also be more likely to pass out of Canadian hands, a matter regarded as more serious by some than by others.

In general, federal interest in northern development has tended to vacillate, and much of the assistance that has been given appears to benefit mining interest in the South rather than the local population. Certain cost benefit studies have been made for internal use (among them a 1965 study by the Stanford Research Institute on the Alaska Highway), but the results are not generally available. While negotiations with particular companies are taking place, the Department of Indian Affairs and Northern Development cannot be expected to release information on its calculations or the investment intentions of companies, but there does not seem to be any reason why such information could not be made public several years after. Without it, there is no way of evaluating the policies which are being pursued. It is worth noting in this regard that although general guidelines are laid down for the granting of aid, a certain degree of bargaining with individual companies does take place.[1]

The policy decision as to how far to make aid specific and automatic is a difficult one. If each case has to be decided on its merits, the overhead costs of investigation will be heavier than they would be otherwise; there are also likely to be administrative delays and charges of discrimination when aid is given to A but not to B. From the standpoint of a firm about to embark on a new enterprise there are obvious advantages in knowing beforehand precisely what assistance can be expected. But there are also dis-

---

[1] Commercial considerations do not necessitate information being kept secret permanently, a view shared by the chief economist in the Department, who considered it reasonable to release copies of agreements after a suitable time period, though he was careful to point out that his views were not to be interpreted as expressing government policy. One such agreement has indeed already been made public, that with the Anvil Mining Corporation Ltd. which was presented before Parliament on March 14, 1968 (Hansard, Vol. VII, p. 7607).

advantages in this approach. The automatic granting of aid can lead to waste. There may be reason to expect one plant to operate successfully in a particular locality, for example, but the presence of two may weaken the prospects of both.

While it is possible to review the various federal programs of northern development in isolation, such programs are, in fact, but one part of a much larger picture in which, as has been seen, a variety of objectives and measures are involved. In the final chapter a return is made to some of the main themes of discussion in an effort to encompass the scene as a whole and to draw conclusions.

# *12. Conclusion*

SHARP DIFFERENCES in income and employment opportunity across the country strike at the very roots of national cohesion and well-being. In recent years an awareness of this fact, coupled with the realization that aggregative measures intended to maintain an adequate demand at the national level do not suffice in themselves to solve regional problems, has led the federal government to take action on a number of fronts.

Part of this action has taken the form of programs set up under ARDA, ADA, and the ADB. Federal expenditures under these programs are increasing rapidly, but they constitute only one part of the total volume of federal aid to the less favoured regions of the country.[1] They are supplemented by various forms of fiscal transfers and by direct support of particular industries and bodies, though the poorer regions are by no means the only ones to benefit from federal subventions, and some federal institutions, among them the Industrial Development Bank, provide much greater assistance to firms in the richer than in the poorer provinces.

In spite of the wide variety of forms of aid provided, incomes in depressed areas remain chronically below the national average and unemployment and under-employment remain well above it.

[1] As this book goes to press, past expenditures and future commitments including those under FRED are approaching one billion dollars. Particular concern is being felt over the rate at which some of these commitments are growing, and once again major changes in policy appear to be in the offing.

The quality of education and other services suffers in such areas, and the lack of economic opportunity continues to breed a sense of frustration and injustice. Where these differences are associated with particular ethnic groups, such as the Indians or French Canadians, the problem assumes a new dimension which further weakens the fabric of Canadian society.

The federal government is now reassessing its regional policies but to some extent solutions lie with the provincial governments, which have often failed to take appropriate steps in fields under their jurisdiction. The Quebec government, for example, gave education much less support for many years than did most other provinces, and federal efforts to participate in this field have met with strong resistance. But even admitting this, there is a limit to what the poorer provincial governments can be expected to do without substantial federal assistance. For one thing, many of them are heavily in debt. There is a striking difference between the levels of provincial per capita net debt across the country, varying from zero in British Columbia to $500 and over in Prince Edward Island, New Brunswick, and Newfoundland. The overriding difficulty, however, lies with the lack of clearly stated objectives and a coherent framework for policy within which the various governments and their agencies can work together rather than at cross-purposes. It was the recognition of this which led in large measure to the creation of the federal department of regional affairs in July 1968. A major reorganization of administrative machinery to deal with regional problems was patently needed.

## The Need for Objectives

Although the federal government is clearly concerned with regional disparities, how far it is prepared to go in securing greater equality across the country is still unclear. It has been very cautious in stating its over-all objectives in precise terms. In spite of an expressed dissatisfaction with high unemployment and low incomes in the Atlantic provinces, for instance, government statements on policy fall short of indicating the degree to which disparities might be acceptable. If 30 per cent is too high a disparity between per capita incomes in the Atlantic provinces and those in the rest of the country, would 20 per cent be an appropriate objective? Or is it enough if incomes there maintain a growth-rate similar to that elsewhere? Understandably, governments do not wish to commit themselves to specific figures until they have some assurance of achieving them and some indication of the probable costs involved in their attainment. Lacking certainty about either of these matters, federal pronouncements on the subject are confined to generalities, but generalities are not likely to satisfy the poorer provinces indefinitely.

Ottawa also remains silent on the question of population distribution, another important issue. Though assistance to individuals is given in approved cases under the manpower mobility program, little or no attempt has been made to determine or influence interprovincial trends. Some indication of the changes that are taking place in the regional distribution of manpower in Canada is furnished by data on increases in the labour force in 1966 and 1967, which averaged an increase of 1.5 per cent in the Prairies, 2 per cent in the Atlantic provinces, about 4 per cent in the central provinces, and about 7 per cent in British Columbia.

It is commonly argued on economic grounds that if rewards for comparable effort are higher in some provinces than in others, labour should be encouraged to move from the lower to the higher income provinces. The same type of argument, however, is often rejected when the subject at issue is the *international* movement of labour because of the deleterious effect of the "brain drain". Those who are indifferent to provincial boundaries do not see the migration of labour in the same light as those who attach importance to them and seek the expansion of output and incomes in individual provinces. But whatever stand is taken on this issue, changes in the distribution of population not only influence the distribution of political power but have far-reaching implications for the economic future of particular regions, inducing a more rapid expansion of output in some and a less rapid expansion or decline in others.

In Canada, as in the Scandinavian countries, low densities of population inhibit development in various regions and add greatly to the cost of providing essential services. The economies of scale that characterize many operations and the advantages that accrue from the concentration of industry in larger centres pose a constant threat to communities in sparsely populated areas. Any gains in bolstering up such communities have to be weighed against the costs and in many cases out-migration from them is the wisest course to pursue. There is a need for policies to facilitate the decline of certain areas as well as the expansion of others. It is a complete delusion to believe that every impoverished part of the country can be restored to prosperity and it would make little sense to try.

Evidence of the extent to which these population movements accentuate or reduce regional per capita income disparities is scant. It seems probable, however, that the movement of younger and better educated people from poorer areas of the country, however desirable it may be on other grounds, benefits residents in the areas to which they move more than those in the areas from which they come. For one thing, residents of the latter may be faced with heavy education and maintenance expenditures they cannot recoup. In this respect the poorer provinces and poorer areas within a province are subsidizing the richer ones, and the fact that education accounts for a large proportion of provincial expenditures makes the situation that much more serious.

The federal government contributes financially to the costs of provincial vocational training programs as well as to university education, but although the contributions are substantial, the poorer provinces have not benefited as much as the others. In the case of manpower training programs, the federal government paid 75 per cent of the total expenditures under the capital-assistance program for the development of training facilities between April 1961 and 1966. The total outlay was over one billion dollars and provided 350,000 new places for students. Of this 350,000, however, Ontario accounted for 180,000 and the Atlantic provinces for a mere 10,000. Alberta and British Columbia, which are wealthy provinces, accounted for another 70,000. Account should also be taken of the fact that the provision of increased training facilities in the poorer provinces will not suffice to increase incomes and employment there. If that is what is desired, there must also be an increase in local employment opportunities. Otherwise such facilities seem likely to lead to a widening of the income gap between the provinces and to an increasing flow of the population towards the richer ones.

A crucial issue, which is far from being resolved, is the determination of the most appropriate boundaries for areas that are to qualify for special assistance. These boundaries cannot be determined, however, until the policy objectives themselves are made more explicit. That this needs to be stressed is a reflection of the widespread confusion that prevails on the subject. Not infrequently attempts are made to establish the perimeter of an economic region as though such a region were a phenomenon existing in its own right, independent of the purpose for its delimitation. It makes a fundamental difference, however, whether the objective is the relief of distress or the development of economic potential.

Those living in the poorest areas are understandably anxious to have the boundaries drawn on the basis of distress. However, if growth rather than the amelioration of distress is the objective, the government must choose boundaries bearing in mind growth potential, dismaying to many though this may be. Either way there is bound to be criticism, especially from adjacent areas that are not designated and that have problems or potentials not significantly different from those that are. By their very nature, area development policies or relief measures favour some areas at the expense of others.

Nor can we escape discrimination merely by increasing the size and number of areas that are to qualify for special assistance, as both ARDA and ADA have indeed been doing. Some limits must be set; but even if most of the country were designated, certain areas would still benefit more than others. Yet a further difficulty in the selection of areas to be assisted is that differences of opinion are bound to arise over the question as to whether or not economic potential does in fact exist. In many cases there will be an element of doubt.

## The Need for a Coherent Framework

Though the possibilities have not been exhausted, many forms of aid are currently available. There is a serious lack of co-ordination among the various bodies concerned, however, and it is often difficult to know who is responsible for doing what. The ADB has concentrated on infra-structure, ADA on tax concessions and later on capital grants to industry, ARDA on physical improvements to land and later on education. Provincial governments have contributed cheap loans and serviced land. The Department of Manpower has assisted with mobility grants and training programs, the Central Mortgage and Housing Corporation with housing. In short, there seems to be something for everybody. But how effective are these various incentives, and what sort of a pattern of regional development is likely to emerge from them? No one is sure. Some effort has been made to ascertain the reaction of industrialists to the incentives ADA is offering them, but to a very large extent the government is still operating in the dark. In so far as growth is the objective, very little is yet known about the steps necessary to achieve it.[1] We know equally little about the inter-relationship of various regions, however they are defined, and there is no indication as to how economic goals that are established for different regions fit into national objectives.

It is difficult to see how much sense can be made of our regional economic policies without a more coherent framework for policy than presently exists. Admittedly, various parcels of aid can continue to be distributed here and there for this purpose and for that, but it is hard to believe that this is the best that can be done. There comes a time, especially during a period of financial stringency, when ministers of finance balk at this sort of approach and ask, reasonably enough, for a statement of objectives and expendi-

[1] Recent studies have added to our knowledge, however. One such is Thomas A. Wilson and N. Harvey Lithwick, *The Sources of Economic Growth* (Studies of the Royal Commission on Taxation, No. 24 [Ottawa: Queen's Printer, 1968]). At the present time much emphasis is placed on the importance of education, but not all educational expenditures are likely to contribute significantly to growth, besides which many people have little ambition to pursue their education beyond a quite modest level.

ture patterns into which the estimates of the various agencies and departments fit, and since regional development typically entails long-run measures, expenditure patterns have to be seen in terms of programs extending over a prolonged period of time. It may well take one or two decades, for example, before significant structural changes can be completed in eastern Quebec or the Atlantic provinces.

It is here that planning can play an important role by determining the strategy of development and outlining the steps for its fulfilment. Half measures or attempts to bolster up declining industries are likely to prove both costly and fruitless. Such attempts have been one of the most wasteful features of both federal and provincial policies in the Atlantic provinces, and they have retarded the whole process of structural transformation. The sums necessary to delay collapse have increased year by year, but to no avail.

One of the main criticisms of ADA's policy is that locational incentives are paid according to a formula based on a criterion of distress, with inadequate regard for an assessment of costs and benefits. If the objective is to encourage secondary manufacturers to locate in specific areas, it is not enough that unemployment exists in such areas and that high enough subventions will induce some manufacturers to settle there. It is necessary to have some idea of the area's potential for development and of the types of activity that are most likely to contribute to its sustained growth, questions to which the ADB is addressing itself.

It is true that if labour located in a depressed area is immobile and cannot be induced to move, or if its transfer elsewhere is not desired and the alternative is unemployment or under-employment, there are obvious merits in encouraging industry to establish in the area. But the most appropriate type of aid does not necessarily lie in encouraging the location of secondary manufacturing industry. Other types of activity may be preferable. By singling out secondary manufacturers for special aid, ADA automatically discriminates against those depressed areas where the main hope for development lies in other types of industry. In any event, aid is likely to be far more effective if it is provided as part of an over-all pattern of development, such as an industrial complex with interrelated plants, not just handed out piecemeal to individual applicants; and if it is made available when the threat of unemployment is first apparent, not when unemployment has become chronic.

ARDA, in its selection of Special Rural Development Areas, has recognized the importance of potential for growth and is spending heavily on measures designed to develop it. It now has a more sophisticated approach to the problems of rural development than characterized its operations at the outset. Its concern with the physical characteristics of land is less than it was, and its concern with upgrading the skills and quality of the labour force is greater. It recognizes that where there are strong underlying forces leading to the economic decline of certain areas, there may be little that governments can or perhaps should do except to smooth the process of transition. The economic demise of many small areas may have to be accepted. In other cases a major restructuring of the area may be indispensable.

But in its efforts to achieve a change in the economic structure of impoverished areas, ARDA is handicapped by the lack of any comparable agency operating on the industrial front. The problems of rural areas cannot be solved in isolation; rural and industrial areas have to be seen in conjunction with each other. Some rural areas are particularly lacking in economic potential, and while miscellaneous measures of a palliative nature might be undertaken in them, the only real hope for the local population is out-migration. The encouragement of such migration, however, cannot be implemented effectively unless adequate opportunities are made available elsewhere.

As has now been recognized, some branch of the federal government is urgently needed with a prime responsibility for examining the interrelationship of various measures and policies introduced by the numerous government agencies and bodies. The fact that provincial governments as well as the federal are active in the promotion of industrial development frequently leads to a conflict of purpose, and sharp differences of opinion often exist on the form that action should take. The problem is compounded by the constitutional division of powers for economic affairs.

So far as provincial incentives to industry are concerned, the richer provinces and municipalities are in a good position to outbid the poorer if they choose to do so. In their anxiety to compete for new industry, some of the poorer provinces and their agencies have been led into making subventions that have cost them dearly. A number of the enterprises which they have supported have failed outright or been kept in operation only with continued subventions. It is beginning to be learned that the scramble for industry can be extremely costly to the participants.[1]

One of the unsatisfactory features of the competition to attract industry is that it is frequently prompted by a municipality's need to increase its revenues, so that it can cover rising educational costs, which constitute one of the largest items in the municipal budget. Poorer areas experience difficulty in providing adequate educational services. Their tax problems may be eased if they succeed in attracting industry, which will contribute more to their revenues because it is taxed at a higher rate, and a municipality that falls under ADA's provisions is in a better position to do this. But is this desirable? What we are doing, in effect, is helping municipalities to meet educational expenditures by policies that steer industry into what seem likely to be less favourable locations. Surely the solution to inadequate municipal tax revenue should be sought in a redistribution of tax burdens, not in policies designed to influence the location of industry. If we are to have effective area development policies, some way has to be found of redistributing the tax burden. It makes little sense for the quality of a child's education to be determined by the success or failure of a municipality to lure industry into its bailiwick.

Unbridled competition for new industry between provinces or areas within a province is most unlikely to contribute to solutions

[1] Here again there are many parallels with other countries. The competition for industry between individual islands in the West Indies has resulted in the granting of concessions which are to the advantage of developers rather than to the economy as a whole.

that are in the national interest, and one of the prime responsibilities of the federal government should be to ensure that the national interest remains uppermost.

Individual provinces, largely if not completely independently of each other, are preparing plans of varying degrees of comprehensiveness. Prince Edward Island recently joined the ranks of the provinces preparing such plans, but it is not clear how far the recommendations of its planning body will be integrated with those of the ADB, which is responsible for the Atlantic region as a whole. There is a strong disposition on the part of individual provinces to go their own way. In general, however, the poorest provinces favour a strong central government which will be able and willing to afford them aid, and the richer provinces prefer to see a greater measure of local autonomy and control over economic affairs, a phenomenon which is not peculiar to Canada.

Interprovincial competition for industry has put the federal government in a difficult position. It has been anxious to avoid taking sides and, given the extensive concern of provincial governments with problems of industrial development within their borders, it might be to the federal government's advantage to allow them to undertake much of the initiative in putting forward recommendations for federal aid, as they do under the ARDA program. There is much to be said for the view that the extent and nature of aid to depressed areas should be conditional upon the province's furnishing an assessment of the area's needs and potentials, and formulating a program for development into which the aid will fit. The federal government could asssist in the preparation of such programs and, as in the case of ARDA, have the power to accept or reject them. The FRED programs provide much valuable experience on which to build both at the conceptual and the implementation stage.

Apart from any other consideration, it may be asked whether the richer provinces are not well able to provide whatever assistance is needed to depressed areas within their own boundaries. It is hard to believe that extensive federal assistance under the ARDA or ADA program is required to enable the governments of Ontario or British Columbia to assist their poorer areas. The federal government might well concentrate its resources on those provinces, where the need for assistance is patently great.[1]

While islands of poverty exist in the richer provinces, it is in the Atlantic region, eastern Quebec, and parts of Manitoba where poverty is widespread and economic opportunities are most lacking. People in these areas are largely cut off from the main stream of economic life. Their opportunities for profitable employment are limited. Many are in a trap in which inadequate education, services, and income create the very conditions and attitudes that inhibit development. Market forces cannot be relied upon to solve their problems and without federal help their future will remain bleak.

In every part of Canada, including the North, government interest in development has waxed and waned. When times are prosperous and unemployment levels have dropped in the depressed regions, attention to their problems tends to decline. This is understandable, but it is not conducive to long-run solutions. Indeed, it is during periods of prosperity that the most effective action can often be taken. Efforts to encourage the movement of people and the establishment of new industry are likely to be more productive when levels of demand are high than when they are low.

What is required is a sustained as well as a comprehensive approach to regional economic problems. There are no quick solutions, nor are there permanent ones. The scene is constantly changing, and the prosperous areas of one period may well become the depressed areas of another. In this sense we are never likely to reach the end of the road, but at least we do not have to travel it alone. A great many other countries are concerned with regional problems too. Depressed areas within Britain, the European Common Market, and the United States have been the subject

---

[1] The mere fact that a province might not receive federal aid should not be interpreted, however, as an indication of federal indifference to its actions. The subsidizing of industry within one province could exacerbate the problems of others. Provincial actions have important national repercussions.

of extensive discussion and action, and their experience can serve as a guide. But what we must do at the outset is achieve closer agreement between the provincial and federal governments on the direction that area policies should take and the roles that individual governments should play in them. This is of paramount importance. Virtually all else depends upon it – the selection of boundaries, the types and extent of aid, and the form and integration of various regional plans. Without such agreement, the task of reducing regional disparities is likely to prove an impossible one.

# Appendix A

T. N. Brewis

## The Data

An effort has been made in recent years to increase the volume and quality of statistics on sub-provincial areas, and to keep it more up to date, but progress has been slow. There are several explanations for this. There is no one concept of a region for which data might be collected, as observed in Chapter 2. Then there is the problem of cost. Collection of data on small areas would call for a great increase in the required sample of data, and even were this done such data might not be published because of the information that might be disclosed on individual firms. Moreover, if our concern is with development, it becomes necessary to collect data on a wide variety of indicators, the relative importance of which will be assessed differently by different observers. In a number of cases no suitable indicator may even exist. There is no way, for example, of measuring regional differences in entrepreneurial talent, though some evidence of such differences may be reflected in profits and bankruptcies.

There is no obvious solution to these problems, but some might be reduced. James Gilmour, for example, has pointed out that the restrictions imposed on publication by the D.B.S. may be needlessly severe. He expresses his conviction "that most firms in an industry know more about each other's operations than D.B.S. could reveal if unimpeded by any restrictions on what it published", and adds that too much secrecy may retard the discovery of social and economic illness.[1] Another deficiency to which he calls attention is the frequency

[1] James M. Gilmour, "The Joint Anarchy of 'Confidentiality' and Definitional Change", *The Canadian Geographer*, X, No. 1 (1966), 40-8. Gilmour's views are not shared by officials in the Bureau of Statistics, who point out that firms are in fact much concerned with questions of disclosure. A combination of data made available by federal and provincial governments makes possible in some cases the calculation of residuals. Thus small area data present a hazard.

and extent of definitional changes. Some of these changes may be unavoidable, but since there are no satisfactory linkages with the past, historical analysis becomes virtually impossible. Any investigator attempting to undertake statistical research on sub-provincial areas quickly becomes aware of both problems.[2]

## Statistical Techniques

### Location Quotients and Coefficients of Localization

Among the more commonly employed statistical measures used in regional analysis are location quotients and coefficients of localization. The former measures the degree of concentration of an industry in a particular region; the latter measures the extent to which an industry is concentrated in the country as a whole.

Using employment as one of several possible bases, the location quotient for an industry is obtained by dividing the percentage a region has of national employment in the industry by the percentage a region has of national industrial employment as a whole. The higher the quotient the greater the degree of concentration. Thus in 1961, when the Province of Quebec accounted for 78 per cent of total employment in tobacco manufacturing and 33 per cent of all industrial employment, the quotient was 2.36, indicating a high degree of concentration and suggesting that tobacco manufacturing would be a source of direct or indirect "exports" from Quebec. The "export" industries are likely to be those most influential in determining the magnitude of regional growth.

The technique can also be used to test linkages between industries. The greater the quotient that results from dividing the percentage of employment in one industry by that in another industry, the *less* the linkage.

The method of determining the coefficient of localization for an industry, using employment as a base, is described below.

|  |  | Regions | | | |
|---|---|---|---|---|---|
|  |  | A | B | C | D |
| (a) | % of national employment in Industry Y | 30 | 10 | 20 | 40 |
| (b) | % of national industrial employment as a whole | 20 | 5 | 40 | 35 |
|  | Location quotient (a ÷ b) | 1.5 | 2.0 | .5 | 1.14 |
| (c) | Differences (a − b) | +10 | + 5 | −20 | + 5 |
| (d) | (c ÷ 100) | .1 | .05 | − .2 | .05 |

2 The official explanation given for the latter deficiency is that the Bureau has felt obliged to concentrate on the provision of current data because of insufficient staff.

The coefficient of localization is the sum of all the positive percentages in line (d) above, namely 0.2. An industry with a heavy concentration will have a coefficient close to unity, and with a light concentration, close to zero, zero and unity being the outside limits.

Location quotients and localization coefficients will differ according to the area selected (indicating once again the importance that attaches to the choice of spatial boundaries), and also according to the degree of sub-classification of the industry in question. Transport equipment, for example, covers a variety of products, and quotients and coefficients vary greatly according to the way in which these are grouped.

There are other points to bear in mind. Given the very heavy concentration of industry in certain areas of Canada, a specific industry in these areas will show a low coefficient of localization when the coefficient is computed using total industrial employment or output as a base even though the industry is concentrated there. The same coefficient could, moreover, reflect very different distributions of industry. To refer to the figure above, a coefficient of localization of 0.2 would also have been obtained had the percentage of employment in Industry Y been 40, 5, 40, and 15 in the four regions respectively. As for the coefficient itself, its magnitude will vary according to the base used, for example employment or value added.

Small, medium, and large plants range from high coefficients of localization to low, but there tends to be positive correlation between size of plant and geographic concentration. The very large plants, those of tobacco manufacture being a case in point, generally show a high coefficient of localization. Somewhat surprisingly extreme concentration also seems to be characteristic of industries with medium-sized plants, the explanation for this presumably being the economies of agglomeration. Industries characterized by small plants tend to be most geographically dispersed, but wood-products manufacture, which is also characterized mainly by small plants, has a high localization coefficient. Extreme care must therefore be used in interpreting data; quite unwarranted impressions can be gained from uncritical acceptance of tables of coefficients.

### The "Shift" Method of Measuring Differential Growth

The "shift" method of presenting data employed by Perloff[3] measures the magnitude of the changes in population, income, job distribution, or other variables among the different provinces or regions of the country as a percentage of national changes. All provinces increased

3 Harvey S. Perloff and Vera W. Dodds, *op. cit.*, Chapter 4.

## Table A:1
## Net Shift in Population by Province
### (as % of the total net shift)
### 1946-1966

|  | 1946-51 | 1951-6 | 1956-61 | 1961-6 |
|---|---|---|---|---|
| Newfoundland | — | + 0.1 | − 5.9 | + 2.7 |
| Prince Edward Island | − 3.2 | − 5.8 | − 3.7 | − 2.9 |
| Nova Scotia | −18.3 | −18.2 | −23.3 | −24.8 |
| New Brunswick | − 8.6 | −15.8 | −14.2 | −14.3 |
| Quebec | +14.5 | −11.2 | + 4.8 | + 0.1 |
| Ontario | +29.7 | +54.7 | +48.9 | +46.4 |
| Manitoba | −17.2 | −17.5 | −19.3 | −26.8 |
| Saskatchewan | −52.7 | −31.4 | −33.7 | −31.2 |
| Alberta | +26.8 | +19.1 | +26.7 | + 5.2 |
| British Columbia | +28.9 | +26.1 | +19.7 | +45.7 |

Note: Population in the Atlantic provinces, Manitoba, and Saskatchewan
has not increased as rapidly as in the country as a whole. Ontario,
Alberta, and British Columbia accounted for almost all the gains
above the national average.

Sources: 1946-61: D.B.S., *Canada Year Book*, various years.

in population between 1946-66, for example, but some very much
more than others. By applying the national growth rate to each area
under study, a norm can be established against which the *actual*
growth can be compared. The deviations from this norm or "expected"
growth are then totalled, and the individual changes are expressed as
a percentage of it. To illustrate, between 1961 to 1966 the national
population increased by 1,677,000, an increase of 9.2 per cent. Four
provinces exceeded this norm by a total of 181,300 and six fell below
it by roughly the same number. Of the 181,300 excess, Ontario
accounted for 46.4 per cent and British Columbia for 45.7 per cent.
It should be noted, however, that while Ontario accounted for the
lion's share of the total shift in population, this does not indicate that
it was growing more rapidly in percentage terms than in British
Columbia, since the population of British Columbia is only one-
quarter the size. In percentage terms, British Columbia's population
was in fact growing at a more rapid rate, 15.7 per cent as against 11.1

per cent for Ontario. As Perloff recognizes, there is no fully satisfactory way of combining percentage and absolute changes to measure differential economic growth, but the "shift" technique which he employs throws into strong relief some of the spatial changes that have been occurring, and is a useful measure of differential growth.

# Appendix B

T. K. Rymes

## Some Comments on Regional Economic Accounts

One of the more modest but none the less important advances in modern economics has been the development of integrated national economic accounting systems.[1] All economists, be they academic researchers or government policy advisers, now use as a matter of course the national economic accounts in their study and work. In some parts of the accounting system, such as national wealth measurement, progress in their development has not been as fast as in other parts, such as the sector income and expenditure accounts. In most countries, certainly in Canada, regional economic accounts, which may be regarded as a disaggregation of the national economic accounts have been, until very recently, virtually non-existent. What are the reasons for this?

Though to some extent the national economic accounts have had a life of their own, one of the reasons for the vast amount of work done on them since World War II has been the increased role of the state in the determination of the level and composition of economic activity. The state and the economy concerned have been the nation-state and the national economy. As a consequence, the principal developments in national economic accounting have been designed, at least principally, if not entirely, to meet the needs of the authorities

---

[1] The expression "social accounting systems" is often used. "Social accounts" tends to imply, however, that other social phenomena besides economic ones are being quantified and recorded in an articulated, integrated balancing system of accounts. Though attempts along these lines are being made (cf. B. M. Gross, *The State of the Nation: Social Systems Accounting* [London: Tavistock Publications, 1966]), the value of the results to date suggests that "economic" and not "social" accounting systems is the more correct, and less pretentious, designation to use.

260

of the nation state who are concerned with the implementation and effects of monetary and aggregate fiscal and commercial policies.

Recently, two developments suggest that "the national accounts" will undergo further aggregation as well as increased disaggregation. First, the need for increased policy collaboration in a world characterized by greater economic interdependence is forcing groups of countries, such as the Organisation for Economic Co-operation and Development (O.E.C.D.) and the Group of Ten, to prepare their accounts along similar lines so that international comparison of the accounting records of the economic performance of the various collaborating countries is facilitated.[2] On this count, then, one may expect to see "international" economic accounts for groups of closely knit economies such as the Group of Ten, the European Common Market, and the European Free Trade Association. Second, in some countries, and this is clearly the case in Canada, the differences among political and regional economic units within the nation state are causing a retreat from economic policies that are imposed mainly at the national level to ones that result from co-operation among national and regional authorities. As a consequence, there is an increased demand for much of the "national economic accounting" system to be reproduced at the provincial or regional level.

Two basic matters should be raised at this point. First, recent work on the economic theory of the optimum constitution[3] suggests that responsibility for economic policies should be partitioned and not shared proportionally; that is, some matters such as the *conduct* of monetary policy should be left in the hands of the national government; whereas others such as welfare and some aspects of redistribution and area development should be more appropriately in the hands of provincial and municipal governments. Yet it is increasingly clear, at least in Canada, that what were thought to be the appropriate lines of division of responsibilities for economic policies are rapidly changing. Certain provinces, if they do not want a hand in the conduct of monetary policy, for instance, certainly want a voice in its formu-

---

[2] Thus, discrepancies in concepts with respect to capital formation and disagreements about the role of imputations in the national accounts are being ironed out, and international agreement as to the basic set of conventions to be followed is being achieved. See, for example, United Nations Economic and Social Council, *Proposals for the Revision of the Standard National Accounts* (New York: United Nations Organization, August 1967). For a review of recent discussions concerning the latest revision to U.N. recommendations regarding national accounting, see H. S. Tice, "Report of a Conference on the Proposals for Revision of the United Nations System of National Accounts", *Review of Income and Wealth*, XIII (March 1967), 36-102.

[3] See A. Breton, "A Theory of Government Grants", *Canadian Journal of Economics and Political Science*, XXXI (May 1965), 175-87, and the subsequent debate in later issues.

lation. Second, since economic information entails both private and social outlay for its collection, processing, and interpretation, the directions in which regional economic accounts are pushed must be chosen to ensure maximum return to this outlay. The lines of such development will partially reflect the policies undertaken by the various governments. Lack of clarity as to which economic policies are most efficiently conducted by the national government, groups of provinces, provinces, regions within provinces, metropolitan regions, and smaller municipalities, and as to the extent to which certain policies can be shared by these authorities, leads to a great deal of uncertainty about how detailed regional economic accounts should be. There is also uncertainty as to in which direction (stocks versus flow, technological versus financial accounts) they should be promoted and how the problems of integrating these various regional accounts with one another and with the national account can best be overcome. On matters of the detail and level of disaggregation, one can contemplate the construction of quarterly "deflated" intra-urban input-output accounts, but it would be far too ambitious to attempt at present to do so. One must select those parts of the economic accounting system which should be developed at the regional level.

In this appendix regional input-output accounts, together with measures of industry outputs and inputs in "real" or "deflated" terms at the regional level, are examined. Many of the problems involved are similar to those found in the national system, though in the regional system spatial aspects of such problems need fuller examination. In choosing to devote most of my attention to these areas, I am implicitly expressing the view that in the near future policy and research related to regional economic problems and development will be concerned most with *production* relationships at the regional level. It is true that such a view is in large measure incompatible with the historical approach to regional economic questions in Canada. In the past, concern with intergovernment transfer mechanisms designed to eliminate gross regional disparities in private and public *consumption* has led to attendant emphasis upon personal income and outlay accounting by region. It is not suggested here that inequality of the interregional distribution of economic welfare is no longer the concern of senior and junior governments in this country. Far from it. Governments now seek to find *explanations* of such inequalities. Collaboration over the appropriate mix of national policies must be achieved so that aggregate demand for the national economy is set at full employment levels. Once this goal has been achieved, a careful examination of the interrelatedness of regional production relationships would then throw light on the remaining sources of inequality among regions.

The importance of studies of the interrelatedness of regional production relationships should be emphasized. It is of limited value to examine the production relationships existing within a region without considering their place in national and international production relationships. For example, the input-output structure of industry in the Maritimes cannot be understood independently of an appraisal of the effects which national commercial (e.g., tariff) policy has had in determining such relationships. Thus, the problems of constructing what may be called "the Production Account" within interregional economic accounts will be stressed here. I shall also show where they fit into the over-all regional and national economic accounting systems so that the place and importance of recording production relationships is not unduly emphasized. I believe that knowledge of such relationships will make a contribution to the resolution of regional disparities in consumption.

## National Economic Accounts

A brief review of most national economic accounts shows that they are divided in two basic ways: (1) some parts of the accounting deal with what are called flows, while others deal with stocks; (2) the accounts may be expressed either in current prices or in what are called constant prices. Thus, we have flow and stock accounts expressed in current and constant prices – four parts in all. Flow accounts measure national production, capital accumulation and consumption, and *transactions* in assets, both real and financial, over various *periods* of time (a month, a quarter, a year, etc.). Stock accounts measure capital stocks by industry, national and sectoral balance sheets, and national wealth at various *points* of time. Customarily, these components of the flow and stock accounts are measured by the national accountant in current prices – that is, in the average prices over a period of or at a point in time to which the measures pertain. Increasingly, components are being expressed in "constant prices" – that is, in the average prices over one particular period for all the periods of time covered by the measures.

The reader should be familiar with the major conventions employed by the national accountants and the major limitations from which national accounts suffer.

First, the theoretical concept of the value of economic production entails the measure of the value of the services of all primary inputs of production – labour, natural agents, and man-made instruments of production – at their implicit opportunity costs, regardless of whether a market with its various possible stages of development and imperfections places a value on the services of such primary inputs. For example, the economic theorist would consider the services of the housewife as part of economic production, as well as the net return to capital such as roadways, which are collectively owned but on which no recorded profit is privately earned. The national accountant is confronted in such cases with a problem. His measures of the value of economic production, which includes the wages and salaries of housewives if they are paid for part-time work in the market-place and the profits of privately operated turnpike corporations, can only, with increasing subjectiveness, be extended to cover the services of primary inputs for which the market is generating no "objective" valuation. The national accountant may extend his boundary-line of measured production by a process known as imputation.[4] The more he relies on this device, however, the more his measures of production reflect his values rather than those of the people making up the economy whose activities he is trying to record. For a country whose regions reflect great disparities both in economic development and in the extent to which economic production receives a market appraisal, the regional accounts for that country, if the same boundary-line of economic production is employed throughout, will be of varying degrees of trustworthiness. In Canada there are regions where the main economic activity appears to be largely agricultural, which raises the attendant problem of imputing a value to food production consumed by farm households. There are also regions where much of the capital accumulation has been undertaken by the state, which raises the attendant difficulty of including in that region's measure of economic production the estimated net return to the stock of social capital within that region. As a consequence, comparisons of the product of the heterogeneous regions making up this country should be made with care – particularly when such comparisons are made over a period when the composition of industrial production and the relative importance of state activity are changing within each region and among regions.

Second, the national accountant must decide what fraction of the expenditures made by transactors (households, governments, and firms) in any economy is final and what fraction represents capital

4 It is sometimes argued that the process of imputation in the national accounts is carried out to prevent measures of national product from fluctuating solely in response to non-economic institutional changes which the national accountant's otherwise limited measure of production would reflect. The classic example of such fluctuation is Pigou's illustration that when a man marries his housekeeper, measured national income falls. This argument is not correct, however. Fluctuations in any measure of economic product will occur in response to non-economic changes. The role which imputation plays is simply to permit the national accountant to bring the measurement of output as close to the comprehensive concept of the economic theorist as criteria of objective measurement procedures permit.

accumulation as compared to current consumption. There is evidence that part of what the national accountant regards as final expenditures by governments are really flows of intermediate input-type services to firms. At present, it is only possible to allocate these governmental expenditures to the industries concerned and to calculate the incidence of such expenditures back to ultimate entities in "net fiscal incidence" studies in a most arbitrary way.[5] Thus, differences among regions and over time in the "intermediate" function of governments must be taken into account in comparisons of regional products. There is growing evidence that the scope of the conventional definition of capital accumulation employed by national accounts, while appropriate for examining the cyclical disturbances of economies, is probably less helpful for the examination of the record of secular economic growth. Broader concepts of capital accumulation, which would include "investments" by households, businesses, and the state in education and medical care, are probably more suitable to the study of economic development – and this would hold for regional economic accounts as well. National accountants clearly recognize the need for such changes, but such difficulties as how to split private expenditures on education into their consumption and accumulation components and how to split the income of households possessing "human capital" into returns to labour and capital services, prevent their easy introduction into the national economic accounts – and again these difficulties would hold for regional economic accounts as well.

It is important to keep these general conceptual problems in mind in turning to the following simple presentation of the standard national accounts. In Table B:1, such accounts are set out for the three main sectors of an isolated economy, households, governments, and business, showing the *ex post* results of the principal economic activities of production, consumption, capital accumulation, and financial transactions. It will be apparent from this table that when the results of economic activity are measured and added up for all the sectors (the total columns), income less consumption equals savings equals capital accumulation. This fundamental national accounting identity, true at the aggregate, is of course not true for any particular sector, and any net *financial* saving (or dissaving) by a

---

5 Consider the following example. Assume that part of the state's capital stock consists of roads. It can be argued, then, that in fact the state "rents" the services of such roads to households and firms. The national accountant, then, can attempt to measure the imputed gross rents and to charge such imputed rents against the households and industries which use such services. Expenditures by households on the products of the industries will contain indirectly such imputed gross rents and will thus be part of the expenditure incidence of governments. The measurement of the imputed gross rents and their allocation to households and industries is extremely difficult – so difficult that it is rarely done at all.

**Table B:1 The Standard Sector Accounts**

| | Households Dr. | Households Cr. | Governments Dr. | Governments Cr. | Businesses Dr. | Businesses Cr. | Total Dr. | Total Cr. |
|---|---|---|---|---|---|---|---|---|
| **Production Accounts** | | | | | | | | |
| Goods and Services | $II_{BH}+CCA_H$ | $C_{HH}$ | $II_{BG}+CCA_G$ | $G_{GG}$ | $II_{BB}+CCA_B$ | $IIQ_{BH+BG+BB}+G+G$ $+\Delta K_{H+G+B}$ | $CCA_{(H+G+B)}$ | $C_{HH}+C+G_{GG}+G+\Delta K_{H+G+B}$ |
| Net Domestic Product | $Y_H$ | | $Y_G$ | | $Y_B$ | | $Y_{(H+G+B)}$ | |
| **Income and Expenditure Accounts** | | | | | | | | |
| Net National Product | | $Y_H$ | | $Y_G$ | | $Y_B$ | | $Y_{(H+G+B)}$ |
| Goods and Services | $C_{HH}+C$ | | $G_{GG}+G$ | | | | $C_{HH}+C+G_{GG}+G$ | |
| Labour Service | $+W_{HH}$ | $W_{HH}+W_{GH}+W_{BH}$ | $W_{GH}$ | | $W_{BH}$ | | $W_{HH}+W_{GH}+W_{BH}$ | $W_{HH}+W_{GH}+W_{BH}$ |
| Capital Service | | $I_{GH}+I_{BH}$ | $I_{GH}$ | | $I_{BH}$ | | $I_{GH}+I_{BH}$ | $I_{GH}+I_{BH}$ |
| Taxes | $T_{HG}$ | | | $T_{HG}+T_{BG}$ | $T_{BG}$ | | $T_{HG}+T_{BG}$ | $T_{HG}+T_{BG}$ |
| Net Savings | $S_H$ | | $S_G$ | | $S_B$ | | $S_{(H+G+B)}$ | |
| **Capital Accounts** | | | | | | | | |
| Net Savings | | $S_H$ $CCA_H$ | | $S_G$ $CCA_G$ $FDS_G$ | | $S_B$ $CCA_B$ $FDS_B$ | | $S_{(H+G+B)}$ $CCA_{H+G+B}$ $FDS_{G+B}$ |
| Goods and Services | $\Delta K_H$ | | $\Delta K_G$ | | $\Delta K_B$ | | $\Delta K_{H+G+B}$ | |
| Financial Savings or Dissavings | $FS_H$ | | | | | | $FS_H$ | |

## Financial Transactions Accounts

| Financial Savings or Dissavings | FS$_H$ | FDS$_G$ | FDS$_B$ | FDS$_{G+B}$ | FS$_H$ |
|---|---|---|---|---|---|
| Bank Deposits | $+M_H$ | $-M_G$ | $-M_B$ | $+M_H-M_G-M_B$ | |
| Bonds | $+B_G$ | $+B_G$ | $+B_B$ | $+B_H$ | $+B_G+B_B$ |

**Mnemonic key to Table B:1: subscript H = the household sector, G = the government sector, B = the business sector.**

$+B_H$, $+B_G$, $+B_B \equiv$ Changes in bond assets and liabilities of the household, government, and business sectors.

$C \equiv$ Household consumption expenditures.

$CCA \equiv$ Capital consumption allowances.

$C_{HH} \equiv$ Household current consumption produced *within* the household sector.

FDS$_G$, FDS$_B \equiv$ Negative financial savings (i.e. dissavings) of the government and business sectors.

FS$_H \equiv$ Positive financial savings of the household sector.

$G \equiv$ Government consumption expenditures.

$G_{GG} \equiv$ Government current consumption produced *within* the government sector.

$I_{GH}$, $I_{BH} \equiv$ Interest and dividend receipts of households from the government and business sectors.

$II_{BB} \equiv IO_{BB} \equiv$ Intermediate inputs and outputs used and produced within the business sector.

$II_{BG} \equiv$ Intermediate inputs used by governments purchased from the business sector.

$II_{BH} \equiv$ Intermediate inputs used by households purchased from the business sector.

$\triangle K \equiv$ Capital accumulation by households, firms, and governments.

$+M_H$, $-M_G$, $-M_B \equiv$ Changes in bank deposits of the sectors.

$S \equiv$ Net savings.

$T_{HG}$, $T_{BG} \equiv$ Direct tax receipts of governments from households and businesses.

$W_{HH} \equiv$ Payments for labour service performed within the household sector.

$W_{GH}$, $W_{BH} \equiv$ Payments for labour service performed by governments and businesses.

$Y \equiv$ Net domestic product.

### Table B:2
### The Production Account for the Business Sector by Industry

| | Industry 1 | | Industry 2 | | |
| --- | --- | --- | --- | --- | --- |
| | Dr. | Cr. | Dr. | Cr. | |
| Goods and Services | $\sum_{i=1}^{n} II_{i1}$ $+CCA_1$ | $\sum_{i=1}^{n} IO_{1i}$ $+\sum_k FO_{1k}$ | $\sum_{i=1}^{n} II_{i2}$ $+CCA_2$ | $\sum_{i=1}^{n} IO_{2i}$ $+\sum_k FO_{2k}$ | . . . |
| Net Product | $Y_1$ | | $Y_2$ | | . . . |

surplus (or deficit) sector[6] is balanced by that sector's *transactions* in paper claims such as the bank deposit and bond examples used in Table B:1. The sum of net financial savings or dissavings for all sectors is equal to zero.[7] The introduction of sectors into the national accounts may be done in a variety of ways. It is usual and useful, however, to divide the economy into ultimate and intermediate entities. Business firms (such as railroads and manufacturing companies) are taken as intermediaries since, in the last analysis, their activities are concerned with the provision of goods and services for the ultimates – the households – of society. The ultimate entities of an economy appear in two basic forms: private families and unattached individuals and collectivities such as churches, fraternal organizations, and trade unions – loosely called "households" in Table B:1 – and major collectivities such as governments. The splitting of ultimate entities unambiguously into private and collective subsectors is not always easy nor is the splitting of the economy into ultimate and intermediate sectors.

6 J. G. Gurley and E. S. Shaw, *Money in a Theory of Finance* (Washington, D.C.: The Brookings Institutions, 1960), Chapter 2.

7 Some economists regard bank money as a component of national wealth (i.e. an asset that is not at the same time a liability) in which case the offsetting transactions in paper claims would be, in the example in Table B:1, limited to bonds alone, while changes in bank deposits would be considered as part of the output and capital accumulation of the economy. See B. P. Pesek and T. R. Saving, *Money, Wealth and Economic Theory* (New York: Macmillan, 1967).

| Industry n | | Total | |
|---|---|---|---|
| Dr. | Cr. | Dr. | Cr. |
| $\displaystyle\sum_{i=1}^{n} II_{in}$ $+CCA_n$ | $\displaystyle\sum_{i=1}^{n} IO_{ni}$ $+\sum_k FO_{nk}$ | $\displaystyle\sum_{i=1}^{n}\sum_{i=1}^{n} II_{ii}$ $+\sum_{i=1}^{n} CCA_1$ | $\displaystyle\sum_{i=1}^{n}\sum_{i=1}^{n} IO_{ii}$ $+\sum_k \sum_{i=1}^{n} FO_{ik}$ |
| $Y_n$ | | $\displaystyle\sum_{i=1}^{n} Y_i$ | |

( $\equiv$ between the Total columns )

A set of national and sectoral balance sheets may also be constructed. Until recently, the formidable problems involved in measuring the value of the stock of such assets as natural agents, privately traded paper claims, etc., and the difficulties associated with valuing the *net* stock of reproducible capital and the revaluation of assets owing to capital gains and losses, have stood in the way of much progress in the construction of such balance sheets.[8]

The Income and Expenditure Accounts in Table B:1, particularly the household sector, show a part of the economic accounting system in which there has been much interest at the regional level. The income of households equals earned income plus net unearned income plus any net transfers from other sectors. That figure is one frequently examined in regional income per caput studies. It could also be taken as net of direct taxes. As indicated earlier, in studies of the effects that government policies have upon the regional distribution of personal "income", allowance has to be made for the per caput regional

[8] For a further discussion of problems in the development of national and sector balance sheets, see R. W. Goldsmith and R. Lipsey, *Studies in the National Balance Sheet of the United States* (Princeton, N.J.: Princeton University Press for the National Bureau of Economic Research, 1963). For some experimental estimates of the stock of reproducible fixed capital in Canadian manufacturing, see D.B.S., *Fixed Capital Flows and Stocks, Manufacturing, Canada 1926-1960* (13-522), (Ottawa: Queen's Printer, 1967). For a discussion of national wealth measurement in Canada, see A. D. Scott, "Canada's Reproducible Wealth" in *The Measurement of National Wealth*, eds. R. Goldsmith and C. Saunders (London: Bowes & Bowes, 1959).

## Table B:3 A Standard Inter-Industry Table

| Outgoings or debits / Incomings or credits | Industries 1  2  ... n | Final Output | Total Output |
|---|---|---|---|
| Industries 1 | $II_{11}$  $II_{12}$ ...  $II_{1n}$ | $FO_1$ | $GO_1$ |
| 2 | $II_{21}$  $II_{22}$ ...  $II_{2n}$ | $FO_2$ | $GO_2$ |
| . | .    .    .   . | . | . |
| . | .   .   .   . | . | . |
| . | .   .   .   . | . | . |
| n | $II_{n1}$  $II_{n2}$ ...  $II_{nn}$ | $FO_n$ | $GO_n$ |
| CCA | $CCA_1$  $CCA_2$ ... $CCA_n$ | | |
| $Y_j$ | $Y_1$  $Y_2$  ...  $Y_n$ | | |
| Total Input | | | |

incidence of indirect taxes, direct taxes levied on the business sector and government current expenditures.[9] Indeed, regional expansion of the Income and Expenditure Accounts for all sectors would be a useful addition to our records since it would show more clearly the interrelatedness of the mechanisms by which national product is *distributed* among the regions. In Canada no comprehensive set of regional sector Income and Expenditure Accounts is available as yet.

Of greater interest from the standpoint of this appendix are the Production Accounts. Further sectoring of these Accounts could be performed along institutional lines. That is, the government sector could be broken into its federal, provincial, and municipal sub-components, and each sub-component into activities such as education, etc.; the business sector could be broken into financial and non-

---

[9] The household sector (called "the personal sector" in the Canadian National Accounts) could also be shown in greater detail so that, with respect to the Production and Capital Accounts, the records for "dummy" industries such as the owner-occupied residential real estate industry are shown explicitly and, with respect to the Income and Expenditure Accounts, the transfers between persons and unincorporated business enterprises are set out separately.

financial intermediaries, etc. All such disaggregations could be dupli-
cated at the regional level.

To examine the Production Account of the business sector more
closely, assume that all production takes place in that sector; that is,
that no national product is generated within other sectors and that the
sector is disaggregated along industry lines. This kind of disaggregation is shown in Table B:2.

The symbol $\sum_{i=1}^{n} II_{i1}$ in the table represents the value of all the
*intermediate inputs* used in Industry 1 which may be obtained from
all the industries of the economy (including Industry 1). The symbol
$\sum_{i=1}^{n} IO_{ni}$ represents the value of all the *intermediate output* of Industry
n which may be used by all the industries of the economy (including
Industry n). The symbol $\sum_{k} FO_{2k}$ represents the value of all the *final
output* of Industry 2 which goes to satisfy the needs of k final de-
manders (i.e., households and governments purchasing consumption
goods and businesses purchasing capital goods); and the symbol $\sum_{i=1}^{n} Y_i$
is the sum of all contributions to net national product originating in
the various industries. For any given industry, the sum of the value of
its intermediate and final outputs equals the sum of the value of its
intermediate inputs, capital consumption allowances, and net income
denoted by Y (i.e. product, or "net value added") originating in that
industry. When this relationship is summed over all industries, the
sum of the value of intermediate inputs and outputs is identical, and
so at the level of the whole economy the sum of the value of capital
consumption allowances and net income equals the sum of the value
of final output – as was shown in Table B:1.

These accounts may be more compactly expressed in matrix form
to reveal the interrelated nature of production. In Table B:3, for
example, row 2 shows the disposition of the total output and column
2 the total input of Industry 2.[10]

These parts of economic accounts are known as input-output
tables.[11] The accounts presented in Tables B:2 and B:3 convey, of
course, the same information, though the matrix presentation reveals
the technological interdependence of production relationships more
vividly. For example, if the final output of Industry 1 is increased
(owing, say, to increased household consumption), Table B:3 will

[10] These accounts are but a sub-account of the whole set of sector accounts. The
Standard Sector Accounts in Table B:1 may also be expressed more compactly
in matrix form as follows:

reveal, given certain assumptions about the nature of technological interdependence, how outputs of industries which supply Industry 1 with its intermediate inputs will be affected. The further impact of changes in the level of economic activity of these industries on yet

| Incomings or credits (Outgoings or debits →) | | Production Accounts | | | Income and Expenditure Accounts | | | Capital Accounts | | | Financial Transactions Accounts | | |
|---|---|---|---|---|---|---|---|---|---|---|---|---|---|
| | | H | G | B | H | G | B | H | G | B | H | G | B |
| Production Accounts | H | | | | $C_{HH}$ | | | | | | | | |
| | G | | | | | $G_{GG}$ | | | | | | | |
| | B | $II_{BH}$ | $II_{BG}$ | $II_{BB}$ | $C$ | $G$ | | $\triangle K_H$ | $\triangle K_G$ | $\triangle K_B$ | | | |
| Income and Expenditure Accounts | H | $Y_H$ | | | $W_{HH}+$ | $W_{GH}+I_{GH}$ | $W_{BH}+I_{BH}$ | | | | | | |
| | G | | $Y_G$ | | $T_{HG}$ | | $T_{BG}$ | | | | | | |
| | B | | | $Y_B$ | | | | | | | | | |
| Capital Accounts | H | $CCA_H$ | | | $S_H$ | | | | | | | | |
| | G | | $CCA_G$ | | | $S_G$ | | | | | | | |
| | B | | | $CCA_B$ | | | $S_B$ | | | | | | |
| Financial Transactions Accounts | H | | | | | | | $FS_H$ | | | $+M_H$ $+B_H$ | | |
| | G | | | | | | | | $FDS_G$ | | | $-M_G$ $+B_G$ | |
| | B | | | | | | | | | $FDS_B$ | | | $-M_B$ $+B_B$ |

Here, Table B:3 is revealed to be but a small part (with the main portion of Table B:3 being, with certain adjustments, a blown-up version of the cell labelled "II$_{BB}$") of the over-all national accounting matrix. It should be noted that Table B:3 is in what is called "gross" form and may be placed, providing the industrial origin of reproducible capital goods is known, on a net basis.

11 For the latest Canadian equivalent of Table B:3, see D.B.S., *Supplement to the Inter-Industry Flow of Goods and Services, Canada, 1949* (13-513), (Ottawa: Queen's Printer, 1960).

other industries which are their suppliers, may be similarly estimated. And so on.[12] Tables B:2 and B:3 are examined in the next section within a regional framework. As indicated earlier, such a survey of only a part of the regional economic accounts is limited. No doubt regional income and expenditure accounts and balance sheets are essential for other purposes of regional analysis, but there are a sufficient number of problems associated with what are called here the regional Production Accounts to warrant this more specialized review.

It should be pointed out that Table B:3 is based on the assumption that each industry produces but one homogeneous good or service. In actual fact, industries are really collections of similar establishments that are generally engaged in many activities resulting in many different goods and services.[13] By way of illustration, many establishments that are primarily engaged in manufacturing, retail trade, etc., will also be engaged in what is called "own-account construction". In Table B:3, the outputs and inputs associated with this secondary activity could be included with those of the primary activities of the establishments and, as a consequence, will appear as part of the outputs and inputs of the manufacturing and retail trade industries rather than of the construction industry. This method of drawing up accounts is called an "establishment collection of outputs and inputs". On the other hand, the data associated with own-account construction could be, so to speak, "pulled out" of the various establishments in which such activity is secondary and included with those establishments in which construction is the primary activity – that is, the establishments customarily making up the construction industry. This would be called an "activity collection of outputs and inputs". It is also possible to look only at commodities and compose a commodity collection of outputs and inputs.

12 In fact, under certain assumptions, a particular pattern of final output (or demand) for the whole economy may be directed against the so-called "inverse" of the matrix of input-output coefficients to "predict" simultaneously the level of industry outputs. For a simple description of input-output accounts and economic analysis, see William H. Miernyk, *op. cit.*; for a description of how such accounts fit into the over-all national accounts, see R. Stone, *Input-Output and National Accounts* (Paris: Organisation for European Economic Co-operation 1961); and for one test of the stability of Canadian input-output coefficients, see Tadek I. Matuszewski, Paul R. Pitts, and John A. Sawyer, "Inter-industry Estimates of Canadian Imports, 1949, 1958" in *Papers* (Canadian Political Science Association Conference on Statistics, 1961), eds. Wm. C. Hood and John A. Sawyer (Toronto: University of Toronto Press, 1963).

13 Multi-activity establishments may be aggregated into multi-establishment firms (or unconsolidated legal entities) and even, finally, into multi-firm enterprises. These latter producer units are more appropriate for use in sector analysis dealing with transactions in paper claims and the study of the results of decision-making with respect to stocks, monetary and real.

## A Review of Regional Production Accounts

Implicit in the concept of social policy-making is the existence of a collectivity; therefore "region" will be taken here to mean a territory which is a political jurisdiction. It need not be territory coincidental with provincial boundaries – as the emergence of bodies such as the Atlantic Provinces Economic Council and the Prairie Provinces Economic Council, which reflect the logic of economic interrelationships, shows. The reader will also be familiar with appropriately defined regions which are smaller than provinces. Clearly, for different purposes, many different ways of classifying regions are possible. The very multiplicity of criteria indicates that regional economics, as a branch of economic analysis, does not yet have a small set of well-defined important economic problems with which to deal.[14] Consequently, the level of detail and disaggregation to which regional economic accounts should be optimally pursued is not at all clear.

Further disaggregation of Tables B:2 and B:3 along regional lines can be done by showing industrial detail by region. Two things have to be remembered. First, as soon as the analysis switches to the regional level, each region, considered as an economy, is no longer isolated. We must distinguish between the domestic product and the "national" product being generated within each region. The difficulty of obtaining estimates of "national" product at the regional level is the main reason why, in regional Production Accounts, the domestic concept of product is virtually always employed. Second, once we consider a region within an economy, we are driven to record flows of exports and imports of goods and services from and to that region. A region's exports can be broken down into two main kinds: the flows of goods and services ending up as intermediate inputs absorbed by industries in other regions; and the flow of goods and services ending up as part of the final consumption of households and governments of other regions. Similarly, we may classify a region's imports as direct imports, those flowing directly into the consumption of the home region's households and governments, and as indirect imports, those taking their place as intermediate inputs in the home region's domestic industries.

By and large, at the present time, we do not have information in Canada on the interregional flows of goods and services on a "from what industry by region to what industry by region" basis. At the level of the national economy we do have information on exports by country of destination and on imports by country of origin – but we

14 See J. Meyer, "Regional Economics: a Survey" in *Surveys of Economic Theory: Growth and Development*, II (New York: St. Martin's Press, 1965).

have to rely to a large extent on the national accountants of other countries or on private researchers to tell us which industries have used our exports and which industries have produced our imports. Preparation of export and import data on the basis of the end use of commodities and their country of destination and origin is a step in the right direction. But aside from some experimental work being performed by professors Tadek Matuszewski for the Province of Quebec and Kari Levitt for the Atlantic provinces, there is no data on interregional shipments of commodities on a region of destination by region of origin basis in Canada – much less with the "to what–from what" industry information added.

Many of the estimates of provincial gross domestic product – and only some provinces (Ontario, for example) prepare such data – are based on the various censuses of industry, etc. These censuses permit the calculation of census value added by region – an approximation to gross domestic product.[15] Little, if any, information is provided in such censuses on the end use of the gross outputs of the industries. From the various census and surveys in Canada, we do have, for some industries, estimates of output for main regions (for example, British Columbia, the Prairie provinces, Ontario, Quebec, and the Atlantic provinces) and for *some* smaller regions, such as metropolitan areas. Thus, the Census of Manufacturers provides regional information, but we certainly do not have reliable estimates of the product originating in, for instance, financial intermediation on a regional basis. In addition, information is periodically provided on the labour force – or, more generally, on some characteristics of the labour input on a regional basis for certain industries and certain occupations. To estimate, for example, "total factor productivity" on a regional basis, however, information by industry by region on the various components of the reproducible and non-reproducible capital stock is also obviously required, and though official estimates by industry of the reproducible capital stock have been prepared at the national level,[16] the reliability of estimates that have been or could be prepared at the regional level can, at the present stage in the develop-

15 Census value added is an approximation to gross domestic product because it does not "net out" such things as intermediate business service inputs. If capital-consumption allowances were deducted from the gross concept, we would be left with net domestic product. In the text two complications – one conceptual and the other institutional – are not taken into account. First, the difference between gross domestic product at market prices and factor cost consists of indirect taxes less subsidies – and this distinction is currently giving rise to some controversy in national accounting literature. Second, at small-region levels, various Statistics acts may have secrecy clauses which prevent the publication of data on an individual industry basis because of the small number of establishments in the industry in the region. Both these complications can be very vexing.

16 See D.B.S., *Fixed Capital Flows and Stocks, Manufacturing, Canada, 1946-1960* (13-522), (Ottawa: Queen's Printer, 1967).

**Table B:4 Schematic Interregional Input-Output Accounts**

| | | Region 1 | | Region 2 | | |
|---|---|---|---|---|---|---|
| | | Industries $1\,2\ldots i\;\; j\ldots n$ | Final Output $FO_1$ | Industries $1\,2\ldots i\;\; j\ldots n$ | Final Output $FO_2$ | $1\,2\ldots$ |
| Region A Industries | 1 2 … i j … n | $x_{i1j1}$ | $c_{i1.1}$ | $x_{i1j2}$ | $c_{i1.2}$ | $\cdots$ |
| | Primary Output | | | | | |
| Region B Industries | 1 2 … i j … n | $x_{i2j1}$ | $c_{i2.1}$ | $x_{i2j2}$ | $c_{i2.2}$ | $\cdots$ |
| | Primary Output | | | | | |
| | ⋮ | ⋮ | | ⋮ | ⋮ | |

ment of regional statistical systems, be seriously questioned. Again, though census estimates and other surveys do provide some regional data on the capital stock, they are not altogether reliable and relate mainly to primary industries such as agriculture. There is little information about secondary industries and virtually none about tertiary. Furthermore, aside from some spatial consumer price indexes, we have in Canada at the present time virtually no price-index data on a regional basis. The data system in Canada, at least on the regional basis, has a long way to go.

These various scarcities or complete absences of data suggest that concern with integrated input-output accounts and constant price measurement at the regional level may be premature. It would be wise, however, to have an over-all view as to where regional economic accounting should be heading.

Table B:4 provides the bare bones of a regional integration of input-output accounts. In order to reduce complexity to a bare minimum, only certain representative entries have been set out. The first entry in the upper left of the table, $x_{i_1 j_1}$, refers to the value of the output of the $i^{th}$ industry in Region 1 used as an intermediate input by the $j^{th}$ industry in Region 1. The entry $x_{i_1 j_2}$ refers to the value of the output of the $i^{th}$ industry in Region 1 used as an intermediate input by the $j^{th}$ industry in Region 2, i.e., it represents an export of the first region and an indirect import of the second region. The entry $x_{i_2 j_1}$, consists of the output of the $i^{th}$ industry of the second region which is used as an intermediate input of the $j^{th}$ industry in the first region – an intermediate import of the first region. The entry $c_{i_1.2}$ represents part of the final output of the $i^{th}$ industry in Region 1 which goes to meet the needs of (say) the households in Region 2. Such imports into Region 2 may be called direct imports. They are similar to the imports purchased directly by households in Region 1 produced by the $i^{th}$ industry in Region 2 ($c_{i_2.1}$). Thus, in interregional economic accounting (just as in international accounting), direct and indirect imports and exports must be taken into account. The degree to which extra-regional products are substitutes of regional ones, that is, the competitiveness and non-competitiveness of imports, must also be considered.

The assumption that there is a one-to-one correspondence between commodities and industries is patently unrealistic. Recognition that there are, in fact, many more "commodities" than "industries" leads to the attempted construction of what are called "rectangular" input-output accounts.[17] In Canada, work on such rectangular accounts is more advanced in Quebec than elsewhere at the present time.

Elaboration of regional Production Accounts along these input-output lines may entail departure in a number of cases from the conventions lying behind the aggregate national accounts. To take one example from the standard national accounts, the economic activity in which governments engage is often recorded by setting up the establishments engaged in such activities as "the Public Administra-

---

17 For a discussion of these matters, see Tadek I. Matuszewski, "Some Remarks on an Econometric Model of a Provincial Economy", *Canadian Journal of Economics and Political Science*, XXXI (November 1965), 552-8; Kari Levitt, "Inter-industry Study of the Economy of the Atlantic Provinces", and G. Rosenbluth, "Comment", in *Papers on Regional Statistical Studies*; Terry Gigantes and Paul Pitts, "An Integrated Input-Output Framework and Some Related Analytical Models", a paper presented to the 1965 Canadian Political Science Association Conference on Statistics; Terry Gigantes and Tadek I. Matuszewski, "Rectangular Input-Output Systems: Taxonomy and Analysis", a paper given at the Fourth International Conference on Input-Output Techniques, January 1968. See also the forthcoming study directed by Kari Levitt referred to earlier.

tion and Defence Industry". In a standard inter-industry input-output table such a treatment is to be avoided since the resulting hypothetical output of the industry has to be deemed as sold to the government, thus breaking the technological link between the user and producer of commodities which it is desirable to show in the input-output accounts. On the other hand, as was previously pointed out, it would be very useful, if possible, to show the various industries that "use" what could be called the intermediate output of "the Public Administration and Defence Industry" to aid in the study of "net fiscal incidence".

Rectangular regional input-output accounts are in their infancy, and a set of interrelated rectangular regional input accounts for Canada at the present time is very much a dream. Yet it is hard to see how answers to fairly sophisticated policy questions can even be approximately obtained if such tools (or at least *parts* of them) are not used. A few examples may help to demonstrate the need for such accounts. In Canada, though there has been much discussion about commercial policy, very little is known about the "effective rate of tariff protection" – that is, the effective protection that a given pattern of simple tariff rates offers on domestic value added or gross domestic product *at factor cost* by industry. Estimates of effective tariff rates cannot be calculated without the set of input-output accounts, at least at the national level, which have been described.[18] Also in Canada, the widely held proposition that Canadian commercial policy has had discriminatory regional effects needs more analysis – and such analysis would be greatly improved if the interrelated regional accounts described were available. In short, decisions by governments at both the national and the regional level which affect the course of regional economic development suffer greatly in Canada from the lack of an adequate statistical knowledge.[19] As the regional economic accounting system expands, top priority should be given to the preparation of regional input-output accounts with the long range plan of ensuring that such accounts be interrelated within the context of a national system of input-output accounts. In my view, this is the general area to which most of the resources devoted to regional accounting should be allocated.

Turning now to an even more speculative area, one of the most notable developments in national economic accounting in recent years has been the construction of a set of national accounts in constant

18 See H. G. Johnson, "The Theory of Tariff Structure, with Special Reference to World Trade and Development" in *Trade and Development* (Geneva: Librarie Droz, 1965).
19 See G. Rosenbluth, *op. cit.*

prices.[20] A correctly "deflated" set of national economic accounts entails the measurement of changes in "total factor productivity" over time.[21] A correctly "deflated" set of regional accounts not only would provide such measures over time at the regional level, but when the "deflation" is performed spatially would provide *some* help in determining differences in "total factor productivity" among regions.

Measuring "total factor productivity" over time for a given domestic economy raises the question of what today's primary inputs would have produced yesterday, under yesterday's technical conditions of production, relative to what they produce today under today's technical conditions. One must be careful in assessing primary inputs, for there has been a great deal of controversy in recent years as to the correct way to measure them. The issue is very important but cannot adequately be dealt with here. The source of much of the difficulty and controversy lies in the attempt to distinguish between "shifts in" and "movements along" production functions.[22] A significant part of this debate centres on the relative merits of neo-classical and Harrod-Robinson measures of technological change.[23] The essential point is that measures of "total factor productivity" must take account of differences (as between times as well as regions) in the efficiency with which economics can reproduce and augment their commodity capital inputs. Such measures of "total factor productivity", if carried out at an industrial level of detail, require the kind of complete "to what–from what" information that can be found in the input-output accounts described earlier. Similarly, measures on a regional basis, which would depict differences in "total factor productivity" as between similar industries over different regions or countries at the same point of time, would require the kind of regional "to what–from what" information outlined in Table B:4. *It must be clearly understood, however, that this information is wanted on a "deflated" basis –*

---

20 From a purist point of view, such index numbers, with all their customary ambiguity and imprecision, are most untrustworthy instruments. How much better it would be to have all the prices and quantities to work with instead of some average – which is what index numbers really are. Clearly, however, some "indexes of performance" are necessary if any discourse at all about economic events is to take place. Index number problems are surely widely understood by now.

21 D. W. Jorgenson and Z. Griliches, "The Explanation of Productivity Change", *The Review of Economic Studies*, XXXIV (July 1967), 249-83.

22 For a discussion of these matters, see L. M. Read, "The Measure of Total Factor Productivity Appropriate to Wage-Price Guidelines", *Canadian Journal of Economics*, I (May 1968), 349-58, and T. K. Rymes, "Professor Read and the Measurement of Total Factor Productivity", *Canadian Journal of Economics*, I (May 1968), 359-67.

23 See J. Robinson, *Essays in the Theory of Economic Growth* (London: Macmillan, 1962) and *The Accumulation of Capital*, (2nd ed.; London: Macmillan, 1965), and R. Solow, *Capital Theory and the Rate of Return* (Amsterdam: North Holland, 1963).

*that is, it must be provided in constant prices both over time and over regions.*

Clearly, the data required at this level of detail is far from what is currently provided – and far from what it is likely to be for some time to come. But, for an understanding of how production relationships interact over time at the regional level, the "total factor productivity" approach or, what is equivalent, the construction of deflated inter-regional input-output production accounts is a necessity. In Canada measures of constant price outputs and intermediate inputs by industry[24] are available at the national level, but there is no national "deflated" input-output set of accounts. To my knowledge there is none of this kind of information at the regional level.

Recent discussions among national accountants indicates that there are some fairly difficult problems involved in "deflation" to which insufficient attention has been paid. For example, most national accountants have argued that, in constant prices, the industry output concept of greatest relevance is gross domestic product at factor cost – obtained by what is known as the "double deflation" method. Considerable doubt has arisen over the meaning of such a measure of an industry's output.[25] This doubt has recently extended to the measure of output in constant prices for the entire economy – when an attempt is made to distinguish between expressing output in terms of factor cost or in market prices. There is also some doubt in the national economic accounting literature as to whether indirect taxes (less subsidies), which are levied not on final demand but on intermediate inputs (which may be called "indirect indirect taxes"), should or should not be excluded from measures of output at factor cost. In constant prices, the ratio of indirect indirect taxes to final output will change with

24 See D.B.S., *Indexes of Real Domestic Product by Industry of Origin, 1935-61* (61-505), (Ottawa: Queen's Printer, 1963). For discussions of some of the difficulties that would be encountered in Canada in producing only part of a set of "deflated" national accounts, see G. J. Garston and D. A. Warton, "Problems in the Estimation of Industry Output in Current and Constant Dollars in Canada", a paper presented to the 1966 National Bureau of Economic Research Conference on Research in Income and Wealth, and B. J. Emery and G. J. Garston, "The Measurement of Constant Dollar Aggregates in Canada", a paper presented to the 1967 International Association for Research in Income and Wealth. Standard measures of "total factor productivity" for Canadian manufacturing may be found in G. Post, N. H. Lithwick, and T. K. Rymes, "Post War Production Relationships in Canada" in *The Theory and Empirical Analysis of Production* (New York: Columbia University Press for the National Bureau of Economic Research, 1967).

25 It has long been recognized in national accounting literature that, with exceptional inverse correlation between intermediate input price and quantity movements, it is possible for such an index to go "negative" – a clearly meaningless result. What has not been clearly recognized is the fact that, strange index number problems or not, the "double deflation" method for measuring industry output in constant prices runs afoul of the attempt to separate out the influences of technological advance and capital (in this case, intermediate input) accumulation. See L. M. Read, *op. cit.*, and T. K. Rymes, *op. cit.*

differing rates of advance in the technology of the industries of a given economy if they are subject to different rates of indirect taxation. As a consequence, measures of the aggregate constant-price national (or domestic) product in terms of factor cost and of market prices will show divergent trends – the difference being, aside from statistical discrepancies, the constant price indirect indirect taxes.[26]

At the present time in Canada, constant price measures of aggregate domestic product may be produced in two ways. The more well-known way is to "deflate" the expenditures giving rise to gross national product and to put the "deflated" trade balance on a domestic basis to arrive at a constant price aggregate called "expenditures giving rise to gross domestic product at market prices". The less well-known industry approach is to sum, over all industries, the "double-deflated" measures of industry output described earlier. In Canada this is done at the factor cost level. To move from constant-price expenditures giving rise to gross domestic product at market prices, via the expenditure approach, to constant price gross domestic product at factor cost, via the industry approach, an estimate must be made, using *current* period input-output relationships, of the constant price indirect taxes (less subsidies) which separate the two concepts.[27]

The basic idea, if we ignore the complications of international income flows and indirect taxes, is, that the two constant price aggregates are identical. It can be argued, however, that the presence of indirect taxes and differences between what are called producers' and purchasers' price evaluation of flows, arising because of trade, transportation, and storage margins, etc., will "unbalance" the constant price production and expenditure aggregates. Recently, it has been argued that

> ... from the point of view of production, an increase in the distance over which goods are hauled, would be an increase in the volume of services embodied in these goods. From the point of view of the user of the goods, however, it will appear to be an increase in price. If the balance [i.e., the identity mentioned above] of the accounts in real terms is to be preserved, it seems essential to treat the greater distance of haulage as an increase in the quantum, not the price, of transport services.[28]

26 For a discussion of these problems, see B. J. Emery and G. Garston, *op. cit.*, and R. Stone, *Quantity and Price Indexes in the National Accounts* (Paris: Organisation for Economic Co-operation and Development, 1956).

27 See D.B.S., *Indexes of Real Domestic Product* (61-505), for a further discussion of this technique. In that publication the constant price indirect taxes were estimated using base period, as an approximation to the desired current period, input-output relationships.

28 See Conference of European Statisticians WG.22/GR.5/2, *National Accounting in Constant Prices*, February 17, 1967, para. 15. The insertion was made to emphasize that it is the non-attainment of an identity which is at issue. Imbalance, in the sense earlier described, of "total factor productivity" estimates arises because of economic progress and is, of course, to be expected.

For regional constant-price Production Accounts, the transportation activity will be extremely important. The quotation, and the line of action recommended in it, indicate the many unsolved problems that confront constant-price regional economic accounting. They also indicate that the application of the production approach in constant-price accounting might artificially "balance" the accounts, making the constant-price accounts virtually worthless, especially for any use such as "total factor productivity" measurement. There are many issues involved in the problem of a balancing set of "real" national accounts, and the development of a constant-price regional economic accounting system should help in their resolution. There is much still to be done.

## Conclusion

Whether it will work out well or not, it seems likely that policy decisions about economic problems in Canada are going to take place at an increasingly disaggregated level. Regional economic accounting has, in the past, been oriented mainly toward Income and Expenditure Accounts, with the stress being placed on recording the effects of inter-government transfers on taxes, subsidies, income, and per capita expenditures in the various regions. The shift of decision-making to lower levels of government should result in more emphasis being placed on the development of regional Production Accounts.

This appendix has set out, in general form, the kind of regional economic accounts to which data systems operated by the different levels of government should be directed. The regional Production Accounts have been stressed because here is where work might most profitably be begun.

The task, however, will not be an easy one. Increased government co-operation will be necessary if the many obstacles are to be overcome and the technical difficulties are to be resolved. Progress is likely to be slow; but if we fail to develop a satisfactory set of regional economic accounts, the policy maker will be left with little light to guide him, and the resolution of regional economic problems hardly begun.

# Suggested Reading

## General

Friedmann, John, and William Alonso (eds.). *Regional Development and Planning: A Reader.* Cambridge, Mass.: M.I.T. Press, 1964.
This book of readings is an excellent introduction to the literature. It lists many of the most important works and journals likely to be of use to the student. In addition to those cited, reference might also be made to *Banca Nazionale del Lavoro Quarterly Review, Lloyds Bank Review,* the *Scottish Journal of Political Economy,* and the *Three Banks Review.*

An extensive 181 page selected bibliography covering the general literature as well as individual country studies has been collected by N. G. Pillai under the title "Area Development, Regional Development, and Economic Growth – Problems and Policies", and has been published in mimeographed form by the Planning Division, Atlantic Provinces Development Board, Ottawa, in March 1968.

## Chapter 1

Camu, P., E. P. Weeks, and Z. W. Sametz. *Economic Geography of Canada: with an Introduction to the 68-Region system.* Toronto: Macmillan, 1964.

Caves, Richard E., and Richard H. Holton. *The Canadian Economy: Prospect and Retrospect.* Cambridge, Mass.: Harvard University Press, 1959.

Denton, Frank T. *An Analysis of Interregional Differences in Manpower Utilization and Earnings* (Economic Council of Canada, Staff Study No. 15). Ottawa: Queen's Printer, 1966.

Economic Council of Canada. *Annual Review.* Ottawa: Queen's Printer, annually since 1964.

Howland, R. D. *Some Regional Aspects of Canada's Economic Development*. Royal Commission on Canada's Economic Prospects. Ottawa: Queen's Printer, 1957.

*Readings of the Resources for Tomorrow Conference, Montreal, 1961*. Vols. I-III, supplementary volume, and Guide to Benefit-Cost Analysis. Ottawa: Queen's Printer, 1962.

## Chapter 2

Cameron, G. C., and B. D. Clark. *Industrial Movement and the Regional Problem* (University of Glasgow Social and Economic Studies, Occasional Paper No. 5). Edinburgh and London: Oliver & Boyd, 1966.

Chisholm, Michael. *Geography and Economics*. London: G. Bell & Sons, 1966.

Estall, Robert C., and R. O. Buchanan. *Industrial Activity and Economic Geography*. London: Hutchinson, 1961.

Greenhut, Melvin L. *Plant Location in Theory and in Practice: The Economics of Space*. Chapel Hill: University of North Carolina Press, 1956.

Haggett, Peter. *Locational Analysis in Human Geography*. London: Edward Arnold, 1965.

Hoover, Edgar M. *The Location of Economic Activity*. New York: McGraw-Hill, 1948.

Lösch, August. *The Economics of Location*. New York: Science Editions Paperback, 1967.

## Chapter 3

Ostry, Sylvia, and T. K. Rymes (eds.). *Papers on Regional Statistical Studies*. Canadian Political Science Association Conference on Statistics, 1964. Toronto: University of Toronto Press, 1966. Especially pp. 27-52 and 75-130.

Smith, Brian C. *Regionalism in England: Its Nature and Purpose, 1905-1965*. London: The Acton Society Trust, 1965.

Thoman, Richard S., and Maurice H. Yeates. "Delimitation of Development Regions in Canada (With Special Attention to the Georgian Bay Vicinity)," a report submitted to the Area Development Agency, Department of Industry, 1966.

## Chapter 4

Brewis, T. N., *et al. Growth and the Canadian Economy.* Toronto: McClelland & Stewart, 1968.

Hoselitz, Bert F. *Sociological Aspects of Economic Growth.* New York: Free Press of Glencoe, 1960.

National Bureau of Economic Research, Conference on Research in Income and Wealth. *Regional Income* (Studies in Income and Wealth, Vol. 21). Princeton: Princeton University Press, 1957.

Perloff, Harvey S., and Vera W. Dodds. *How a Region Grows: Area Development in the U.S. Economy.* New York: Committee for Economic Development, Supplementary Paper No. 17, 1963.

Tiebout, Charles M. *The Community Economic Base Study.* New York: Committee for Economic Development, Supplementary Paper No. 16, 1962.

Wilson, Thomas A., and N. Harvey Lithwick. *The Sources of Economic Growth* (Studies of the Royal Commission on Taxation, No. 24). Ottawa: Queen's Printer, 1968.

## Chapter 5

Economic Council of Canada. Annual Review. Ottawa: Queen's Printer, annually from 1964.

Fishman, Leo (ed.). *Poverty and Affluence.* New Haven, Conn.: Yale University Press, 1966.

Myrdal, Gunnar. *Economic Theory and Underdeveloped Regions.* London: Methuen, 1963. (First published by Duckworth in 1957.)

Royal Commission on the Distribution of the Industrial Population. *Report.* London: H.M.S.O., 1940 (Reprinted 1963), Cmd. 6153.

U.S. Department of Commerce, Area Redevelopment Administration. *Area Development Policies in Britain and the Countries of the Common Market.* Washington, D.C.: Government Printing Office, 1965.

## Chapter 6

Buckley, Helen, and Eva Tihanyi. *Canadian Policies for Rural Adjustment: a Study of the Economic Impact of ARDA, PFRA, and MMRA* (Economic Council of Canada, Special Study No. 7). Ottawa: Queen's Printer, 1967.

Tremblay, Marc Adélard, and Walton J. Anderson (eds.). *Rural Canada in Transition.* Ottawa: Agricultural Research Council of Canada, 1966.

The Department of Forestry and Rural Development in Ottawa has published a good many studies of various aspects of the problems of rural areas and the policies associated with them. They constitute the largest single source of information on the subject.

## Chapter 7

Barzant, Sergio. *The Underdeveloped Areas within the Common Market*. Princeton, N.J.: Princeton University Press, 1965.

Boote, Maurice J. "Area Development Policy in the United States: 1955-65". Ottawa: Area Development Agency, Department of Industry, 1966 (mimeographed).

Hirschman, Albert O. *The Strategy of Economic Development* (Yale Studies in Economics No. 10). New Haven, Conn.: Yale University Press, 1958.

Klaassen, L. H. *Area Economic and Social Redevelopment: Guidelines for Programmes*. Paris: Organisation for Economic Co-operation and Development, 1965.

Wilson, T. "Financial Assistance with Regional Development", a report prepared for the Atlantic Provinces Research Board, 1964 (mimeographed).

———— *Policies for Regional Development* (University of Glasgow Social and Economic Studies, Occasional Paper No. 3). Edinburgh and London: Oliver & Boyd, 1964.

## Chapter 8

Atlantic Provinces Economic Council. *First Annual Review: The Atlantic Economy*. Halifax, N.S.: APEC, 1967.

———— "Submission to the Royal Commission on Taxation". Ottawa: 1963 (mimeographed).

Cairncross, A. K. *Economic Development and the Atlantic Provinces*. Fredericton, N.B.: Atlantic Provinces Research Board, 1961.

Donald, J. R. *Report on the Cape Breton Coal Problem*. Ottawa: Queen's Printer, 1966.

Howland, R. D. *Some Regional Aspects of Canada's Economic Development*, a report to the Royal Commission on Canada's Economic Prospects. Ottawa: Queen's Printer, 1958.

The Atlantic Provinces Economic Council publishes pamphlets on various aspects of the economy of the Atlantic region.

## Chapter 9

Boudeville, J. R. *Problems of Regional Economic Planning*. Edinburgh: Edinburgh University Press, 1966.

Isard, Walter, and John H. Cumberland (eds.). *Regional Economic Planning: Techniques of Analysis*. Paris: Organisation for European Economic Co-operation, 1961.

Lewis, W. Arthur. *Development Planning: the Essentials of Economic Policy*. London: Allen & Unwin, 1966.

Lilienthal, David E. *TVA: Democracy on the March*. London: Penguin Books, 1944.

Skeoch, L. A., and David C. Smith. *Economic Planning: the Relevance of West European Experience for Canada*. Montreal: Canadian Trade Committee, the Private Planning Association of Canada, 1963.

Tinbergen, Jan. *The Design of Development*, a publication of the Economic Development Institute, International Bank for Reconstruction and Development. Baltimore: Johns Hopkins Press, 1958.


## Chapter 10

Brann, W. Paul, *et al*. *Community Economic Development Efforts: Five Case Studies*. New York: Committee for Economic Development, Supplementary Paper No. 18, 1964.

*Development Plan for the Pilot Region: Lower St. Lawrence, Gaspé and Iles-de-la-Madeleine: A Summary*. Ottawa: Department of Forestry, Rural Development Branch, 1967.

*Establishment of Industrial Estates in Under-developed Countries*. New York: United Nations, Department of Economic and Social Affairs, 1961.

Gilmore, Donald R. *Developing the "Little" Economies*. New York: Committee for Economic Development, Supplementary Paper No. 10, 1960.


## Chapter 11

Advisory Committee on Northern Development. "Government Activities in the North", 1966. Ottawa: Department of Indian Affairs and Northern Development, 1967 (mimeographed).

Jenness, Diamond. *Eskimo Administration*. Montreal: Arctic Institute of North America, Technical Paper No. 14, 1964.

*The Northwest Territories Today*, a reference paper for the Advisory

Commission on the Development of Government in the Northwest Territories. Ottawa: Queen's Printer, 1965.

Phillips, R. A. J. *Canada's North.* Toronto: Macmillan, 1967.

Quirin, G. David. *The Economics of Oil and Gas Development in Northern Canada.* Ottawa: Queen's Printer, 1962.

# Index